The Americans and Philosophy

Popular Culture and Philosophy® Series Editor: George A. Reisch

For full details of all Popular Culture and Philosophy® books, visit www.opencourtbooks.com.

To the memory of
Sir Roger Moore (1927–2017).
He wasn't a real spy
but he played one on screen.

Popular Culture and Philosophy®

The Americans and Philosophy

Reds in the Bed

EDITED BY

ROBERT ARP AND
KEVIN GUILFOY

OPEN COURT
Chicago

Volume 112 in the series, Popular Culture and Philosophy®, edited by George A. Reisch

To find out more about Open Court books, visit our website at www.opencourtbooks.com.

Open Court Publishing Company is a division of Carus Publishing Company, dba Cricket Media.

Printed and bound in the United States of America.

The Americans and Philosophy: Reds in the Bed

This book has not been prepared, authorized, or endorsed by the creators or producers of *The Americans*.

ISBN: 978-0-8126-9971-5

Library of Congress Control Number: 2017948527

This book is also available as an e-book.

Contents

Contents

From Russia with Malice and a Little Love

When the events in *The Americans* unfolded, the two of us were about Paige Jennings's age (and still are, of course, if she has survived).

We remember the confusion on the TV news when President Reagan was shot. And the fear when General Alexander Haig was "in charge" at the White House. We also remember watching Reagan's "Evil Empire" speech. We had the same response as Paige to these events—something along the lines of, "Oh my God! Are we all going to die in some kind of nuclear apocalypse?"

It's nostalgic—and perhaps a bit unsettling—for people of our generation to watch *The Americans* and relive these fateful moments. Like Paige, we watched *The Day After* with our parents. The threat of nuclear holocaust can focus the mind on the truly important questions, such as "Are we ever justified in killing a few to save many?" or "Should we *even consider* killing hundreds of thousands for the sake of national dominance or security?" These kinds of questions happen to be the kinds of questions you'll find answered in this book, actually. It remains to be seen whether Paige will be around to hear Reagan demand, "Mr. Gorbachev, tear down this wall!" because it looks as if Paige is going to give the family business a try.

Paige, along with Henry, Philip, Elizabeth, and other characters on *The Americans* are confronted with many interesting philosophical problems and challenges on a regular basis throughout the show (for example, "Is Mail-bot a conscious being?" or "Can we truly be happy while leading a double life?" which are just two of the questions answered in this book).

Philosophy is not very good in hand-to-hand combat—no one has ever literally been crushed in the grip of logic. Granted, the middle of a field operation is not the best time to be questioning everything, but when the Jennings duo is not killing for Mother Russia, they're often struggling to resolve deep questions that confront the *dusha* (душа), the soul. When you find yourself asking "Is this suitcase big enough to hold a body?" it's time to sit down and have a really good re-think about where your priorities lie and what you're doing with your life. We all have to make some sacrifices to achieve our goals, but Philip and Elizabeth probably take sacrifice to a whole different level. There is just about no one they won't sacrifice—which seems to be a philosophical issue in itself.

And who hasn't looked at their spouse, or a loved one, or a close friend, and thought: "Who the hell are you?" We all have private, even secret, parts of ourselves. We all have public faces that we construct, some real, some fake, some even we don't know. Philip and Elizabeth literally put on faces, and wigs, and accents, and new names, and even they don't know who they are. Is Clark really just make-believe? Who is the *real* Philip? What's Elizabeth's *true* identity? Again, more philosophical musings.

Philip and Elizabeth are better spies than philosophers. Fortunately, the contributors to this book are here to help. As you read the chapters, you will come across issues in ethics, metaphysics, epistemology, social philosophy, and other areas of philosophy that plot lines and dialogue in

The Americans address with a fair degree of thoughtfulness and humanity. So join us, comrades, for some interesting insights.

KEVIN GUILFOY AND ROBERT ARP

I

Pledging Allegiance

1
They Get Them When They're Children

SETH M. WALKER

It's a typical, peaceful evening in Falls Church, Virginia. The kids are upstairs in their bedrooms, winding down for the night. You're taking advantage of the post-dinner lull to catch up on some laundry and a little spy banter with your husband. As you make your way through the house, dropping off everyone's clean clothes, you startle your young, teenage daughter. Caught off guard, she quickly hides whatever she was reading and nervously accuses you of barging into her room. *What could she possibly be hiding?* you wonder.

As she withdraws the book from under a pillow, your jaw drops: a Bible?! The hardline Marxist in you cringes in parental failure. "What is this?!" you desperately ask. *She's been attending a church as well?* You worry your daughter has been lost—brainwashed by some naive group of people who think their beliefs and aspirations are more than just fantasy, that the work *they're* doing, and the young people *they're* indoctrinating with their values, will make the world a better place. *She's so not like me.*

Well, the obvious kicker here is that these two aren't all that different. Paige and Elizabeth Jennings are more alike than they think. As Elizabeth starts to realize, Paige's involvement with the church—and Christian theology, more specifically—is influenced by the right kinds of urges; she's just looking for what she wants in the wrong place. But, couldn't Paige say the same thing about her mother—even after she finds out who her parents *really* are? Aren't we just dealing with different forms of indoctrination and belief? On the surface the conflict seems to be about Paige's behavior, but political ideology can have religion-like qualities—what theorists call "civil religion."

People Who Get It

As we all know, Paige's "conversion" experience didn't start with some charismatic preacher luring her into his bedazzled flock; it began with a lonely afternoon bus ride ("The Walk In"). A young girl about Paige's age named Kelli strikes up conversation with her during the long, otherwise uneventful trip to Pennsylvania. Kelli, who is on her way to visit her father, has the dysfunctional family Paige fears she's getting ready to have as well. Kelli shares some insight and advice for Paige as the two hit it off, ultimately inviting her to give her a call sometime if she ever wants to hang out with her and other people "who get it."

We don't actually see what she meant by this until the following episode ("A Little Night Music"), when Paige discreetly meets up with her for the first time at the Reed Street Church's youth group. Kelli was employing a classic recruitment strategy on that bus: locate the vulnerable target, relate to the target by drawing on shared sentiments and emotional turmoil, and present the "solution" to life's problems.

There are many models of religious recruitment, and even though we're often left with mixed results when those models are applied to particular examples, the models *do* offer some insight into these scenarios. Sociologists John Loftland and Rodney Stark offered one such model of conversion back in 1965. And Lorne L. Dawson, another sociologist, did his best about thirty years later to outline some generalizations based on empirical evidence supporting Loftland and Stark's model. We can outline Dawson's generalizations to more broadly capture religious conversion:

- People tend to join groups when they know people already involved

- The *quality* of interaction with others in the group is crucial

- That interaction also needs to be fairly intense so that members don't lose interest

- Like any social commitment, having the time and freedom to be involved are important factors

- Those who aren't already "religious" are more likely to join

- Individuals interested in joining have been thinking about life's "big questions" and have maybe even done a little preliminary reading about them on their own

- Group members can expect some sort of *reward* by joining—whether it's positive vibes and warm, fuzzy feelings, or in the form of monetary aid.

Paige never had a chance, huh? Well, she only met Kelli right before joining (and where did she go after Paige started attending?), but everything seems to be pretty straightforward in her case: the church is very accommodating and outwardly compassionate; there are always events taking place during the week—from services to preparing material for protests—Paige is young, without any real serious commitments that might distract or prevent her involvement; she was clearly *not* a practicing Christian—or even generally "religious"—prior to joining; she was seemingly struggling with making sense out of her family life (suspecting a possible love affair involving one or both parents), general adolescence, and her place in the world; and she feels like the church is giving her life purpose, mostly by allowing her to express and actualize things important to her (like making the world a better place).

It's no surprise, then, that Kelli's recruitment was a success. The last two points in that outline above become specifically argumentative throughout the series. In "The Deal," Paige confesses to Elizabeth that this new outlet and group is helping her make sense of her "crazy life." Paige, quite literally, gives her the "It's not you, it's me" to help her mother—who reacted negatively when first seeing Paige with a Bible in the previous episode ("A Little Night Music")—cope and understand that this new aspect of her life has nothing to do with anything Elizabeth may have done (umm . . . whew?). But, this clash between her parents' Soviet ideology—which includes a very critical understanding of religion—and Paige's newfound Christianity never truly goes away, no matter how accommodating they try to be to their daughter's personal values and beliefs.

She Was Praying, Philip—Praying!

When Elizabeth and Philip first catch Paige with a Bible—and yes, *catch* is exactly how it went down, as Paige knew that she was doing something her parents wouldn't like—they're noticeably alarmed and confused. When pressed, Paige explains to her mother that her new friend Kelli has "a messed up family" and the Reed Street Church is where she goes to help her deal with things and be "happy." "But *you* don't have a messed up family," Elizabeth responds.

It's easy to empathize with both parties here—the parent who'd like to be involved in the *correct* development of her child's values and interests, and the teenager who's trying to make sense of the world around her. I think most of us would agree with Paige. She may not know all the details of her parents' double life, but her family is pretty messed up.

The conflict grows as Paige's involvement with the church continues. Elizabeth and Philip regularly criticize Paige's use of prayer—from their discreet smirks during the first time we witness it at the dinner table, to the concern they express later in the episode: "She was praying, Philip—praying!" ("A

Little Night Music"). They make mocking remarks while sharing a strong, Afghan joint: "She's living in a fantasy world" ("Born Again"). They ridicule her request to get baptized: "She's gonna wash her old life away and make herself clean for Jesus Christ?" Elizabeth sarcastically asks Philip ("Dimebag"). But, they do admit, "She's got some passion in her" and "she wants to do something good," even if they feel it's being misdirected. "I wish I could tell her about the real heroes," Elizabeth says to Philip. "People sacrificing themselves for this world—not some stupid children's story about heaven" ("Echo").

Elizabeth and Philip have deeper objections as well. "This is what happens. They get them when they're children . . . Philip, you and I, we know who we are. We have values. But these kids, what do they know? We're failing them. We're failing to help them stand up to the distractions, the consumerism. Look at this country. Church, synagogue—I mean, that's what's holding it all up. The opiate of the masses" ("A Little Night Music"). Unsurprisingly, Elizabeth quotes Marx. Marx's criticism of religion—the theistic, other-worldly sort—was rooted in his understanding of how higher social classes keep the lower, working class in a complacent rut.

If some sort of paradise is waiting for us on the other side of this wretched, miserable existence, the reasoning goes, then why bother exerting the energy to dig ourselves out right now? If embracing Christian theology, for instance, leads to that mindset, then hey, that's a pretty strong incentive to keep people with their heads bowed while they trudge back to work. Marx referred to the feeling religion stirs as an illusory form of happiness, an opiate for the masses. That remark Paige makes about Kelli going to church to feel "happy" should come to mind again here. For Marx—and good Russian socialists like the Jenningses—a revolt against that "happiness," in demand for *real* happiness, was needed in order to break that hold and live a fulfilling life. A forced, statewide atheism was, unsurprisingly, a very significant part of official, Marx-influenced Soviet ideology.

You Respect Jesus? But Not Us?

Elizabeth repeats her concerns over Paige's upbringing to Philip—who is also concerned, though far more reserved about it. She would rather risk Paige getting into hard drugs or alcohol than trust someone else with her mind ("Yousaf"). But, maybe we should say that Philip is *usually* more reserved about it than Elizabeth. It's hard to forget his reaction in "Martial Eagle" after finding out that Paige donated $600 she had been saving to the church, lying and disrespecting her parents in the process—giving the *church* a bit more *reward* than seems reasonable: "You respect Jesus? But not us?" he yells, after tearing pages out of her Bible and throwing it against the floor.

The episode ends with Philip going to the Reed Street Church—dressed in all black, with gloves that look perfect for some late-night strangling—and confronting Pastor Tim. But, "I want you to stay away from my daughter" is all we get out of Philip—which is surprising, really, given Tim's poorly chosen response: "The best thing you can do for her is find a way to deal with your anger" (doesn't he know you never tell an angry person to calm down!?).

But Tim is right: Philip is definitely angry. And maybe those *est* lectures really *are* helping him deal with that anger. But, Philip is no teenager; *est* isn't going to break his Soviet allegiance, even if it's a little hokey and seemingly *illusory*. Paige, on the other hand, is a prime candidate for this sort of illusion, following Dawson's outline, and Elizabeth *won't* let her "be indoctrinated by the church" ("Stealth"). "They get them when they're young," she reminds Philip. "It's what they do. You know it's what they do." But, are *they* the only ones who do that sort of thing?

When I Was Called, My Mother Didn't Hesitate

In various flashbacks we're able to see Elizabeth's and Philip's KGB recruitments. Elizabeth was recruited at the age of sixteen ("Baggage"), officially joined the KGB at seventeen ("Gregory"), was paired up with Philip at nineteen ("Pilot"), and arrived in the United States with him at twenty-two ("Gregory"). Sixteen years old is very young to be dealing with serious politics—giving up the only life you've ever known and risking it for the new one every single day. It's unlikely that most sixteen-year-olds—especially those living under the type of regime established by the Soviet Union—dealt with those politics all on their own.

Paige isn't that much different in age when she is first *recruited* either (around thirteen or fourteen years old). But, the point is that, while they're obviously in opposition to each other, Paige's Christianity and her parents' Soviet ideology both depict instances of indoctrination. With that in mind, it's easy to catch some of the irony in Elizabeth's rant earlier in this chapter as well.

It's no secret that indoctrinating adolescents and young adults is far more successful than attempting to mold the minds of those who have been around the block a few times. More broadly, as deplorable and morally questionable as things like militant children's armies, disposable children soldiers, and the training of new generations of followers to replace current ones are, they've been a very real part of human history for a long time—from the Nazi Party's Hitlerjugend, the Soviet Union's Young Pioneers, Saddam Hussein's "Lion Cubs," and the Lord's Resistance Army in Africa, to the Islamic State's "Cubs of the Caliphate" and far rightwing Christians such as those depicted in documentaries like *Jesus Camp* (2006).

State or social pressure (sometimes at the threat of violence) often encourages parents to support these types of recruitment efforts as well—something Elizabeth's mother appears to have demonstrated: without even blinking an eye, Elizabeth tells Philip, her mother told her to go and serve her country when she was first approached by the KGB ("Baggage"). But, what if she *had* blinked an eye?

Dawson also points out that when recruitment is successful, it's because opposition was either weak or non-existent.

Paige really didn't have any other options on the table to compete with what had been thrown her way. And Elizabeth's mother didn't *really* have that option either. If there had been room for competition among different ideologies then things may have gone in a much different direction. Maybe Paige would have become a socially engaged Buddhist or Elizabeth a gung-ho capitalist! We'll never know. But, the point is that there are noticeable similarities between the two—both in practice and in conversion. Successful movements are those that offer us a way to fulfill or deal with some sort of deep longing, urge, or troubling issue (sort of like what's going on with Philip and *est*, too). Political and religious movements are notorious for presenting themselves in this way. And sometimes, it's hard to even draw a hard distinction between the two.

Taking Marx's criticisms to heart and purging the old tsarist regime of its ties to the Orthodox Church left a *religious* gap that needed to be filled. The Soviets filled this gap with the cult of personality. Vladimir Lenin (1870–1924) and Joseph Stalin (1878–1953) became objects of veneration. Government ideology gave them larger-than-life qualities, and sanctified their writings. Their actions became parables.

Those leadership cults display features of nationalism and civic pride that are very similar to common understandings of "religion." Building on Jean-Jacques Rousseau's notion of "civil religion," the famous sociologist of religion Robert Bellah has outlined some of these features. According to Bellah, state political systems have symbols, rituals, holidays, admired places and texts, prophets, martyrs, and so on that have *religious* qualities and are a deep part of national and civic identity. The busts and portraits of Lenin we see scattered throughout the Rezidentura (and the lapel pin Nina Sergeevna prized as a Young Pioneer) are subtle indicators of how Soviet leadership cults functioned in this reverential sort of way; it's easy to notice how interchangeable the cross Paige wears around her neck all of a sudden becomes from this perspective.

She's Just Looking in the Wrong Place

Elizabeth knows that she and Paige are alike. "Paige is like me," she tells Philip. "She wants to make a difference in the world. She's just looking in the wrong place" ("Stealth"). When they find out about Center's "second-generation illegals" program, Elizabeth and Philip object. But Elizabeth eventually tells Philip that Paige "does need something. She's looking for something in her life. What if—what if this is it?" (as opposed to the worldview Reed Street is peddling, of course). Elizabeth seems to have forgotten the promise she and Philip made to let their children live their own lives and never let them know who they are. Philip hasn't: "We swore. We swore we would never—It would destroy her," he responds ("Echo").

Elizabeth's more *devout* commitment starts to break down that promise more and more as Center continues to push them to start developing Paige. Recalling that last point in Dawson's outline, we could probably trace the first indication that Paige might warm up to the notion of working with her parents to the end of Season Two. After returning from her nuclear arms protest with the Reed Street Church and Pastor Tim, she passionately declares to her parents how moved she's become by the symbolic level of Jesus's sacrifice: "This moved me. Okay? I mean, this is the whole point of the church. It's not all about just Jesus and the Bible. It's about what he represents. That he was willing to sacrifice himself . . . he was willing to sacrifice himself for the greater good. And that inspires me" ("Echo"). We can imagine that Philip and Elizabeth see themselves sacrificing for the greater good on a daily basis. So, what's so different? Are these congruent ideologies, differing only in specific content but not general aim and form?

Well, there's the more obvious and immediate physical danger associated with Elizabeth and Philip's work that separates the two. Knowing how things panned out with Jared Connors—with him killing his entire family when they got in his way of becoming a KGB agent ("Comrades")—

Elizabeth and Philip can't help but keep that risk in mind, too. Center is obviously aware of this as well. But, the strange thing is that it *is* willing to risk another Jared incident with Paige. "If you bring her into this, anything could happen," Philip lectures Gabriel ("Open House"). Perhaps, Center is also well aware of that fundamental perk of getting them "while they're children": it's much easier than dealing with adults who've already started developing some messy values and worldviews that push them to question those in charge.

Ideologically, She's Open to the Right Ideas

After an entire season of her knowing her parents are Soviet spies, we still don't really know what's going to happen with Paige. Her faith doesn't exactly seem to be unraveling—even if her interest in Reed Street is—but she is starting to show signs of a possible . . . "doctrinal shift," we might say. The everything-is-all-right performance Paige puts on for Tim and Alice, along with the strange, unsolicited "reports" she starts to provide on Matthew Beeman, are arguably instances of her *working* for her parents.

And we can easily link this to some of Elizabeth's initial groundwork, before Paige even finds out about them—like when she takes her to Gregory's old stomping ground ("Born Again"), telling her that their civil rights activism "wasn't always legal, but it was right," and, in full recollection of what moved Paige so deeply about Jesus's sacrifice, that "It was right for the greater good." *They* were some of those "real heroes," in other words.

But, even though Philip isn't too thrilled about the whole thing, he eventually starts to go along with it. Maybe he begins to realize that this truly *is* what Paige needs. Or, maybe, just like Elizabeth, he knows he needs to unquestioningly do whatever his government demands—regardless of whether or not it's in the best interest of his daughter.

But, we can't forget: Paige *is* going to have a choice about whether or not she'll officially cross that doctrinal divide and follow in her parents' footsteps ("Open House"). As Elizabeth indicates, "Ideologically, she's open to the right ideas" ("EST Men"). We'll just have to wait and see if cutthroat socialism and stringent atheism start to look more appealing to her than those "cute boys cooing about Jesus" ("A Little Night Music").

2
Clash of the Faiths

Matthew Brake

People who believe in God always make the worst targets.

—"The Clock"

Philip Jennings utters these words to his wife and KGB deep-cover partner Elizabeth about a woman named Viola, the housekeeper for Secretary of Defense Casper Weinberger. Philip and Elizabeth blackmail Viola into placing a bug inside a clock in Weinberger's office. They infect Viola's son with a virus for which only they have the cure; however, Viola has difficulty following through on her assignment despite the danger to her son's life. Viola is a devout Christian, and through her faith, she finds the strength to temporarily resist Philip's threats even though it would cost her son's life. While she eventually gives in and plants the bug (and later informs the FBI that she did), Philip's words above set the tone for the Jenningses' negative attitude toward religion and their difficult relationship with it throughout the series.

When Faith Comes Too Close to Home

In Season Two, the topic of religion becomes much more entangled in the Jenningses' family life. Their daughter, Paige, meets a girl named Kelli who takes Paige to the Reed Street Church youth group (funny side note: this happens because

Paige was investigating her suspicions about her parents' double life, so her exposure to religion is a little bit their fault, no?).

Paige becomes interested in religion and begins to read the Bible, a fact that she attempts to hide from her mother. Elizabeth, however, finds out, catching Paige in a lie. Angry over Paige's deception, Elizabeth complains to Philip later that the entire consumerist culture in the United States is propped up by religion. Quoting the famous saying from Karl Marx, Elizabeth tells Philip, "Church. Synagogue. That's what's holding it all up. The opiate for the masses" ("A Little Night Music"). She considers religious organizations to be deceptive, stating, "This is what happens. They get them when they're children. They indoctrinate them. With friendship. With songs. With cute boys cooing about Jesus." As far as Paige's parents are concerned, she is "living in a fantasy world" ("Born Again").

Elizabeth and Philip's concerns seem to stem from what they perceive to be a sense of misplaced loyalty on Paige's part because of her Christian faith. When Philip and Elizabeth attend Paige's church for the first time, they discover that Paige has donated all of her savings to the church. Neither of her parents are happy, and in a heated exchange, Philip takes Paige's Bible, begins thumbing through it, and proceeds to become irate, tearing out pages and asking if "this book" told her to lie to them, finally screaming, "You respect Jesus but not us?" ("Martial Eagle").

More concerning for Elizabeth is that Paige's devotion is focused in the wrong place. Over time, she comes to see Paige's commitment to her faith as a sign that Paige simply wants to make a real difference in the world. As she bemoans to Philip, "I wish I could tell her about the real heroes, people who sacrifice themselves for this world, not some stupid children's story about heaven" ("Echo"). For Elizabeth, the cause of Communism and the Motherland is worth living and dying for, and unlike religion, it doesn't require the deception of young, vulnerable minds, as her conversation with Philip indicates concerning Paige's conversion: "We know who we are. We have values. But these kids, what do they know?" ("A Little Night Music").

The Cause Comes Too Close to Home

As Paige explores her growing faith, a tragedy strikes Philip and Elizabeth. The Jenningses are forced to confront worries about the safety of their own family when two of their friends and fellow spies, Emmett and Leanne Connors, along with their daughter, are found dead in a hotel room with only their teenage son, Jared, left behind as a survivor. Throughout the season, Philip and Elizabeth believe that the man responsible for the deaths is Andrew Larrick, a Navy SEAL officer. He had been a KGB informant for Emmett and Leanne, who had been blackmailing him because he is gay.

As the season ends, Philip and Elizabeth discover that not Larrick, but the Connorses' son Jared, killed them. The Soviet government had targeted and recruited him for a new initiative involving second-generation illegals. First-generation illegals like Philip and Elizabeth are indeed able to effectively infiltrate the US and ingrain themselves in the cultural fabric enough to blend in and perform covert operations, while remaining above suspicion; however, the backstories of the first generation aren't fool-proof and might contain holes in their histories that would rouse suspicion should they ever apply for a high-ranking job in the US government. The kids of these illegals, being natural-born citizens, would lack the holes in their backgrounds and would have the potential to infiltrate the highest offices of the country.

It turns out that Jared killed his parents, not because of orders, but because they discovered that the Center recruited him, which led to a heated argument. In the heat of the moment, he killed his family. Adding fuel to Jared's passion was the fact that Jared had actually fallen in love with Kate, his KGB recruiter and handler, who had promised that they would be able to be together. Discussing the situation with Claudia, their former handler, Philip and Elizabeth learn about the second-generation program, and to their horror, they learn that the Center wants to recruit Paige.

Let's rework a quote from Elizabeth earlier and see how apt it is for this situation, while altering some of the words: "This is what happens. They get them when they're children. They indoctrinate them . . . with cute [girls] cooing about [Communism and the Motherland]."

This interchangeability of terms is weird, right?

The Separation of Church and State or the Migration of the Sacred

The twentieth-century political theorist (and sort-of Nazi-ish) Carl Schmitt is famous for having said in his *Political Theology: Four Chapters on the Concept of Sovereignty* that the modern state relies on theological concepts that have been secularized. In a way, even purely secular politics might be thought of as religious in nature. Typically, people in the Western world think of religion and politics as being two separate spheres, which need to stay very far away from each other; however, Schmitt's quote indicates that they might have a closer relationship. Then again, Schmitt did dabble with Nazism, and that might hurt the credibility of any argument that draws upon Schmitt's ideas.

Thankfully, there are also non-Nazis we can turn to as we think about the relationship between politics and religion. Simon Critchley (not a Nazi) challenges the idea that history has proceeded from a superstitious, religious past to a secular and enlightened modern age. This understanding has been referred to by scholars as the "secularization thesis." Instead, Critchley claims that the changing of political forms in history actually represents a transformation of the sacred. In other words, the sacred has changed forms but not gone away.

In speaking of the sacred, we are talking about that mysterious "something" that seems to require our loyalty, devotion, and respect rather than our questions, suspicion, and interrogation. Another word for the sacred might be "the holy." It is something that shouldn't be touched, a foundation that gives us the motivation to uphold whatever institution or cause to which we give our loyalty. It is a sacred fiction or narrative that guides our social lives. Regarding the relationship between religion and politics, William Cavanaugh (also not a Nazi) describes the relationship as a migration where the responsibility for the care of the holy is transferred to the state from the church, which almost makes it sound like a bad custody battle. Being the caretaker of the sacred or the holy then allows the state to demand our sole devotion and loyalty to its narrative. Instead of being committed to a religious narrative like Paige "making herself clean for Jesus Christ," the state calls on us to adhere to its sacred narrative and tells us to consider its importance above all else. More than religious institutions. More than family. More than personal conscience.

Center Comes First

When Philip and Elizabeth confront Claudia about the second-generation program and learn that Center wants Paige, they make it clear to her that Paige joining their ranks is not an option. After all, she is *their* daughter. Claudia's response, however, is quite telling if we keep in mind the idea that the sacredness of the state legitimizes its demand for our sole loyalty: "Paige is your daughter, but she's not just yours. She belongs to the Cause. And to the world. We all do. You haven't forgotten that have you?" ("Echo"). They have orders to recruit Paige. If a viewer is paying close enough attention, they can begin to see the cracks in Philip and Elizabeth's logic concerning religion as juxtaposed to the operations of Center.

The need for choice played a strong role in Elizabeth's critique of religion. She feared that religion didn't give teenagers a choice. Instead, religion seeks to manipulate youths into giving their full devotion to religious faith. Elizabeth and Philip supposedly made a free choice to join Center, and they "knew" what their values were. Surely Center wouldn't use the manipulative methods of religion to encourage the young to join their ranks.

Philip and Elizabeth request Claudia's transfer and are reunited with their former handler Gabriel. Paige's recruitment remains a source of friction, particularly between him and Philip. Philip reminds Gabriel that he and the Jenningses made a choice to join Center, but Gabriel assures Philip that Paige will have a choice. However, we can't help getting the impression that it is the type of choice that religious heretics have been given in the past between getting burned at the stake or submitting to the will of a religious institution.

While still debating who is manipulating his own daughter, Philip receives one of his most disturbing assignments: to seduce a fifteen-year-old girl in order to bug her father's briefcase. Recognizing Philip's lack of ease with the assignment, Gabriel attempts to comfort him while also reminding Philip of his priorities: "When people's lives intersect with our operations, it's the operation that's crucial. And when the person involved is so young. You have a conscience, Philip. There's nothing wrong with that. But conscience can be dangerous" ("Salang Pass"). The sacred call of Center sometimes requires you to give beyond what your conscience can bear. As Gabriel tells Philip, "You should trust the organization" ("Do Mail Robots Dream of Electric Sheep?"). Don't question. Just believe.

Boys Cooing about Jesus

Center wants Philip to sleep with the girl, Kimmy, in order to ensure that he will have long-term access to her father's briefcase, Philip delays having sex with Kimmy. One night after Kimmy gets out of the shower, it seems like there's no way out for Philip. He must sleep with Kimmy for the sake of the operation until he has a moment of inspiration and tells her that he likes her, but he can't sleep with her because he has gone back to church. He expands on this story later and tells her that he just found out that he has a son (that part is true), and instead of sleeping together, he asks Kimmy to pray with him. After they do, she responds, "That was amazing" ("Born Again").

Having been raised in Christian youth groups with horny teenage couples sublimating their sexual desires through spiritual activity with each other, I am not at all surprised that this worked, and I think it is quite a viable long-term strategy for Philip. The irony here is not lost on anybody. Philip becomes one of the features that he and Elizabeth criticized about the church: a cooing boy talking about Jesus.

Understanding modern political history as a migration of the sacred as opposed to a strict separation of the religious/ non-religious or sacred/secular allows us to ask the question concerning modern political structures: if something acts like a religion, what really distinguishes it from religion? The sacred never went away. It just found a new home.

America and the Sacred

Some readers are probably thinking, "Well sure, you can say that the Soviet Union demanded a similar kind of loyalty that religion demands. Both are irrational and tyrannical. Damn Christians, damn commies!" But is the US really so different? Even if we remove Christianity's complex relationship with politics in this country, we're still left with tokens of the sacred.

In the very first episode of the show, I was struck by the irony of Philip reciting the pledge of allegiance at a school function with his son ("Pilot"). As Critchley notes, political affiliation requires truth, not a proposition but an act of "being true to" or fidelity, and truth requires religion or "a framework of ritual" in which people can believe. Even those who don't believe need this framework for practicable political solidarity. Remove traditional conceptions of religion from politics, but effective politics will still have religion. The sacred has changed, but it hasn't gone away. It is present in the pledge of allegiance as a way to socially form a community around an understanding of the sacred. This is equally true for the atheist and the theist.

On an undercover op posing as a security official, Elizabeth interviews a man named Adam Dorwin. She asks him the following question, "Do you believe in the American system of government?" ("Comint"). This is an interesting way to phrase the question, isn't it? Would there even be a way to convey the same idea without using such sacredly charged works like "believe," "devoted," or "committed." It seems politics is unable to work without a basic level of faith.

Nina, Love, and the Sacred State

One of the most tragic figures in *The Americans* is Nina Krilova. Caught smuggling items back home on the black market, Stan Beeman turned Nina into a double agent for the FBI. Over time, Stan and Nina had an affair, Stan falling heavily in love with her. However, Stan betrays her trust by killing one of her friends and fellow agents, and she becomes a triple agent working for the Russian Rezidentura and developing a relationship with one of her colleagues, Oleg Burov.

Despite Nina coming clean with her superiors, they give her a mission to retrieve sensitive material using her relationship with Stan. Should she fail, she will be sent to the Gulag. Stan comes very close to betraying his country, but in the end, he leaves a note, "Tell Nina I'm sorry" ("Echo"). Nina is sent to the Gulag, but that doesn't stop Oleg from attempting to persuade his father, the Minister of Railways, to ensure her release. Oleg's father considers it, but only if his son will return home. Ultimately, Nina is executed.

As she told her cellmate in prison, "In America, I had two lovers. One Communist. One capitalist . . . but at the end, they loved their countries more than they loved me" ("Born Again"). Such is the loyalty that the sacred demands!

Which Sacred?

As long as we live in political communities with others, it seems impossible to escape the influence of the sacred. Philip and Elizabeth thought their own government was above the tactics of religious organizations, but apparently, being non-religious isn't enough. In fact, that may not even be possible, for Critchley notes that any politics that actually works seems to require a religious or sacred dimension.

But there are so many sacred narratives out there. How do we know which is the correct one?

Here, the thinkers we've looked at might not be helpful in helping us make a determinate decision. Schmitt, as I point out, was kind of, sort of Nazi-ish. Cavanaugh believes that the answer to the question of the sacred lies in what he calls the Eucharistic politics of the church. Critchley believes in an unstable "infinite demand of love." So there are many, many ideas of the sacred ranging from the very specific and sometimes scary to the vague and sentimental.

Or maybe the most we can hope for from the sacred in this life is that it is an indication that there is something more, something worthy of our devotion, even if its specific nature remains an open question for us for the indefinite future.

3
Freedom with Benefits

KEVIN GUILFOY

In the episode "March 8, 1983," Philip and Elizabeth Jennings watch Ronald Reagan denounce the Soviet Union as "the focus of evil in the modern world." In June 1987 Reagan stood in Berlin and demanded "Mr. Gorbachev! Tear down this wall!" In 1989 the Berlin wall fell and took the Soviet Union with it. Elizabeth and Philip are working for the losing side as a new world order is born.

In the 1950s no one would have predicted that the Soviet Union would collapse under internal economic pressure without a shot being fired between the US and the Red Army. Back then there was fear that the Soviet planned economy worked. The Soviet system claimed to provide economic prosperity for ordinary people while only "hurting" the rich. In the West, *laissez-faire* capitalism had done the opposite. The Soviets could manufacture more steel, produce more grain, and mobilize more soldiers than the West.

The Soviets also *claimed* greater political and economic equality. Every schoolchild, East and West, knew about Jim Crow. Nina tells Stan "They tell us terrible things. You oppress people" ("The Walk-In"). The truth about the Gulags was only rumor until the 1970s. Children of the 1990s wonder why anyone would be a Communist. But the characters in *The Americans* are children of the 1950s. From their perspective market capitalism had led to depression and world war. By many accounts Soviet-style socialism was better.

The West responded with the Kuznets curve. Theoretically, poverty and inequality grow in the early years of capitalist development but eventually taper off. In the long run everyone benefits. But, as Keynes pointed out, in the long run we are all dead. The defenders of capitalism had one thing to fall back on: freedom.

Milton Friedman argued that freedom is an absolute value and should never be sacrificed for utilitarian or political benefit. F.A. Hayek argued that compromising freedom for social benefit sends us down *The Road to Serfdom*. These thinkers, and others, framed a stark choice. We could choose the freedom of capitalist markets and accept the resulting poverty and inequality; or we could choose socialist control and more equal prosperity. They chose freedom. Soviets chose prosperity. In the larger cultural narrative, Soviets learned America was a place of inequality, poverty, and racism. Americans eventually learned Russia was a totalitarian nightmare. This is the world Elizabeth and Philip Jennings, and Stan Beeman grew up in.

Economic freedom differs from other freedoms and is often overlooked. Freedom of thought or conscience can't be taken away from you. You can be punished for believing something but your ability to believe it can't be removed. Freedom of speech is slightly different. You can be prevented from saying or publishing what you believe. Freedom of thought combined with freedom of speech make the core of political freedom.

For Friedman and Hayek, without economic freedom, political freedom is meaningless. The great Enlightenment thinkers who defined political freedom had one thing in common. They were all rich. They could support themselves as they exercised their political freedoms. The options are different without economic freedom. A believer in capitalism in the Soviet Union can think what he wants. The government might even allow him to say what he wants. So what? Where would he get money to print his subversive pamphlets? Which state-owned industry would hire him? Which state-owned printer would take his order? By contrast, at the height of Joe McCarthy's communist witch-hunts, the highest paid writers in Hollywood were blacklisted communists. The freedom to sell your labor and engage in trade provides the liberty to engage in free thought and speech.

As the Soviets see it, Paige does not have economic freedom. Claudia is explicit about Center's attitude, "Paige is your daughter, but she is not just yours. She belongs to the cause, and to the world. You haven't forgotten that, have you?" ("Echo"). Paige is not a free individual at liberty to choose her life's path. Paige may find value and meaning in the life of a spy. But if she doesn't she is not free to follow her parents into travel planning. In hindsight becoming a travel agent is a terrible career choice for a teenager in 1983. The internet will have killed that business just as she turns forty, making her unemployable. Russian spy, on the other hand, is now a growth industry. Center may have accurately predicted employment trends, but Paige is still not free.

"March 8, 1983"

On this date Ronald Reagan delivered a speech that reshaped the moral framework of the Cold War. Far from being out-produced, the West was overflowing with consumer goods. The crimes of Joe McCarthy's Communist witch-hunt could not possibly counterbalance what was now known about the Gulags, slave labor camps, and the forced starvation of millions of peasants. Reagan's speech acknowledged America's history of racism and inequality. With typical naïve optimism he declared those days over. The West now had freedom and prosperity. The Soviet Union had neither. Philip and Elizabeth are pulled out of their ordinary life by Reagan's characterization of the Soviet Union:

> Let us be aware that while they preach the supremacy of the state, declare its omnipotence over individual man, and predict its eventual domination of all peoples on the Earth, they are the focus of evil in the modern world.

Philip and Elizabeth turn to each other and seem to realize that the nature of their war has just changed. Reagan continues to identify the source of Evil:

> it is conceived and ordered (moved, seconded, carried, and minuted) in clear, carpeted, warmed, and well-lighted offices, by quiet men with white collars and cut fingernails and smooth-shaven cheeks who do not need to raise their voice.

The clean-shaven bureaucrat was supposed to be the symbol of efficiency and order. His job was organizing the system that took from everyone according to their ability and gave to everyone according to their need. In Soviet practice, the dominion over the individual by the clean shaven bureaucrat in his committee meeting had become the embodiment of evil.

Nina is quickly and cleanly executed by a clean-shaven clerk, at his desk, after a perfectly official procedure ("Chloramphenicol"). This method of execution was seen as a humane way of dispensing with people, and is described in numerous sources from the Soviet era. When we finally see Philip's son, he is in a mental hospital. His mental illness? Doubts about the war in Afghanistan ("Persona Non Grata"). The complete subjugation of the individual to the state is finally clear.

By contrast, in Reagan's West we could have it all. There was no longer a trade-off between prosperity and freedom. People who had defended freedom, warts and all, in the 1950s became market triumphalists in the 1980s. Friedman and Hayek became court-philosophers to Ronald Reagan and Margaret Thatcher as these two led the West from a market economy to a market society.

There is no disputing the fact that the Western economy brilliantly provided consumer goods. Gabriel and Claudia, meeting in a diner, are confronted by twenty different kinds of omelet and twelve kinds of hamburger. Overwhelmed by abundance they try to order tea only to be confronted with Earl Grey, or English Breakfast or . . . "Just tea!" They scream. "This is the brilliance of America" Claudia mutters ("I Am Abassin Zadran").

But this is brilliant! Twenty types of omelet seems strange to me because I only like type 9—extra bacon. Someone else likes type 3—veggie. Someone likes each one of the available omelets. If they like omelet 21 there is another diner eager to have their business. This is what Friedman celebrates and Hayek predicted. An organized government program to provide omelets could not provide the abundance of options available in a market where each person can pay a price corresponding to their desire for a particular omelet. This only seems stupid and wasteful because we do not share the desire for the nineteen other omelets. The West has come a long way since Henry Ford promised consumers that they could have whatever color car they want as long as it was black.

The benefits of prosperity are impossible to ignore. The Western economy had provided the average person with a material standard of living higher than at any other point in human history. The visual contrast between the Jenningses' suburban home and over-crowded badly-wired, plaster-peeling tower block where Philip's son visits his grandfather is enough to drive that home.

Drowning in Omelets and Tea

Abundance can bring problems. A market economy can overwhelm people with the variety of consumer choices. But is this good? I will unequivocally defend the abundance of omelets. Sure, breakfast with someone who can't make up their mind is hard. A market economy subjects us to the torture at the hands of the indecisive and the wishy-washy. There are always tradeoffs. But what about cell phone plans? Or health insurance?

Developing the ideas of Herbert Spencer, Ha-Joon Chang argues that our market society provides too many options for us to rationally evaluate and choose between them. We need to understand and evaluate too much information to be well informed. When we are presented with twenty different options of phone plan we just don't understand all the relevant technological matters. We cannot evaluate the truth of claims we cannot understand. So we adopt intellectual or emotional shortcuts. I pick the company that has funny commercials. The consequence of choosing a phone plan badly is more severe than choosing the wrong omelet. That's why people are much happier with their local diners than they are with their cell plans. Before the Affordable Care Act the health insurance market provided a dizzying array of options, coverages, and prices. The consequence of choosing the wrong health insurance can be catastrophic.

Chang does not argue that people are short-sighted, ignorant, or simply prone to bad decisions. It's just that we have a finite amount of intellectual capacity. When confronted with so many options we are eventually tapped out. We lose the capacity to engage in the informed voluntary exchanges that are the moral foundation of economic freedom. No one reads the full description of twenty different types of omelets. They look at three or four and select from that edited list. They are then disappointed when their companion orders something that that didn't see on the menu. With omelets we get over it. When they try to eat their friend's omelet and need health insurance that's a different matter.

The shift to a market society does more than just provide an abundance of consumer goods. A market society assigns a market or monetary value to everything. In a market society all values, all culture, and all social conventions are subject to market-based voluntary exchange. The depth of a person's personal values is measured in how much a person is willing to pay. Friedman has hope that racism and bigotry can be eliminated in a market society simply because they are expensive. (Also because even the most despised minority is free to sell their labor and engage in trade.) Sure, some people may choose to pay a premium for their racism and bigotry. But this is their own free choice and they are literally paying the price for it. We can hope that the price would be too high. Any perceived unfairness is not the result of social structures, it is the natural result of voluntary exchange between free people. In a market society the results of a voluntary exchange between free people is by definition just.

I'll Have an Order of Jesus and a Side of Marx. To Go

When the logic of supply and demand seeps into areas traditionally thought of as matters of ethical value not monetary value, the market society becomes even harder to navigate. The desire to find value and meaning in the world becomes a shopping trip. Henry buys video games. Paige buys religion. Philip test drives the values of a market society. Elizabeth and Stan stick to the secular civic virtue of their youth.

Agent Stan Beeman is a sad case. He lives the collapse of the civic and social order he grew up with. He rents some *est*, but in the end he sticks to the old values. Stan is ill suited to a market society. He does what he has been always told is his duty, and he expects to live in social and material comfort. From Stan's perspective the market provides consumer goods. But moral values should be outside the market and not subject to the innovative forces of creative destruction.

People like Stan expect to have a reasonable standard of living, in a community of people who share their values. When those social values are shaped by market forces instead of the other way around the grounding truths that provide meaning to people's lives are lost. They can be replaced, but it's hard for a person to see their core values as the equivalent of omelet 9. Extra bacon is good, but it is not a foundational truth on which to build your life. At this point in his life Stan is lost. His wife has left him. He has no relationship with his son. He expected his wife and family to have similar devotion to the old civic virtues he grew up with. They have freely chosen other values.

The Americans is a show about family, and family involves children. But what are the values involved in choosing to have children? For Stan, having children is almost a duty.

It is just what he was expected to do. For Philip and Elizabeth having children is a duty also. They have a duty to do everything that "normal" Americans do. Normal Americans, like Stan, have children. Things are different in a market society. Friedman describes having children as just one of many ways people can choose to spend disposable income. Some people buy boats. Some people buy kids. The depth and meaning of the social purpose Stan attaches to having children is lost when children are just another lifestyle accessory.

These children, Paige and Henry are raised in this market society. In an attempt to blend in and appear normal they have been swept along in the dominant social culture of their time. Henry loses himself in video games and movies. He is a person who doesn't really seek values or meaning. He is happy with shiny things that bring him short-term pleasure. Elizabeth is right when she tells Paige that Henry may never be engaged enough to wonder about his parents' real identities. Henry has a bit of Philip in him.

Paige shops for meaning and value. The whole "Will she, won't she?" drama with Paige is just a trip to the moral shopping mall. She rejects consumer culture. Stan's American civic virtues have lost their appeal. She is shopping for the right fit. Elizabeth's revolutionary values are an option. She buys Jesus. Paige has selected a value system from the market, but what has she bought? She is baptized with the claim that becoming a member of the dominant religious and cultural group in the most powerful nation on Earth is her "most defiant act of protest yet!" ("Baptism of Fire"). She has purchased a sense that she is a difference maker in the world. She writes letters to the president and goes to organized protests. And now she is baptized. "In your face powers of evil." I was Paige's age in 1983. I bought a Ramones T-shirt and a pair of biker boots. We both got a sense of purpose at an acceptable cost.

Elizabeth is mortified. Full confession, before I became a punk rocker I also joined a Protestant youth group. To the best of my knowledge my parents were not Soviet spies but they were just as upset. They were afraid I would be lured away from "the responsibility and commitment of Catholicism to easy, hippy, feel-good, Jesus." Elizabeth feels the same way. She deeply feels the sense of sacrifice and commitment that comes from her commitment to the Cause. She has devoted her life to fighting against a society that allows this choice. But her anger is not just because she is a Communist. In his own way Stan is fighting against a market society too. For these two, values are not a choice.

Elizabeth is firmly committed to the secular values she grew up with. Unlike Stan she is not home to watch that world crumble. She gets to watch her enemy slip into a culture of vacuous, easy consumerism. But she'll be damned if it gets her daughter. She tells Philip: "You and I, we know who we are. We have values. But these kids? What do they know? We're failing them." They are failing to help the kids stand up to American culture, the distractions, the consumerism, and especially the Christianity ("A Little Night Music"). Elizabeth is fighting for the revolution, and she's fighting to not lose Paige to America.

Philip, on the other hand, sees the American glass as half full of good beer. From the very beginning Philip is drawn to American material prosperity. He questions whether it is not time to defect and enjoy life ("Pilot"). He buys himself an icon of 1980s superficial affluence: a bitchin' Camaro. Elizabeth does not approve:

PHILIP: Is it the car?

ELIZABETH: [*smug half-smile*] I just want you to be happy.

PHILIP: [*shrug*] Come on Elizabeth. Don't you enjoy any of this? Sometimes? This house, those clothes, all those beautiful shoes?

ELIZABETH: [*pulls face and sighs*]

PHILIP: It doesn't make you bad at what you do, it just makes you a human being. Don't you ever like it?

ELIZABETH: That's not why I'm here.

PHILIP: But don't you ever like it?

ELIZABETH: We have to live this way for our job, for our cover. Five miles from here there are people who are living . . .

PHILIP: Do you like it?

ELIZABETH: You know how I grew up. It's nicer here. It's easier here. It's not better. [*walks away*] ("New Car")

This is an ongoing tension between the two. Philip sees the benefits of economic freedom and consumer culture. In a scene immediately following this exchange Elizabeth watches a CIA officer slowly strangle a young pie-eyed revolutionary, Lucia. Lucia is an obvious representation of Paige. Elizabeth pimps her out and sells her life for the CIA agent's co-operation. Elizabeth is fully committed to the Cause, undistracted by shiny cars or shiny ideals. When Elizabeth wavers, it's from exhaustion not temptation. Philip is tempted from the beginning.

In their fight for influence over Paige Elizabeth takes Paige to the impoverished neighborhood where Gregory lived. She introduces Paige to the depth and sacrifice of meaningful commitment to enduring values. She does not mention Lucia. Elizabeth has done more than march for the Cause.

To win Paige's favor, Philip lets her drive the Camaro. Why even pretend about sacrifice? This is an awesome car.

For himself, Philip seeks meaning from *est* trainers in hotel ballrooms (see Chapter 6 in this volume). Philip is attracted to finding meaning and purpose as an individual and he is shopping for options. Like Paige he is looking to actualize himself in a meaningful way at a cost he is comfortable with. Unlike the traditional values of Stan or Elizabeth, *est* is a product marketed to individuals. The *est* training provides a return on your investment in you. It offers a value system that can be purchased in discrete units adaptable to your individual desires. We might be tempted to see Philip as shallow compared to Elizabeth. But I think this is wrong.

Freedom with Benefits

Philip is just more open to the shopping mall of values. When we remember Lucia and think of Paige, I'm not sure that Elizabeth should be praised for her commitment to core values no matter what.

4
Is Elizabeth Free to Choose?

CHARLENE ELSBY AND ROB LUZECKY

From the beginning of *The Americans,* Philip expresses his interest in giving up life as a spy. Philip has kids and likes stuff, and he's grown a little distant from his roots in Mother Russia. He doesn't see why he and Elizabeth should continue living as if they hate America when they seem to be doing just fine living in America.

Paige, meanwhile, is expressing too many American values for Elizabeth's liking—she's going to church, giving her money away, and confiding in Pastor Tim as if he weren't just some misguided American who uses just another form of deluded dedication to a universal in order to negate his own freedom. But is Elizabeth's continuing dedication to the cause a result of her own free will?

In the ever-increasing body of literature on the topic, philosophers have questioned whether the debate over free will and determinism even makes any sense. For example, David Hume thought that if we just defined our terms accurately, we would find there is no debate at all. The two terms, "free will" and "determinism" are defined relative to one another and, if asked the right questions, a lot of people will assert that they believe absolutely in *both*.

If you ask someone if they believe everything has a cause, they will agree. At the same time, if you ask someone if they believe that they make choices, they also agree. So where's the debate, exactly? The question comes down to what the definitions of these terms are, and whether the things they describe can exist at the same time. (It seems that they can.)

So perhaps we *are* asking the wrong questions. Perhaps a better question is what constitutes the "free" part of free will? There are several ways of conceiving of freedom of the will, and Elizabeth Jennings exemplifies a kind of radical freedom in the face of constant pressure to conform—a freedom that *is* just the human capacity to recognize what comes next in the chain of causality and then to reject it outright. Elizabeth's rejection of her husband's suggestion that they give up on everything they believe in demonstrates her authentic dedication to a personal ideal. In short, Elizabeth embodies everything the existentialist would like to be—she consistently enacts radical freedom in the face of a society that would have you sit back, relax, and buy another sofa.

The Limits of Freedom

The philosophical debate on the limits of freedom strays far from the discussion we've all heard about on the news in relation to American politics. Elizabeth herself derides the American notion of freedom. Discussions abound as to what freedoms people are willing to give up in the name of freedom—the freedom to correspond privately, for instance. These abstract freedoms exist on a level far above the basic, necessary freedom Elizabeth has in her relation to the world. The way we use the word "free" is various and, through careful analysis, we should be able to pick out this more basic level of freedom that we both admire and fear in Elizabeth Jennings.

The US Constitution, for instance, guarantees the American people several sorts of freedom. The freedom of speech, the freedom to bear arms, and all such freedoms that American citizens take as foundational values to their society, connote an abstract sort of freedom that is guaranteed in the legal sense, but not necessarily in the more basic, fundamental sense of "freedom." Someone may have freedom of speech, but that doesn't necessarily mean that any individual is necessarily *completely free* to speak their minds whenever they so please. People whose jaws are wired shut do not seem to be able to speak as freely as others, nor can people without tongues. That kind of freedom, instead of legal or political freedom, indicates some kind of *physical* freedom.

According to Aristotle's concept of voluntariness, any kind of act that originates due to us moving our own body parts is a voluntary act. At the same time, we can recognize that all sorts of actions are constrained by all sorts of limitations, and we can base a sliding scale of freedom loosely on the kind of limitations imposed upon our freedoms. At the basic Aristotelian level, you are free to do anything your body is capable of doing. That is a physical (some might say biological) sort of freedom, the constraints on which are supplied by the specifics of your physical form. It is possible for some, but not others, to touch their toes, for instance. It is impossible for humans to fly without the aid of some machine, on the other hand.

I am also physically not free to move my body from Russia to America without, in the course of traveling, also traversing all of the space in between the two countries. The human form allows us all sorts of freedoms—the freedom (for most) to move our legs to walk from one place to another, use our hands to grapple with objects, and yell at people we don't like.

Limitations on our physical freedom tend to come in the form of constraints. When Nina sends money back home and is imprisoned, the Russian government is limiting her physical freedom. At the same time, her physicality is not *completely* limited; she's still free to walk from one end of the cell to the other. Nina's lie detector test is an interesting example of physical freedom, because the test is supposed to measure precisely *involuntary* responses. But by engaging in a certain amount of training, Nina is able to subject these so-called involuntary responses to her will, and by doing so, the definition of freedom shifts to include, specifically, her voluntary control over her heart rate.

Open-Minded

Another sort of freedom would be the psychological freedom. It seems that some people are more "open-minded" than others. Elizabeth, for instance, is not open-minded to Paige's insistence that she just give the church a chance. By giving the church a chance, what Paige means is that Elizabeth should consider the possibility that perhaps the Pastor is not an evil bastard set out to indoctrinate her daughter and to enslave her under the dictates of Christianity.

Does Elizabeth have the psychological freedom to do so? We believe yes, she does. Elizabeth has freely considered and rejected the idea that her only hope for happiness on Earth is Jesus. Paige, on the other hand, does not have all of the information she needs to make an informed decision regarding her place within the church and within her family. Elizabeth recognizes this constraint on Paige's psychology, and pressures Philip to let her fill Paige in, to give her all of the information she needs to make an *informed* decision. A limit on psychological freedom, then, is the amount of information we have when we consider possibilities and attempt to make informed decisions. (Aristotle agrees that *ignorance* is a possible source of non-voluntary actions.)

And then there are *social* freedoms. There are the considerations that come into play when we takes into account *other people*. According to Jean-Paul Sartre's play, *No Exit*, "Hell is other people", and other people certainly do limit our freedoms. You might consider yourself physically and psychologically free to decide to walk outside without pants—after all, cats do it all the time, and they seem pretty on the ball—but you will quickly find yourself socially limited.

It's not a physical or psychological limitation that prevents Young Hee's husband Don from sleeping with Patty. He has functional genitals, and she's hot. But in addition to physical and psychological freedom, there is a kind of social freedom that makes it incredibly shameful for him to do so. Don is, therefore, not *socially* free to bang Russian spies and also maintain a healthy marriage with Young Hee. Social and cultural limitations to freedom are closely related—the idea of marriage (cultural) prevents Don from freely engaging in extramarital affairs, but the real effect of his flouting this limitation is that *his particular marriage* would collapse in the face of his perceived transgression.

There are also the specific freedoms we are afforded (and denied) due to a law or political dictate. Elizabeth's and Philip's arranged marriage isn't *illegal* in America, but it is against the norm. Therefore, they must come up with some sort of story for how they met, fell in love, had children, and opened a travel agency together. It is illegal, on the other hand, for them to have assumed the identities of Elizabeth and Philip Jennings in order to engage in missions in America collecting information to report back to Russia. This additional limitation sometimes blends with the social—people often try to make things illegal that are against their personal values. Sometimes, there's a clearer distinction between the cultural and the political. It is culturally forbidden to engage in anti-American dialogue with your children over their school assignments, but it is within the limits of political freedom—there is no official system in place to forbid such an act. There is an official system in place to prevent Elizabeth from sending plans for a submarine propeller system back to Russian authorities.

Elizabeth constantly defies all sorts of limitations to freedom. She does so because, in spite of the pressures against her to give in to the American way of life, and in spite of the fact that she has very little information coming in from her homeland, she consistently makes the psychologically free choice to continue in the mission, follow it through, and everything else be damned.

Elizabeth the American

Elizabeth Jennings is constantly vigilant to discern possible threats against her political freedom. She disdains the American people for either explicitly or implicitly giving up their freedom to think for themselves, work for themselves, and on the existentialist line of thinking, to create themselves. The basic tenet of existentialism is that "Existence precedes essence," and Elizabeth's choices reflect her desire to *create* both herself and the world in which she would like to live. I think she would agree with Simone de Beauvoir, who writes:

> And certainly the proletarian is no more naturally a moral man than another; he can flee from his freedom, dissipate it, vegetate without desire, and give himself up to an inhuman myth; and the trick of 'enlightened' capitalism is to make him forget about his concern with genuine justification, offering him, when he leaves the factory where a mechanical job absorbs his transcendence, diversions in which this transcendence ends by petering out: there you have the politics of the American employing class which catches the works in the trap of sports, 'gadgets', autos, and Frigidaires.

Elizabeth's constant battle with the American system of "sports and Frigidaires" flies in the face of the intentions of her husband. In order to continue her mission, Elizabeth often has to defy social limitations on freedom by defying her husband's wishes. At the same time, she is preserving her own freedom and aims to secure the freedom of entire peoples by doing so. Elizabeth's existence is a constant battle to preserve freedom in the face of persistent limitations. In each of her missions she defies all sorts of these limitations on her freedom, perhaps even the physical.

When we examine Elizabeth's life from the outside, cut into little snippets where we observe her behavior and not, in general, her thought process, it's easy to forget that each and every moment is one that she has to *live through*. To live through all of these moments, in an unfamiliar society, where even her husband doubts her primary motivations, she has to maintain an inflexible stance in the face of constant doubt, derision, and loneliness. Her stubbornness, as we see especially in her interactions with Paige, doesn't seem to be the kind that just maintains some dogma. That is, she doesn't maintain her value system just because she's oblivious or unreceptive to alternative viewpoints. Her stubbornness is instead a kind of resistance. In the face of constant forces attempting to displace her convictions in what is right, she has to constantly, actively resist. With Paige, we can see where she gets a lot of her motivation for doing so. She believes she must raise her children ethically, and to her, ethically means resistant to the temptation to conform to American society.

It's obvious how Elizabeth flouts the law. She's a Russian spy living in America who sometimes murders people and sometimes drugs others, and occasionally she provides the means to transport samples of biological weapons out of the country. These are illegal acts that defy the limitations on her political freedom—she breaks the law, and therefore shoves the boundary between freedom and limitation far away from what politics considers within the realm of acceptable action. To "break" the law, in Elizabeth's case, is to demonstrate its inefficacy to bind her actions to within the acceptable realm. Were there an actual limitation on her freedom, she shouldn't be *able* to poison any college students with an umbrella ("The Clock"), but then *she does*. The sense in which you *can't* just walk around poisoning people doesn't apply to Elizabeth.

Elizabeth also has the opportunity to defy all social conventions. At the same time, she must demonstrate a mastery of them. In order to avoid detection, Elizabeth must adhere to strict social norms that constitute the guidelines for living the American way. We can see how her knowledge of American norms guides her own actions on a regular basis.

On the other hand, her learned mastery of social norms also allows her to manipulate other people into playing the roles she needs them to play. By predicting their conditioned responses to certain behaviors, Elizabeth can control the behavior of others. Don, for instance, couldn't just leave a woman abandoned on a street corner when she calls to ask for help. He also can't deny her request that he come inside and help her move an armoire, because she's just too feminine to do it on her own. He also can't deny her offer of a glass of wine, especially since she's already opened the bottle. Where the situation goes is what Elizabeth always intended—she drugs him and feigns an extramarital sexual encounter—and he can't avoid falling victim to her plan, because of the simple fact that *he doesn't want to be rude*. Elizabeth's knowledge of the limitations on social freedoms is what allows her to so effectively manipulate the behavior of others to fit her plans.

We might think that the hardest part of Elizabeth's job is to avoid psychological limitations. It is all too easy to fall into the American way of thought, when that is what she is constantly exposed to as she goes about their business on a daily basis. It's not a revelation to declare that thinking differently tends to be subject to admonishment by the world at large. Even in the face of her isolation from her family and her home, Elizabeth maintains a belief in the fundamental values for which she believes she's fighting—to maintain the dignity of mankind and to free them from the constraints of American indoctrination.

Elizabeth's mission is closely related to the notion of psychological freedom. While we like to think that we can believe whatever we like, the very concept of "indoctrination" assumes that it's possible to affect someone's thinking to conform to a certain set of beliefs. Philip, especially, as Elizabeth's assigned partner and co-conspirator, is a threat to Elizabeth's psychological freedom. He seems to remind Elizabeth continuously of the alternative scenario to her present life, the one where she simply *gives up* and lives as if American values were correct. She maintains a strict divide between life and thought that must be incredibly difficult to maintain. On the one hand, she must do everything she can to appear as if she believes one thing, while if she actually did, it would constitute a failure of her life's work. This is Albert Camus's idea of the existential crisis—the divorce between a person and their lived life.

Even at the level of physical freedom, Elizabeth often seems to defy expectations. She is, when all is said and done, limited by the same constraints to which all humans are subject. At the same time, the normal human perceives someone of her physical form to be much more limited than she in fact *is*. Elizabeth learns this lesson in "Dinner for Seven," when a couple of intimidating figures threaten her daughter. While these intimidating figures assume Elizabeth is limited by her slight physical form, they then learn something about how far her physical freedom really extends.

A Conflict of Freedoms

Is Elizabeth Jennings the perfect existentialist? Probably not. She does embody the enactment of freedom just for the sake of it that is highly valued by both Jean-Paul Sartre and Simone de Beauvoir. At the same time, there are some other ideals of existentialism that she can't maintain—or can she?

One source of concern is the fact that, according to Sartre, by acting in any particular fashion, we necessarily imply that *everyone* should act that way. Existentialism asserts that there are no absolutes. There are no universal rules, laws, or even conventions. When a person chooses to act they are establishing that action as the thing to do. If Beeman gets a divorce, that necessarily implies that he thinks divorce is just fine. But if everyone were a spy like Elizabeth, the universe as we know it would collapse.

This objection, in the end, doesn't hold up. By spying on the Americans, Elizabeth isn't committing herself to the idea that everyone should be a spy. She is committing herself to the implication that her values can be everyone's values, and the values she holds are ones she definitely thinks other people should have as well. She believes in human dignity, freedom from American indoctrination, freedom from capitalist debt-slavery, and also in the idea that sometimes it's okay to off someone if they get in the way of your mission. When Elizabeth wakes up Paige to clean the refrigerator, she gets an idea of to what extent Elizabeth thinks her values should be universalized.

Another source of concern is that Elizabeth, in the course of ensuring that her own freedom is maintained, occasionally oppresses the freedoms of others. In her attempts to raise her children as she sees fit, she attempts to limit Paige's psychological freedom to believe whatever she likes. More often, we see Elizabeth exercising her freedom to limit the physical freedom of others. One of the most obvious examples of her capacity to limit the freedom of others is when the Jennings kidnap Timoshev ("Pilot") and keep him in the trunk of their car. This example demonstrates what can happen when various sorts of freedoms conflict.

The Jenningses believe that Timoshev was not free to defect as he did. They therefore react by taking away his physical freedom to exist outside of the trunk of their car. Philip attempts to convince Elizabeth that they also have the freedom to defect, as Timoshev did. She explains how Timoshev, during her training, took away her freedom not to be raped, and the situation concludes when Philip decides to take away Timoshev's freedom to continue being alive. Was this the existentialist thing to do? The problem is beside the point—in the grey areas, the existentialist has to decide for everyone what is right, and that's what the Jenningses did.

So should we all aim to be Elizabeth Jennings? Perhaps not in the sense that we should all steal propeller plans on behalf of the Russians. On the other hand, her dedication to individual freedom and her persistence in the face of all those who would aim to limit her, are certainly admirable.

II

Fake Lives

5
Living a Lie

TALIA MORAG

Philip and Elizabeth take themselves to be living a life of pretense and disguise. They are Americans, but they are *really* Russian spies. They are friendly neighbors to Stan Beeman the FBI agent, but they are *really* his mortal enemies. They have friendships as well as love and sexual relationships, but *really* they are just using them to get information. They are married to each other, but their loyalty *really* is to the KGB.

Really?!

This question is one of the main themes that emerges from *The Americans*.

Phillip and Elizabeth have a few identities: their old and repressed Russian identities with their ongoing role as KGB agents known only to their KGB handlers; their American identities as Phillip and Elizabeth, travel agents and parents of Paige and Henry; and multiple other identities that they put on and off as frequently as they switch wigs and disguises, which they present to their unsuspecting sources of information.

Only their Russian identity as KGB agents is their true identity, or at least that is what they think. For example, Philip's name is not Clark (it's actually not Philip either, but I'll call him Philip all the same), he does not work for the FBI, he does not live in his own apartment, he does not have a mother called Alexandra and a sister called Jennifer. These are lies that Philip tells Martha, a secretary in the counter-intelligence division of the FBI, in order to make their relationship possible, a relationship through which he manipulates Martha to give him information.

But Philip doesn't just lie about his name, occupation, biography, and address. He sustains over time an elaborate and all-encompassing lie about what he feels and wants, about his engagement with Martha, about what he does with her, such as sex, breakfasts, watching movies in bed, laughing, talking, and sharing stories and opinions. Philip doesn't just lie with words about his legal status, he needs to pretend that he loves Martha, that he is attracted to her, that he enjoys spending time with her.

This emotional and sexual dimension of the pretense is what makes Martha trust him and steal information for him. If Philip's displayed emotions toward Martha were real, it would be extremely difficult to do his job, perhaps even impossible. So an ideal spy would be able to engage in these activities as role-playing or make-believe, to pretend that his heart is where his mouth is, while keeping those clearly separate.

Has Anyone Ever Really Known Me?

The ideal spy is what philosophers call "instrumentally rational," operating in order to achieve goals. His actions are means to an end—to get information—which is in turn the means to another end, the political and national ideals for which he became a spy in the first place. Those ends are the reasons for his actions, reasons that guide and justify his actions. As the philosopher Elizabeth Anscombe emphasized, when we are instrumentally rational, when we are motivated by reasons, we are aware of those reasons and know what we are doing. And as the philosopher Christine Korsgaard claims, our identity—our values, ideals and self-worth—is implicated in our rationally motivated actions.

Being completely self-aware and feeling great about it may be the psychological ideal some philosophers have for us. But when it comes to spies, knowing what they're doing and why they're doing it would amount to a very lonely life! The ideal spy would have a handler who knows something about his idealistic motivations but very little about his daily activities. And the deceived lovers and friends of that spy would be interacting with him, but without knowing what actually motivates him. A person like that would have no-body in the world who actually knows him.

There is such a person in *The Americans*, William, and he describes his situation on his deathbed as having been "in-visible," like a ghost ("Persona Non Grata"). As the philoso-pher Stanley Cavell often said, to be a person at all we need the acknowledgment of others, we need them to see us as the persons we are, to understand us as we understand our-selves. We all have our secrets, but without *any* such ac-knowledgment, we might as well indeed be ghosts.

At least Elizabeth and Philip have each other. Only a spy can really see another spy, as Stan understands when he reflects on his relationship with Nina, the KGB agent ("A Little Night Music"). But even the relationship Eliza-beth and Philip have with each other suffers from some un-reality. It's only after years of being married with children, that they finally become truly intimate, romantically close to one another. Season One is largely about Elizabeth fi-nally reciprocating Philip's love, about them becoming a real couple after years of a mere "arrangement," as their elder handler Claudia calls it, when she warns Elizabeth against thinking of her marriage as real ("Mutually As-sured Destruction").

Philip and Elizabeth reflect about the reality of their rela-tionship, gradually turning their arrangement into a real mar-riage. But when it comes to their relationships within their other, more temporary, fake identities, they seem ruthlessly unreflective. For most of the first three seasons, they take themselves to be instrumentally rational, engaging with people under pretended identities, as their friends, lovers, even spouses, in order to succeed in their KGB operations. They take themselves, in other words, to live a life of constant betrayal, of using people's emotions and sexual desires in order to get them to do things they would otherwise never do, including stealing information and risking their lives.

Your Body Talks Too

As we watch *The Americans* we get to know Philip and Elizabeth very well, as we do all TV-show characters. We spend a long time with them, learning their mannerisms, their shticks, their tells, and we can see aspects of them they don't see or refuse to see. As the show progresses we learn that Philip and Elizabeth are actually not ideal spies. Nobody is! *The Americans* is implicitly making a philosophical point, that is, that people are not merely instrumentally rational. And who we are is not just about what we think to ourselves in private.

To begin with, it's actually not so easy to separate how we behave from what we think and feel and want, as if our bodies were puppets or marionettes that our desires and goals operate, as the philosopher René Descartes claimed. In fact, many of our daily activities do not require any thinking at all. Walking, riding a bicycle, or simply twiddling our thumbs, are obvious examples of basic skills, actions that we just do unreflectively. But even more complicated actions, such as going through the motions when having meaningless sex, having typical arguments with our partner, or rehearsing old excuses to alleviate a guilty conscience—actions that we often see on *The Americans*—can become a matter of routine.

Acting out of habit does not require reasons. Habits are self-motivating; they have a life of their own. And as the pragmatist philosopher John Dewey said, habits embody our characters. Who we are and what we value is reflected in our habits of action. Dewey goes as far as claiming that it doesn't really matter if our thoughts and beliefs contradict our habits. Who we are is what we do—no matter what it is that we're thinking. We could perhaps accept a more modest claim—we are what we do at least as much as if not more than we are what we think. And if these two identities conflict then we just have to accept, as Freud famously did, that people are not rationally unified, that people live a much more challenging and exciting life of conflict and contradiction.

And so, although Philip is not exactly in love with Martha, he is nevertheless Martha's husband. He spends a lot of time with her, and he knows her very well. In fact, she knows him quite well too. She can tell when he is about to ask her to do something for him ("The Oath"), she knows he has a toupee, and even more surprisingly, Philip hasn't suspected that she knows about it. Philip or Clark visibly appreciates and enjoys that fact, almost finding it sexy ("Operation Chronicles"). Importantly, when Elizabeth acknowledges Clark's independent existence, when she demands to have sex with him—with Clark—she's disappointed to discover that "it's the same" ("Behind the Red Door"). Martha has been having sex with Philip, not with some make-believe person, no matter how disguised Philip is with her.

Does this mean that Philip *is* Clark? That he's in love with Martha even if he thinks he's not? Can he fake it until he makes it? Perhaps this is going too far. But at the very least, as Dewey said, we get attached to our habits. Watching *The Americans* carefully, we can detect quite a few moments where Philip shows us that he feels close to Martha. "You're a kind person, Martha," he tells her sincerely right before he has (has to have) sex with her ("Safe House"). He feels bad, even if only momentarily, when he picks a fight with her instead of spending a "lazy romantic morning" with her ("A Little Night Music"). He's shattered when he offends her so terribly with the tape he faked where he manipulates the words of Martha's boss to say that she is ugly ("New Car"). And there are further examples of this gradually growing attachment. At some point it becomes clear that it is not just that Martha trusts Clark and loves him no matter who he actually is. Philip also trusts Martha, as he tells Elizabeth toward the end of Season Three ("Divestment"), and genuinely cares about what happens to her when she finally gets exposed by the FBI in Season Four ("The Rat").

We Can't Be Emotional to Do This Job

This brings us to a third way in which actions can be motivated. Once Philip is attached to Martha, he's motivated by feelings for her, and does all he can to save her. This is so obviously the case that Elizabeth even thinks Philip is really in love with Martha, that he would want to leave with her to go to Russia ("Travel Agents").

The attachments caused by habits and the emotionally motivated behaviors they engender conflict with the harsh instrumental rationality that was meant to govern these supposedly fake relationships such as the one *Clark* has with Martha. Most of us would find it difficult to exploit and endanger those we care about, no matter how much we care about the ideals that rationalize this exploitation. This difficulty is acknowledged by the KGB. Gabriel, Philip's handler, tells him: "It might be confusing . . . It's difficult for all of us to keep in mind . . . that it's the operation that's crucial" ("Salang Pass").

The head of the FBI counterintelligence division, Gaad, also admits that "things get personal." The advice he gives to Stan is: "You can't forget who they are" ("Covert War"). Who *they* are? What Gaad is saying is actually—you cannot forget who *you* are. Whatever feelings you have, whatever habits you've formed, you are *really* working for your country as a spy.

Back to the question with which I started. *Really?!*

Not exactly. If we take seriously Dewey's idea that our habits embody our character, or if we acknowledge that involuntary emotions are just as important as our avowed values, then spies like Philip and Elizabeth have conflicting identities.

Spies who see themselves as "really" *only* spies, as "really" having only one identity, deceive themselves. In order to not forget who they "really" are, spies need to forget who they really are. They need to lie to themselves constantly and consistently that they are not confused or conflicted, that their national ideals and interests crush all other personal relations.

The question now arises, how can this self-deception be achieved? As philosophers since Kant have asked, if lying means that we know the truth about which we are lying, then how can we lie to ourselves? How can we both know and not know the truth? That would be paradoxical! The possibility of self-deception is a difficult conceptual question and yet clearly it has some kind of an answer, since people obviously succeed in deceiving themselves on a regular basis. We all know people who deny loving someone when they clearly do or who deny being angry when their behavior demonstrates otherwise, and who seem genuine in their denial of feelings that are otherwise apparent, especially to those who know them well.

As a TV series, which presents us with the daily life-situations of characters, *The Americans* is uniquely positioned to explore this question. As viewers, we are also a bit like spies, in the sense that we engage in the surveillance of the lives of Philip and Elizabeth over a long period of time. We see them in more or less similar situations, their routine of killing and stealing, the routine of their relationships and of their deception and manipulation of those they pretend to love as lovers or friends, further pretending to themselves and to their superiors not to care that they live a life of constant betrayal of such people.

Through the serial structure of TV drama, we can begin to identify within the repetitions and variations patterns of behavior. Each such behavior plays a very marginal role in any given episode; sometimes it is hardly noticeable. But these moments accumulate over time, showing us the characters' subtle habits and emotional patterns. This is how we get slowly exposed to Philip's tender feelings towards Martha, and then when they explode and receive major focus, when he makes the grand effort to save her in Season Four, we're not so surprised. And this is how we can also gradually come to recognize Philip and Elizabeth's patterns of self-deception.

Talia Morag

That's Non-Experience

They have two favorite techniques. The first is what the philosopher Kent Bach calls *evasion*, which means simply not thinking about what you don't want to know about yourself.

Elizabeth is the main specialist in evasion. In the first three seasons, she basically does not talk about what bothers her in her spy work. Bach claims that we evade disturbing thoughts without telling ourselves that this is what we're doing. If someone asked us what we were doing, we would not answer, "We are evading this or that disturbing thought or emotion." If we could describe our evasion in this manner— then we would know that we are evading a thought or an emotion and thereby fail to evade that thought or emotion. This is how Bach solves the paradox of self-deception, echoing Sartre's words that "Bad faith does not speak its name."

Elizabeth may not tell herself in any given situation that she is evading what's bothering her, but there are moments where she allows herself to reflect on this practice. Sometimes she speaks about it in riddles, as when she says to Philip that their job "requires being a certain way" ("Comint"). But other times she seems perfectly clear on her strategy. For example, after she instructs Lucia, her younger colleague from Nicaragua to kill her informant and lover she says: "First time I had to resolve a situation in such a painful way, I tried not to think about it. The moment came, it was fast, I went home, wrote my report and went to bed. I would advise you to do the same" ("Behind the Red Door").

Elizabeth seems to be able to maintain her habit of evasion, yet every now and again she can stare at it with striking clarity. Bach would probably claim that this clarity would make the maintenance of this habit impossible. But Elizabeth seems to go back to her habit of evasion fairly quickly. Or does she? Are these rare moments of clarity, that accumulate as the show progresses, what eventually cause Elizabeth to fail evading and to acknowledge and mourn the loss of her supposedly-instrumental friendship with Young Hee Seong in Season Four?

The second self-deceptive method that Philip and Elizabeth frequently use is that of rationalization. Instead of acknowledging what they hate about themselves, they give reasons for their behavior, justify it, pretending that they do what they do for good reasons, pretending that they stand behind their actions. Instrumental rationality, so it turns out, is itself a tool of self-deception. Elizabeth never tires of rehearsing Communist ideals to justify herself. Philip, on the other hand, knows this is total BS. When he talks to his Pakistani reluctant informant Yousaf who confronts him about his spy life, he interrupts his own idealistic justifications and says frankly: "I feel like shit all the time" ("March 8, 1983"). Philip can say that because he has been disillusioned with the cause from the very first episode. He then wanted to defect with Elizabeth, expressing the desire to live "the life we've been living, but just *really* living it, just being us . . . We *are* Philip and Elizabeth Jennings" ("Pilot").

Philip's rationalization is different. He does what he does because this is what a KGB agent does and he cannot defect from the KGB—not without Elizabeth. He does what he does, in other words, for Elizabeth and for their children. This is evident in a few of his patterns that emerge throughout the show. For example, he often volunteers to do the dirty work for Elizabeth, to spare her from it—sometimes with disastrous results ("The Colonel").

Philip also has a typical fleeting facial expression of hardening against the guilt he feels toward his "fake" relationships, with those that he actually does care about, like Martha or his informant and lover Annelise. For example, we see that look momentarily when Philip apologizes to Annelise for getting her to sleep with Yousaf for information, or after he ruins a lazy romantic morning with Martha. That look communicates something like: "*I know very well* that that's terrible and I wish I didn't have to do this, *but still*, that's life as a KGB agent, and there's nothing I can do about *that*." When Philip joins *est* for some kind of a group therapy, he says precisely that—he cannot leave the job he hates because people depend on him ("Glanders"). Many of us, as the psychoanalyst Octave Mannoni discovered, use this "*I know very well . . . but still . . .*" structure. We use it as a cover up, as a self-deceptive excuse that allows us to ignore and set aside what we know very well.

Philip and Elizabeth keep turning to their KGB identities for excuses for behaviors that actually make them unhappy, granting that identity a higher degree of reality than that of their other social roles and relationships. But this prioritization is misguided and is used as a cover-up, as means to turn a blind eye and to harden themselves to the misery they cause others and especially themselves. *The Americans* demonstrates a particular kind of self-deception, that is the prioritization of what we think over what we do, of our ideals and self-image over our embodied habits of action.

The show takes a very clear stand about who Philip and Elizabeth *really* are. It's called *The Americans*—not *The Russians,* or *The KGB Agents*. Philip and Elizabeth *are* Americans, because they live as Americans, and because people are what they do in their embodied lives.

6
Cults of Authenticity

DAVID LAROCCA

I had begun to wonder if aged sixty was too late to change my life not that I had any choice.

—JIM HARRISON, *The English Major*

In "EST Men," the Season Three premiere of *The Americans*, Philip Jennings and Stan Beeman find themselves at an *est* (Erhard Seminars Training) meeting, a self-help-meets-human-motivation-and-potential gathering aimed to convey the teachings of Werner Erhard. That Erhard himself was born in 1935 as John Paul Rosenberg, and therefore, operates with a dual identity, is one of many resonances we might explore when asking what the characters in this show might want of *est*.

While the entire series is preoccupied with the identity status of Elizabeth and Philip (and many other characters)—Who's who? Who's a spy? Who's Russian? Who can you trust? Who am I married to?—the *est* scenes are philosophically informative because they localize and clarify these larger, longer, season-over-season queries. For one thing, consider how Stan relates to the movement, and in the company of Philip. Stan attends ostensibly as a bid to appease (or win back) a wife he's losing; meanwhile Philip, at his side, seems troubled by his own divided life, split personas, conflicting commitments to himself and others. Here "breaking up"

(Stan) and "breaking down" (Philip) share a space of common inquiry. Perhaps without being aware of the term, Stan and Philip are exploring the meaning and practice of authenticity. Moreover, the notion of authenticity is predicated on a faith in an *essential* self. The name *est* also derives from the Latin *est* ("it is"), which implies accepting reality, being aware of the present moment, and thus practicing to be your true or authentic self from moment to moment, in an endless series of "nows." As we think of *est* in relation to being and essential traits, *est* (the organization) also addresses "breaking down" in order to "build up." Does it really move these people closer to a realization of their own authenticity?

For millennia philosophers have been asking questions familiar to *The Americans*: Are we all not secret agents to ourselves? Maybe even double agents? Do our secret lives, our inner lives, truly align with what we say and do? Are we hypocrites and fakers and liars, deceiving others and ourselves along the way? Even the title of the show invokes the sense of role-playing, of being (an authentic) American. Part of the dramatic edge of the series for viewers lies precisely in the fact that *we know* Philip and Elizabeth are not (authentic) Americans. Our fascination with the show involves seeing how successful (or not) they are at seeming to be Americans, "passing" for authentic. What it means to be an American is usually thought of in political terms (nativism, immigration, citizenship), but this show insists that it's also an *existential* matter. What does it mean to *be* an American? And what does it mean to be *oneself*?

Some People, They Just Don't Get It

We begin in an anonymous hotel conference room outfitted with de rigueur crystal chandeliers. Chalkboards are filled with concepts (Truth, Integrity, Authenticity, No Fear, Direction, Clarity, Letting Go, Communication, Action, Productivity, Creativity, Transformation), claims (The truth does not mean anything. It just is), and existential reflections (Rocks are hard, water is wet, and you're feeling so sad you don't get to vote on the way it is). A crowd, including Stan and Philip, has gathered before Lawrence, a charismatic (smug?) leader for Erhard Seminars Training, whom they listen to intently:

> LAWRENCE: I can tell you what's wrong with you. It's simple. You assholes haven't had a single real experience your entire lives. You're living in the realm of non-experience, which is why your lives don't work.
>
> NICHOLAS: [*raises his hand, and when called upon asks politely, with a stutter of meekness and confusion*] What is the realm of non-experience? How can there be non-experience?
>
> [*Back to the teacher, who speaks directly to Nicholas, and crudely:*]
>
> LAWRENCE: Let's say you're balling a woman. You're banging her good, and you want her to have an orgasm, right?
>
> [*The audience, which includes many women, laughs nervously. Nicholas smiles and replies: "Sure."*]
>
> LAWRENCE: When you're thinking about her orgasm, are you experiencing?
>
> NICHOLAS: Um, I guess not.
>
> LAWRENCE: [*snapping his fingers*]: That's non-experience.
>
> [*At this point, Stan looks at Philip skeptically.*]
>
> LAWRENCE: And sex is one of the few things we have—almost getting killed is another—that can jolt us into feeling fully alive. If you want to actually experience life, then you've got to stop being so reasonable all the time. You've got to stop hoping things are just gonna get better, and you've got to accept what you've got.

Almost getting killed can jolt a person into "feeling fully alive." Philip and Elizabeth seem to be living that jolt on a regular basis. But to what end? Enduring a perpetual series of life-threatening scenarios is dangerous, but perhaps it's even more perilous for them to change their lives—to escape the lives they have created for themselves. Yet, first, you must know who you are in order to become someone else.

After the seminar, Philip is driving his white Camaro, and Stan looks at him: "Well, thanks." "You bet," replies Philip. And then we catch up with the conversation they've been having: "It's not a very good plan, though. I mean, what am I gonna tell her? 'It's the stupidest thing I ever heard in my life'—?" Philip laughs: "Yeah, that's—that's a problem." Stan sarcastically applies some of the lessons he's just learned: "According to these idiots, I probably should say that." And then he pantomimes the speech he'll give his estranged wife: "Honest. Hey, sweetie. I went to *est*, and I think they're all insane. Can we get back together now?" Philip too is lost for advice, "Greveys?" he asks in reply. Stan smiles: "Yeah, let's go get a non-beer."

In a later scene, a scene from a marriage, Stan visits Sandra at her suburban home—a symbolic red Mercedes-Benz coupe stands out against the gray day, and gray house, and Stan's government-issue black car.

SANDRA: Thank you so much for bringing this stuff by.

STAN: Yep. No problem.

SANDRA: Are you gonna pick up Matthew next Thursday night?

STAN: Yeah. Absolutely. Yeah, I'm sorry about last weekend.

SANDRA: We both know your work's important.

STAN: Yeah, it wasn't really work. I, uh, I actually took the first weekend of *est*.

SANDRA: Why?

STAN: I don't know. I guess . . . you got a lot out of it. I thought I should see what it was all about.

SANDRA: That's, um, interesting. What d'you think?

STAN: It was pretty good stuff.

SANDRA: You know, if you'd really been listening the first weekend, what you might have gotten was that it was about honesty.

STAN: I just told you I went.

SANDRA: No, it's okay. You know, some people, they just don't get it.
STAN: What . . . Sandra?

SANDRA: Stan, this was the big problem in our marriage, you know. You were always yessing me to avoid conflict and—and—disagreement, and then you weren't being yourself.

STAN: Okay. You want the truth? I thought it was stupid. Total bullshit.

SANDRA: I'm glad we got that cleared up.

The Americans is also, compellingly, about the marriage of Philip and Elizabeth. Indeed, the authenticity of that relationship forms a through-line of reflection from the first episode onward: what kind of marriage is this? Theirs is a variation on the challenges of the "arranged" marriage: is love in a marriage created after the fact of the "arrangement"—say, something the couple has created by learning to talk with one another? Stan and Philip's spiritual odyssey at *est* raises other questions: what precisely are one's duties to one's spouse (and children), especially if the civil contract of marriage gets in the way of "feeling fully alive"?

The *est* seminars emphasize truth and honesty (and Authenticity is on the chalkboard!) but against what criterion? Philip—as Elizabeth, as Stan, and so many others—are questioning their fidelity to marriage (within that contractual arrangement) and also to work, and thus to themselves as individuals. The questioning of faithfulness to these missions—that is, with the specter of faithlessness in view—forces a person to ask about what really is the case. Is my marriage authentic? Is my work real? Do I know who I am? If the marriage and the job and the self is a surface, what lies beneath? What is the true, real, essential substrate that might conjure my loyalty? The *est* training is the sort of instruction that presumes there *is* an authentic self one can be faithful to.

Becoming Who You Are

When Simon Critchley and Jamieson Webster describe our contemporary situation, they see an evolving cultural trend: how "a postwar existentialist philosophy of personal liberation and 'becoming who you are' fed into a 1960s counterculture that mutated into the most selfish conformism, disguising acquisitiveness under a patina of personal growth, mindfulness and compassion." Critchley and Webster call this phenomenon "passive nihilism," and declare "Authenticity is its dominant contemporary expression. . . . Authenticity, needing no reference to anything outside itself, is an evacuation of history. The power of now." The last bit is a dig at one of the self-help industry's most prominent proponents, Eckhart Tolle, and his millions-selling book.

In Philip's experience, one of the themes outside of the *est* classroom, is the way in which *deception*—not truthfulness, not honesty—is the criterion of doing one's job well, of being happily married, of "being oneself." Authentic feeling is *acted* feeling. Philip and Elizabeth are actors inhabiting roles. Being true to your country, your Cause, your wife (or wives) is authentic. Being a Russian spy is an authentic identity. Yet all of this authenticity is based on the art of playing a role well—becoming a simulacrum.

As Stan saw when he spoke "honestly" to Sandra, the raw truth may be unkind, unloving, the very thing one should *not* say. Philip's crisis of faith—his search for his true self, misses the ways in which his life is *permeated* by authentic being and doing in the form of his commitment to these roles and responsibilities. Whether those activities are *moral*, however, is more pressing (one thinks of the casualness and calmness with which Philip and Elizabeth murder people), even as that concern draws us away from the existential and metaphysical pressure of *est* and Philip and Stan's investigations of themselves.

We could ask: does Stan's failure with Sandra prove that *est* is "stupid," is "bullshit,"—or does his failure to rekindle his wife's affection with honesty show something else: that he just doesn't get it? Stan's lack of comprehension may signal his inability to appreciate *est*. Sandra's rebuke may be a sign of her indifference to his attempts. Again, who's being honest, true, authentic? And how would we know? The collapse of Stan's marriage—somehow ratified there on Sandra's suburban lawn when she concludes that their marriage failed because "You weren't being yourself"—points up the inside-outside divide so familiar to a cult. There are those who "get it" and those who don't. Inspired religions call this "faith," but is *est* a religion? Or is it more like a "program"— not a divinely granted set of edicts but a practical method aimed at achieving discernable goals? The difference may not matter. What does matter is the claim that some people can see things clearly and be themselves (truly, authentically) and others . . . cannot.

The *est* training may be on the wrong side of history. Not long ago, people could legitimately claim to be (in the Marxian sense) "alienated" from their work. Since the late seventies, "the distinction between work and nonwork is harder and harder to draw," as Critchley and Webster note. The seemingly facile observation has profound relevance for our thinking about *The Americans*, since Philip, Elizabeth, and Stan appear representative of this phenomenon: in short, they are *always at work* (even domestic life for Philip and Elizabeth is an act—a performance for the children), and always working on their marriages. (And for Philip, he has to work on *two*!) Don't forget that we're in the early 1980s, when exercise became work—one more fad to impose new demands and expectations on daily life.

In our age, "work is no longer a series of obligations to be fulfilled for the sake of sustenance . . . it is the expression of one's authentic self," say Critchley and Webster. To be at odds with your *work*, therefore, means to be at odds with your *self*. The isomorphism of labor and identity has created a modern individual who interprets value and meaning in direct relationship and equivalency to some perceived—or believed— interior, subjective truth, some core self.

The people who seek out support and advice from *est* feel that something is not right in their lives. Things feel out of order, misaligned. A person is, in the wonderfully telling phrase, "at odds" with himself or herself; oh, to be "at evens"! The promise of *est*, and the rest, is the promise of reordering and realignment. This may come in the form of seeing things more truly or clearly, or of activating some new reserves of will. The common denominator of such programs must be a two-step process: 1. the identification of an authentic self and 2. the capacity to activate and express that true self. Does *est* attract people who *already* believe in this two-step logic (and therefore may join because they've found a doctrine that reinforces their hunch), or does it indoctrinate them—in effect, persuading people to "sign up" for a certain (more promising) picture of the way things are. In every case, we have to ask ourselves "Do I get it, or not?"

Life Changes Things, You Change, or— or Something

In the Season Four finale ("Persona Non Grata"), Philip returns to *est*, this time on his own. At home, in Philip's absence, Paige asks her mom where her dad is. Elizabeth says he's at a class. Paige looks quizzically at her mother. "It's called *est*. Uh, it's like a seminar in . . . thinking about yourself," Elizabeth explains. This exchange shows how mother and daughter seem to be trying to understand the legitimacy of what Philip is up to. What exactly is *est for*?

We're back to the hotel conference room with chandeliers, blackboards, a tray of donuts, and a sign suggesting Philip's advancement in the training: "Tonight. EST. Graduate Series." Philip stands before the attentive crowd and offers up a soliloquy encoding his experiences over the entire arc of the events since his first meeting with Stan. Every phrase and hesitation lends itself to a double and triple layering of euphemisms. Philip is, in short, speaking to us—his knowing audience—since we know what he knows.

PHILIP: Travel agent is pretty much the only job I've ever known. Uh, it—it suited me. I—I like to travel, see new places and . . . meet new people. But, I mean, you choose a job before you really know if you'll like it, right? I mean, when you're young, you don't . . . know anything—who you are, what you wanna do, be. You pick something because it fits what you like, what—what you need. But life changes things, you change, or—or something. And then one day you wake up, and you don't want to go into the office. You don't want to make arrangements for people you don't know and don't give a shit about. You don't wanna do it. You just don't. Every morning, I wake up with this sick feeling in the pit of my stomach.

The teacher, sensing an ending, says "Okay." And asks a follow-up question: "So, why don't you quit, find a new job?" Philip sighs: "I can't." "Why not?" comes the incredulous teacher. "Because I have commitments," says Philip, "I've made promises." "To who," asks the teacher. "To people who trust me and people I love." The teacher follows up by filling in: "And you don't wanna let them down?" "No," says Philip. And then the teacher turns away from Philip and addresses the class: "But it's okay to let *yourself* down? Do you think your family would no longer love you if you quit? Do you think the world would stop spinning? 'Cause I got news for you: you ain't that important."

While Philip calmly ponders the teacher's sophomoric analysis, we might reflect on what we saw on the chalkboard this time:

You do not have to get there.

You cannot get there.

You only have to 'realize' your self.

As you do, you are satisfied.

I'm not trying to minimize *est*'s effectiveness; this chapter is not a product review. Rather, I'm inquiring after the kind of philosophical beliefs and claims that underwrite such seminars.

One of the many presumptions *est*—and similar cults of authenticity—make is the degree to which a person can be "causative." One of the constants of the self-help, or self-transformation, industry is that an individual is *free* to change; fate is anathema to agency. We are encouraged to practice "mindfulness," to "get out of our own way." Virtues and values are expressed in pithy accounts of potency and potentiality ("Be all that you can be"), genuineness ("Be yourself"), and endogeneity ("Be original"). Platitudes have been corralled into a series of directives, each one more digested and stripped down than the last. For many, Twitter is a platform for the apotheosis of this approach. We shall live and die in 140 characters or fewer.

Today some may regard psychoanalysis as just another antiquated scheme for assigning meaning to human life. But Sigmund Freud had little faith in individual freedom: "We are lived," is how he put it. Firmin DeBrabander glosses the idea by saying that "conscious autonomy is a charade." Freud's concern was that we "typically—wrongly—ignore the extent to which we are determined by unknown forces and overestimate our self-control." On this front, "self-reliance is a fallacy," and "radical individualism" is a myth.

DeBrabander directs our attention further back to Baruch Spinoza: "To be human, according to Spinoza, is to be party to a confounding existential illusion—that human individuals are independent agents—which exacts a heavy emotional and political toll on us. It is the source of anxiety, envy, anger—all the passions that torment our psyche—and the violence that ensues."

La Merde Arrive

After listening to Philip's lament—a narrative in which we find our protagonist struggling with his decisions, or more pertinently, his sense of estrangement from them—we can think anew about what *The Americans* can teach us about the possibility (or not) of changing our lives. One doesn't have to believe in fate—for example, in a fixed destiny filled with meaning—if one doesn't believe in free will. As the iconic Eighties bumper sticker declared: "Shit happens."

The Americans creates a palpable tension around the question of personal change. Will Philip and Elizabeth remain married? Will they retire? Will Center leave them alone if they do? We can begin our replies by asking what has changed for them, or by them, in the seasons we have seen thus far? As Philip and others *contemplate* changing their lives—getting a different job, a different spouse—can we say that they have been part or party to that change? And so, in this light, we listen again to Philip's lament: "But, I mean, you choose a job before you really know if you'll like it, right? I mean, when you're young, you don't . . . know anything— who you are, what you wanna do, be. You pick something because it fits what you like, what—what you need. But life changes things, you change, or—or something."

But now, in relative maturity, does Philip know what kind of job he would really like, what kind of wife he would want to be married to? Does he, in fact, "know anything"—or anything *more* that might avert a future existential panic and vocational crisis? Perhaps we should learn from—and linger on—Philip's elliptical speech, how he goes from declaring that "life changes things" to "you change" to "or—or something." The trailing off of certainty, the lessening or lack of conviction (the stuttered "or—or something") may be our best insight yet into the way we go about changing our lives, being authentic: we do not seek to outsmart ourselves (say, an older version trading in a younger version), but rather to dwell in our incomprehension, in our ignorance, in our absence of mastery and control, and—against the grain of passive nihilism—to say to ourselves, like Socrates so many millennia ago, I know only that I don't know.

Then, perhaps, we can say that we have seen things clearly and truly. Such a perception would be worthy of our claims to authenticity.

7
Secrets and Lies

GREGORY L. BOCK AND JEFFREY L. BOCK

Should we always tell the truth? Is it wrong to keep secrets? It's said that honesty is the best policy—but maybe not all the time.

Think about national security. During the Cold War, the United States and Soviet Union threatened to annihilate one another in a global nuclear apocalypse. Each side engaged in espionage and concealment, which helped save the world, but what does this mean? Is deception a virtue now?

Secrets Are Everywhere

The world operates on secrets. For instance, what's the recipe for the Colonel's fried chicken? You don't know, do you? It's a secret and an important one. If the secret were revealed, KFC's competitors would quickly put them out of business.

In her book *Secrets: On the Ethics of Concealment and Revelation*, Sissela Bok (no relation to us) defines secrecy as "intentional concealment." She says there's nothing inherently wrong with secrecy; it depends entirely on the situation. She says, "Secrecy may accompany the most innocent as well as the most lethal acts; it is needed for human survival, yet it enhances every form of abuse." Each kept secret must be evaluated independently in light of the circumstances and with regard to its costs and benefits. What dangers does it involve? What advantages?

A trade secret like the recipe for fried chicken doesn't harm anyone and is quite useful as an entrepreneurial incentive. Secrets may also protect human autonomy. As Bok says, secrets "concern protection of what we are, what we intend, what we do, and what we own." However, secrets have a dark side, too. In government, secrecy may foster corruption and injustice and undermine democratic institutions by hiding the actions of the state from the citizenry. The military might conceal weapons programs or operations that would be found objectionable to the general public if they came to light; on the other hand, the loss of military secrets could threaten national security and render a country vulnerable to attack.

Philip and Elizabeth are secret agents, pretending to be busy travel agents. Their secret allows them to live inconspicuously among Americans, all the while infiltrating deeper and deeper into the layers of secrecy in nearby Washington DC. They're careful to conceal their true identities from their FBI neighbor, Stan Beeman, and their secret is even kept from their children. It's only when Paige gets older that she learns the truth. In this context, we see the dangers of secrecy.

Perhaps the Jenningses' secret is similar to the secrecy of many other government and military jobs in which special clearance is required. For such jobs, employees are required to keep their personal and professional lives separate, hiding their work even from their families. However, the Jenningses' job differs from typical careers of this sort in that Philip and Elizabeth kill people, too. Philip even kills an innocent busboy in a restaurant because the busboy witnesses Philip killing two Afghans in a weapons deal ("Comrades"). Killing innocent witnesses may protect secrets, but is such killing morally justified?

Philip believes he is working towards a greater good. A utilitarian would decide that what is right is what brings about the greater good. If killing one innocent busboy to keep a secret is for the greater good, then so be it. However, this is deeply troubling and constitutes the main objection against utilitarianism. If this were the right thing to do, then we would be justified in killing people anytime their deaths would benefit society. What if Henry or Paige were in the busboy's situation and witnessed a political assassination? Would Philip and Elizabeth agree that their deaths were justified? Probably not.

On a different mission Philip and Elizabeth are discovered by an elderly bookkeeper while they are bugging Mailbot. Elizabeth talks to her hostage too much for her safety. The bookkeeper realizes that she is not going to live to see the morning and asks why:

> ELIZABETH: To make the world a better place.
>
> BOOKKEEPER: You think doing this to me will make the world a better place?
>
> ELIZABETH: I'm sorry, but it will.
>
> BOOKKEEPER: That's what evil people tell themselves when they do evil things.

If an ethical theory based on the greater good can justify killing innocent people in order to keep secrets, then there is something wrong with the ethical theory.

Don't Lie to Me, Clark!

Everybody lies, but should they? In her book on lying, Bok defines a lie as "any intentionally deceptive message which is stated." A lie isn't just a falsehood; it is intentionally false and meant to mislead. She says, "Such statements are most often made verbally or in writing, but can of course also be conveyed via smoke signals, Morse code, sign language, and the like." Oleg Igorevich's view of lying is in line with Bok's definition when he says the following to Nina ("A Little Night Music"):

OLEG: I'm just saying, our jobs are all about deception. And maybe it's not so hard to deceive with the eyes, the smile, the things we say, but the body—those parts of the body that can love—they want to tell the truth. When we train them to lie, that's hard on the soul.

NINA: My soul is fine, Oleg Igorevich. How's yours?

The Golden Rule supports a presumption against lying. We don't want others to lie to us, so we shouldn't lie to others. Most liars, it seems, are reluctant to grant the same liberty to others that they take for themselves and become angry or hurt when they find themselves on the other end of the stick.

Immanuel Kant (1724–1804) defends an absolute stance against lying. There are no exceptions. Lying is even wrong when people's lives are on the line. For example, imagine an SS officer knocks on your door and asks: "Got any Jews?" Kant thinks you shouldn't lie. Perhaps you should tell a misleading truth or try not to answer the question, but when it comes right down to it, Kant thinks that we aren't responsible for the immoral actions of others, only our own. So, if someone chooses to murder someone else using facts you provide, it isn't your responsibility. What's most important to Kant aren't consequences but the moral law.

Almost everyone thinks Kant's view is extreme. Certainly, we ought to tell the truth on most occasions, but sometimes other considerations take precedent. Truth-telling is a *prima facie* obligation. Honesty should be our first impulse, but we should think about it first. Bok describes three conditions that might justify a lie:

1. There are no honest alternatives

2. The reasons for lying outweigh the reasons against it, and

3. Society would accept it if they knew about it.

Would Philip and Elizabeth's lies satisfy these conditions?

Philip must lie to Martha in order to get her to plant a bug in Agent Gaad's office. Philip develops a relationship with her by telling her he's in love with her, flattering her at every turn. These lies compound over time as the innocent wallflower, Martha, develops a need for Philip's affection. He's forced to deepen the lie as the information she provides him becomes more and more valuable. When Philip asks her to place the bug, she balks. This would be a tremendous risk, and a betrayal of her boss. Philip promises to marry her if she'll do it. The lie of love pushes Martha into a deep well of risk and paranoia from which she never recovers. Eventually the bug is found. Philip must then compound the sin of lying with murder—itself an act of deception—to ensure that someone else takes the fall for her indiscretion. Martha slowly unravels. Philip's deceptions are not real. She has nothing to grasp on to and becomes despondent. The truth of her supposed husband's actions tears into her psyche. Philip, in developing Martha as his informant, has developed empathy for her and her situation. Rather than allow Center to remove Martha as a threat (execute her), he convinces them to let her defect to Russia. She is not happy, but what American would be? She accepts, knowing that the alternative is certain death for her and her family.

Go back in time. Philip is recruiting Martha and asks himself, "Is this a good time to lie?"

Condition 1: Are there honest alternatives? Certainly, he could tell her the truth about his identity, but Martha is less likely to spy for a foreign government than for another US agency. Perhaps there are other means of acquiring the information: wiretapping, eavesdropping, or stealing files from Mail-bot. These methods don't put anyone's life at risk, but they are less effective.

Conditions 2: Do the reasons for lying outweigh the reasons against it? From the perspective of the KGB, the access to Gaad's office and the strategic advantage this gives them outweighs the dangers to Martha. A utilitarian would sacrifice one person for the greater good, but as mentioned above, this is disturbing. Should small advantages in intelligence gathering justify destroying the life of an innocent administrative assistant?

Condition 3: Would society be okay with Philip's lies? This would come down to perspective. The people of the Soviet Union might be okay with Philip's actions, but not with a CIA agent using the same methods inside the Soviet Union.

So, the answer is no; Philip's lying to Martha isn't morally justifiable.

Elizabeth lies, too. For example, she befriends Young Hee Seong to gain access to her husband Don, but her friendship with Young Hee becomes real. She discovers that the cost of lying to her friend is almost too much to bear. She asks her handlers for any way out of the hole she's dug for herself, but eventually it becomes clear that the only way forward is to continue with the deception. She tricks Don into believing they've slept together, demoralizing a loyal and innocent man. Then she creates another deception, telling Don she's pregnant and that he needs to leave Young Hee and support her. He refuses to comply, as his loyalty and love for his wife are clear.

This leads the spies into their next deception: Patty (Elizabeth's alias in the con) has killed herself out of sorrow over Don's rejection, and now the family (Philip, Gabriel, and another Soviet agent) have shown up at his work, demanding he cover the costs of her funeral and of transporting her body back to California. The toll on Elizabeth and Young Hee are clear. They've lost a real friendship. Young Hee leaves a message on Elizabeth's machine, asking where she's gone and explaining how oddly Don is acting lately. Elizabeth can never again be Patty, can never again spend time with her friend. The cost of lies runs deep.

Applying the same three conditions, it seems that Elizabeth's lies are not morally justifiable. First, there are other alternatives to lying. Philip and Elizabeth have already proven quite capable of turning US government employees to their side. Does a certain love-struck administrative assistant ring a bell? Why not do the same in Don's organization? Second, the reasons for lying don't outweigh the reasons against it. The deception could destroy both Don and Young Hee; moreover, if the secret were to get out, it could result in bloodshed on both sides. Third, society wouldn't be okay with her lies. The Soviets might benefit from her lying to the Americans, but if an American agent were to do the same in Russia, they would disapprove.

I Love You, but Can I Trust You?

Perhaps national security justifies a certain level of lying and secrecy, but what makes the Jenningses' situation even more troubling is that their children are part of the deception, even though they don't know it. What's more, to keep up the ruse, Philip and Elizabeth must lie to them daily. Parents may lie to their children from time to time about little things like whether Santa Claus is real or whether any cookies are left in the house, but the number of lies that Philip and Elizabeth must tell in order to maintain their secret is mindboggling. Lying to a child about something as foundational as their identity, as their family's identity, can be devastating. Bok explains why:

> Those who learn that they have been lied to in an important matter—say, the identity of their parents, the affection of their spouse, or the integrity of their government—are resentful, disappointed, and suspicious . . . They see that they were manipulated, that the deceit made them unable to make choices for themselves according to the most adequate information available, unable to act as they would have wanted to act had they known all along.

Parents desire honesty and openness from their children as well, not only because they want their children to grow up to be honest adults, but also because they want a healthy family and a close relationship with them. The Jennings family has several heated discussions that are perfectly normal in most families but very different in theirs:

ELIZABETH: You're hiding something.

PAIGE: A book for school.

ELIZABETH: If it's for school, why are you hiding it?

PAIGE: It's for this course about the Bible.

ELIZABETH: You're not taking a course on the Bible. Why are you lying to me? Paige, what is this?

PAIGE: I'm reading the Bible.

ELIZABETH: What is the Reed Street Church?

PAIGE: I met this kid Kelli, and she's really nice, and this is where she goes, like a youth group, and she's got a messed up family, and it makes her happy.

ELIZABETH: But you don't have a messed up family.

PAIGE: Do we have to talk about this? . . .

PHILIP: What's going on?

ELIZABETH: Paige thinks she's in a messed up family, and she's been going to some youth group she doesn't tell us about. ("A Little Night Music")

Elizabeth may be concerned her daughter is becoming religious, but she's more concerned with the secrecy. She tells Paige, "I don't care what you're reading. I just don't want you hiding things" ("The Deal").

The lying and secrecy also wear on the Jenningses' marriage. You'd think that having the woman you love seduce other men would drive a wedge between the two of you. You'd think that your husband marrying someone else would spell the end to your marriage, but this is mostly business as usual for the Jenningses. The source of stress in Philip and Elizabeth's relationship isn't the sexual aspect of their job; it's the lies they tell and the secrets they keep from one another.

In the episode "Duty and Honor," sex, lies, and secrets drive a wedge into the marriage. Philip is assigned the task of working a job in New York City with Irina, another agent and Philip's old love interest. They sleep together. Irina tells

Philip they have a son together. He lies to Elizabeth about the sex and keeps secret the existence of his son. The truth comes out, however, when their handler, Claudia, tells Elizabeth. Claudia says, "This isn't an easy life we've chosen, but there's no way to get through it without the truth." Claudia is just being her manipulative self, but this disclosure threatens to undermine Philip and Elizabeth's growing intimacy and love for one another, and they separate, if only temporarily. Elizabeth confronts Philip:

ELIZABETH: I asked you not to lie to me.

PHILIP: I made a terrible mistake. Can we please just start over?

ELIZABETH: No, we can't. ("Mutually Assured Destruction")

Can they find a way to trust each other again?

I Can't Lie to Everyone!

So, where do we stand? Maybe some level of lying and secrecy is unavoidable in a Cold War world of espionage and nuclear technology, but this doesn't mean we shouldn't work for a better world, one in which the amount of lying and secrecy is reduced along with the incumbent risks. In fact, this may be the only way to avoid another Cold War—a serious concern these days.

While there are complex political dimensions to this discussion, these issues are also personal. In *Lying*, Bok says there is a way for individuals "to influence the amount of duplicity in their lives and to shape their speech and action." People can choose to "rule out deception wherever honest alternatives exist." The choice may have been removed from the playing field long ago for Philip and Elizabeth. For them, honesty comes with a far greater cost than we (those of us who are not spies) will ever have to face. They've been raised in the Soviet world of secrecy and deception, and they've become a part of that deception, like it or not. Now they live with the dangers they've built up for themselves, and they've brought into that world two children and a circle of relationships that are affected daily by their choices. The ability to remove themselves from the dangers may no longer be a viable option, if it ever was one.

However, if they desire happiness for themselves and intimacy with the ones they love, they must find a way to maintain trust because honesty and openness are essential for close personal relationships.

8
How to Keep On Denying and Love Being a Spy

ROB LUZECKY AND CHARLENE ELSBY

Over the course of *The Americans*, Philip and Elizabeth have denied a lot of things. They have denied that they are Russian agents. They have denied that they are American citizens. The have denied the importance—and validity—of their marriage bond. They have denied their relationships with a larger community. Denial defines every register of their lives. Philip's and Elizabeth's all-encompassing denial is the sort of nihilism that is most often identified with Gilles Deleuze's elaboration of Friedrich Nietzsche's thought.

Deleuze asserts that Nietzsche identifies two different types of nihilism: "reactive nihilism" and "passive nihilism." Reactive nihilism is characterized by the devaluing (or negating) of a value through the process of performing any set of negative actions. An example of this sort of nihilism is found in the destruction of freedom that comes from the awareness that your neighbor across the street is, in fact, trying to get you, and there is very little in this suburban life that you can or should trust.

As bad as this seems, passive nihilism is, in fact, much worse. Passive nihilism is what emerges when the negativity that defines nihilism starts to cannibalize itself. Deleuze identifies reactive nihilism as implying a sort of affirmation of your capacities to act in a situation, which initially presented as the denial of all values. Passive nihilism is what is evidenced when you realize that you're nothing but a pawn in service of higher values—that are themselves worth nothing.

Both types of nihilisms are expressed in *The Americans*. When we deny everything, we discover a fundamental denial of passive nihilism, and this is realized as our capacity to affirm our choice to continue being spies.

Two Ways to Destroy Everything You Value in Life

When Philip is talking about his wife during the first few seasons of *The Americans*, we really aren't sure who he is talking about. It would be easy to assume that he's talking about Elizabeth (who is, after all, the mother of his children), but this would be too quick. The marriage certificate (the document which legally denotes the legitimacy of the marriage) is, in fact, a fake. In this sense, the married life of Philip and Elizabeth is a complete sham, and whatever Elizabeth might be, she is not Philip's wife.

We might say, on the other hand, that Philip's wife is Martha. Though this might be a bit jarring to Elizabeth, it seems to be a bit closer to the truth, in the sense that Philip and Martha were married by a person with the legal power to sanctify the ceremony, and the marriage certificate was not forged in the bowels of some dingy sub-basement at KGB headquarters.

The ambiguity of the concept of marriage is analogous to an ambiguity involved with the concept of nihilism. In his reading of Nietzsche, the French philosopher Gilles Deleuze identifies two kinds of nihilism: 1. one kind of nihilism is identified as a reactive rejection of all values, and; 2. another kind of nihilism is identified as a rejection of the value of the very thing that devalues life.

The first type of nihilism is already pretty extreme, and takes a bit of thinking to get your head around. Right off the bat, we should be clear that nihilism can't really be reduced to any one action, though some actions—especially when they are repeated—imply nihilism much more strongly than others. Doing something like stabbing Agent Amador and letting him die ("Safe House") might seem cruel and unnecessary, but it's still a long way from being nihilistic. Nihilism (in both its senses) involves attempting to destroy what Deleuze refers to as the "supersensible" world. There isn't too much "super" about the supersensible, except that usually used to identify the world of concepts (all those ideas and relations among ideas that most certainly exist even though they don't have fleshy bits). We can see hints of a nihilist denial of the value of the supersensible in Philip's and Elizabeth's tendency of lying, to each other and agents of the American government.

Like a single action of killing, a single lie doesn't imply too much, but the Jenningses' constant lies to pretty much everyone in their lives implies an assault on the supersensible idea of the truth. Pastor Tim would most certainly tell us that anyone who is not a nihilist at heart would feel some degree of guilt when they tell a lie. When we encounter someone who spends most of their life lying without any sense of guilt, this person is explicitly nihilist, in the sense that they don't think of the truth as something that has any value. If either Philip or Elizabeth thought truth was valuable, then they would at least feel some modicum of guilt when they constantly tell Stan that they work as a travel agents, but whatever emotion Philip and Elizabeth feel when they talk to Stan, guilt is not it. The Jenningses' lies imply a nihilism, in the sense that all claims about the existence of the world are crucial components of the world, and as soon as we devalue these claims, we devalue a very significant portion of the world. When the Jenningses repeatedly treat the truth like some corpse they just murdered, they are completely devaluing one of the essential values of life, and this is what makes them nihilists.

It is simple enough to recognize that nihilism is negative, but it seems sort of weird to think of it as reactive. Why on Earth would we characterize any sort of nihilism as reactive? That a nihilist is engaged in enterprises that involve negation and have negation as their aim is self-evident. Negating the value of the ideas that shape our world is a process that is about as far from positive as is a spy mission which involves killing a grandmother while your partner installs a listening device on Mail-bot ("Do Mail Robots Dream of Electric Sheep?").

The reactive aspect of this sort of nihilism hinges on the recognition that most of Philip's and Elizabeth's nihilism might be explained as responses conditioned by a set of beliefs, or, perhaps, unconscious habits developed during years of training, beatings, and rapes at the hands of their KGB instructors ("Pilot"). Reactive nihilism is something a bit different—a bit more refined—than simply that which is evidenced in a series of actions that involves—or results in—some sort of devaluation of life.

While it certainly is the case that reactive nihilism involves the devaluation of one or many aspects of life, reactive nihilism is distinct from the typical kind of nihilism, in the sense that it is based on a fundamental concept of something that is valuable. When the world seems all out of joint, when you're a spy living in a hostile land that just elected to the office of President a mostly washed-up actor who might or might not be a sex-offender, and who seems to have very little grasp on reality, you might feel like engaging in some negative activities of your own.

Perhaps you feel like protesting. Perhaps you feel like taking a single great stand or performing many subversive actions to fight for and protect those values that you believe to be right. The presupposition behind all of this is that there is something of value, and all your negative actions (whatever they may be) are reactions against the corruption of a country that has in a very real sense failed. Philip and Elizabeth are precisely reactive nihilists every time they perform a negative action or series of negative actions that are in service of some higher value.

Though it is negative, and certainly does involve destructive (often violent) types of actions, reactive nihilism does not seem to be all that bad. Sometimes spies have to become really dark and stab some guy in the throat in the dingy alleyway that all too often can be found in the dystopian hellscape outside any food pantry in any urban center in America. Elizabeth only stabbed the would-be muggers after they intimated that they were going to assault Paige ("Dinner for Seven"). While not the exactly manifesting the height of the higher values, Elizabeth's action isn't completely terrible, because at least she meant well. But good intentions never seem to be fully adequate as justifications for negative actions.

We can see the ideological support for Philip's and Elizabeth's reactive nihilism begin to collapse in all sorts of ways. With the collapse of this support, we witness the tragic emergence of passive nihilism, in which the destruction of values takes on a whole new level of negativity, one that is no longer driven by the appeal to a higher power. Reactive nihilism differs from passive nihilism both in terms of its object and in terms of its degree of negativity. Passive nihilism takes as its object the very entity that was devaluing values in reactive nihilism. In the sense that passive nihilism takes the person who is devaluing values as its object (because passive nihilism is quite literally a self-destruction), it is more nihilistic than reactive nihilism.

Passive nihilism emerges in both Philip and Elizabeth as they grow more and more disenchanted with their lives as spies. That Philip grows to despise his life as a spy is evidenced in his open criticisms of the plans of Directorate S and in his explicit threats to Arkady ("Echo"). Perhaps even more revealing of Philip's passive nihilism, is his continued attendance at those damn *est* seminars. At least when Philip was killing the soldier at the training camp, he knew why he was putting a knife into a body ("Martial Eagle"). In the lame 1980s decor of the *est* seminar room Philip shows himself to be a man who is fundamentally lost. There is nothing so pathetic as the figure of Philip when he sits in a folding chair desperately seeking a reason to exist in all the noise of *est*'s bankrupt, pseudo-philosophical, self-help mumbo-jumbo.

Philip identifies himself as a spy. Being a spy is the cornerstone of Philip's sense of self. We see the erosion of Philip's sense of self (the triumph of passive nihilism) when

Philip realizes how creepy (not to mention borderline inces-
tuous) his seduction of Kimmy is ("Dimebag"). We see a similar awareness that the self has been destroyed in the dead
look of despair on Elizabeth's face when she puts down the
phone, walks into the apartment and drugs Don ("The Day
After"). Like an utterly passive machine, like a robot with no
sense of self or animating soul, Elizabeth followed orders:
she stripped herself naked and destroyed the lives of maybe
her only friends. The destruction of her friendship erodes her
belief in the goodness of her mission and her self-identifica-
tion as good Russian spy. Moment after moment, day after
day, negative acts abound and all attempts to appeal to the
higher values or a sense of self fade out like the dying
strands of some 1980s glam-rock tune.

At least when they were reactive nihilists Philip and Elizabeth knew what they were doing. Their lives had a purpose
bequeathed to them as orders from the outside. When they
destroyed some value, they did so deliberately. Passive nihilism involves nothing so pleasant as joyfully reacting
against a country that manifests a whole host of values you
deeply and truly hate. Passive nihilism comes into being at
the coldest of moments on the nights when, alone, you come
to the utterly depressing awareness that you are spiritually
lost. Passive nihilism emerges from reactive nihilism at that
terrible (and seemingly irredeemable) moment when you
come to the creeping realization that the higher values you
were fighting for are actually nothing but lies. You are in the
grips of passive nihilism when you discover that are you are
nothing more than a pawn whose very sense of self has been
destroyed by the fight against the very values you thought
were worth destroying. This is what has happened to William
Crandell. It is happening to Elizabeth.

Transvaluation of Values

Being a spy is exhausting work. Being a spy for fifteen years
is terrible. A person has to be always on guard, always lying,
and always denying. Though Gabriel recognizes that Direc-

torate S is pushing its spies too hard and asking too much of them, the "vacation" he offers them is defined by its utter inadequacy ("The Magic of David Copperfield V: The Statue of Liberty Disappears"). How can you take a break from fearing for your life with every breath? How can you take a break from lying to your colleagues at your cover job? How can you take a break from knowing that you can kill, have killed, and will kill again? Just like waving your hands, dropping a big curtain, and rotating a platform doesn't make the Statue of Liberty vanish, staying at home and spending some time with friends and family doesn't make nihilism disappear. Parlor tricks and false smiles do nothing to stop the devaluation of values. As paradoxical as it seems, stopping nihilism involves embracing its negativity most fully.

Deleuze identifies the acceptance of the negativity as the essential moment which starts the transvaluation of values that ends nihilism. In order to understand how something so simple as accepting your negativity will destroy nihilism. When you transvalue values you are doing something much more significant that merely deciding to value things differently. News flash: Bruce Dameran thinks that "Ronald Reagan doesn't care" and he attempts to assassinate some executives of the World Bank, because they are a bunch of technocratic jerks who are ruining the world ("The Walk In"). Had Dameran suddenly decided that Reagan really cared and that the executives from the World Bank were really a bunch of swell guys, these would not have been instances of the transvaluation of values.

Changing your mind about values is *not* transvaluing them. The transvaluation of values involves a much more fundamental change. Transvaluing values involves a change in the very way you comport yourself to reality. The valuing person is the element that gives value to values, and changing the way a person gives value to values is a hell of a lot more substantial than them merely changing your mind about the particular value of a thing or group of things at a given moment. For a person to change the way they value things, they have to bring some very fundamental *affirmation* into their bleak view of the world.

But what sort of affirmation could a spy bring to bear on their world view? Pastor Tim would probably say that that affirmation tends to involve some sort of confession. Pastor Tim probably never read Nietzsche. He certainly couldn't handle life as a KGB spy. Philip and Elizabeth wouldn't be affirming anything if they invited Beeman over for supper, served a casserole and Jell-O salad, cracked open a few beers, and joyfully confessed to him that they are spies. The most terrible aspects of these actions are not the possible out-comes. Though the possibilities that Philip and Elizabeth would end up in prison for the rest of their lives and that poor Paige would be condemned to live with Pastor Tim and his ever-so-self-deluding little family of religious zealots would be terrible, these would pale in comparison to the sense of failure that would accompany the act of surrender-ing to Stan Beeman. The sense of complete loss that accom-panies such a giving up would make the pain and suffering that characterize the snow-covered streets of Smolensk feel like Disney World.

The Jenningses are devaluing—denying or negating—so much, so often, so completely, that it's not an overstatement to say that their lives are nihilistic. They should keep it up. They should embrace it. The only way to bring any sort of af-firmation to the nihilist's life of devaluing is to affirm this devaluing. Such an affirmation of devaluation is precisely not a contradiction, in the sense that affirming devaluation implies embracing it in all its instances. Perhaps the most important implication of the affirmation of devaluation is that it involves none of the self-negating mopiness that de-fines passive nihilism. Whereas passive nihilism comes about from following orders—until every sense of the self that decides what it is going to devalue has been destroyed—an affirmation of devaluing is a celebration of the self that critiques the values of Cold War America.

Were the Jenningses to affirm their critique of values, this would not get rid of the negative aspects of their cri-tique—the absolutely essential "no" that defines the life of spies)—but this affirmation would make this negativity logically secondary to a fundamental acceptance of what they are. Were the Jenningses to affirm their own critique of values, they would be doing it as themselves (not merely as KGB agents who were following orders)—they would no longer be merely acting as spies trapped in nihilism. When Philip and Elizabeth accept what they do, when they affirm who they are (with all the negation it involves), then they will be acting people who make the active to choices to be spies, and to continue to be spies. An affirmation of the negativity that everybody feels as they gaze out to the banality of the suburban streets found in every American neighborhood is precisely the affirmation at the Philip and Elizabeth must make. Affirmations like these will bring an end to the long and tragic story of American nihilism.

III

Terrible
Parents

9
Yes, Paige, There Is a Santa Claus

Daniel P. Malloy

Philip and Elizabeth Jennings lie a lot. They're spies, after all. Espionage is not a field that rewards honesty. They lie to their neighbors, their friends, their employees, their clients, their contacts, and to each other. They also lie to their children. Philip and Elizabeth are hardly alone in lying to their children. Most parents do. Just like spying, parenting requires lying sometimes.

But when? Spies lie whenever the truth will jeopardize their missions or their lives. But when parents should lie is complicated. Parents lie for a lot of different reasons—to keep secrets, to reassure children, to help them grow into good adults, to avoid awkward conversations. Philip and Elizabeth also have to lie to Paige and Henry to maintain their cover. As Paige demonstrated, kids can be little blabbermouths.

Taking a closer look at what parents do and why they do it will help us better understand the role of lying in parenting. Parenting, like spying, serves a purpose. If lying is a reasonable parenting method, then parents can sometimes be justified in lying to their children. If not, then the Jenningses' long list of lies to Paige and Henry make them strong contenders for the worst parents ever.

A Hard Job

Philip and Elizabeth Jennings have a hard job. I'm not talking about international espionage or even their high-stress careers as travel agents. No, the toughest job the Jennings have taken on is the job of parents.

There are a lot of reasons why parenting is the toughest of their jobs. There's no training for it and no licensing. And it would actually be a bit weird to have training or licensing for parents. The thing about parenting that makes it so different, and the reason you can be trained and licensed to be a travel agent or a spy, but not a parent, is that there isn't a clear set of goals involved in parenting. Oh, sure, there are some basic things: make sure your offspring doesn't die, for instance, but that's relatively easy stuff. Beyond that, things get difficult.

Even what parents should hope for their children can be controversial. Do good parents want their kids to be happy? Or successful? Or simply good people? Ideally, perhaps, parents would want all three for their children, as well as a few others. But these multiple goals don't always go hand in hand, and sometimes even conflict. Becoming a good person, for instance, often means forgoing opportunities because they are unethical and sacrificing your own happiness for the sake of others. Philip and Elizabeth, for example, are frequently in conflict about what is best for Paige—should they encourage her to do what will make her happy, or should they push her to become like themselves, and sacrifice her happiness in service of the cause? Philip places Paige's happiness above everything else, where Elizabeth thinks it is more important for Paige to be good person (in a certain very loose sense of the word).

There is no easy solution to this problem, and the Jenningses will likely face it again when Henry gets older. But even if we set aside the Jenningses's unusual hopes for their children, there are two goals at the heart of parenting that simply cannot be reconciled. As philosopher David Archard points out, parents must both protect their children from harm and foster their ability to make their own choices—that is, to be independent, autonomous beings. Protecting children means guiding and directing them, sheltering them from threats and dangers of every variety. In spite of their risky occupation, Philip and Elizabeth go to great lengths to keep Paige and Henry safe. But protecting children in this way undermines their ability to make choices. Letting children make choices means accepting that some of those choices will put them in harm's way. But not allowing them to make any choices keeps them children forever, unable to live lives of their own or become their own people. How to balance these goals is difficult to decide. How to achieve them is perhaps even more difficult.

Mischa and Nadezhda Had a Baby

So, even typical parents have multiple agendas regarding their children. Philip and Elizabeth have further agendas imposed by their life as spies. They must keep their real identities a secret from their children, while at the same time grooming them to at least understand why they've done what they've done, if not to become spies themselves. In the service of these various agendas, parents have a variety of tool and techniques available to them. Parents may punish or reward children to discourage or encourage certain behaviors—as when Henry is punished for breaking into the neighbors' house to play video games. Parents can regulate their own behavior to set the appropriate example, as when Elizabeth swallows her ill-will toward religion to make peace with Pastor Tim. On the flip side, parents can point to bad examples as warnings to their children. And, of course, parents can lie.

That may seem questionable. There's no denying that parents do in fact lie, but it's reasonable to ask whether they should. Lying is supposed to be immoral, and so, at the very least, parents set a bad example by lying to their children. At worst, they take advantage of the trust inherent in the parent-child relationship and potentially damage the child's ability to trust people in the future. And that doesn't even get into the ethics of lying itself.

Is lying wrong? Most people, and most philosophers, seem to think that it is in most cases. Few would claim that it's always wrong. Even some who do could make exceptions for children. Immanuel Kant (1724–1804) famously argued that lying is never justified. Kant went so far as to claim that if a murderer were hunting your friend, you should not lie to protect your friend. Lies are always means for manipulating one another—we lie in order to make people act in ways they wouldn't if they had the correct information. As such, when we lie to anyone, we fail to treat that person with the respect they are due as a person.

Even Kant might make an exception for lying to children. The presumption in Kant's argument is that the person lied to is a fully rational being, capable of making free choices and being responsible for their actions. But children don't meet these conditions. So, lying to children can be justified.

When we claim that lying is justified, we generally offer one of three justifications: either the lie led to some good result, or was motivated by some good intention, or was directed to someone who, for whatever reason, doesn't deserve or need to be told the truth. I discuss the first two justifications in the next couple of sections, but here I want to look at the last one, because it is the most common justification for lying to children.

Parents, teachers, and other authority figures that deal frequently with children will often claim that they're justified in misleading kids because the kids wouldn't understand. So, when children ask how babies are made, for example, we tell them fairy tales about storks instead of getting into the biology of human reproduction. Implicit in this sort of justification is the idea that a child, as a child, is not deserving of the truth. People think that because children below a certain age lack certain reasoning abilities there's no harm in telling them falsehoods. There's an element of this sort of thinking in Philip and Elizabeth's reasons for lying about themselves to their children. Impressing the need for secrecy is hard enough when Paige is a somewhat mature teenager—imagine trying to explain it to a toddler.

This line of reasoning, common though it is, is flawed. The problem is that if we accept this blanket justification of lies told to children, then there is no way of distinguishing when we should tell children the truth rather than a lie. There are many things children lack the cognitive capacity to understand—for that matter there are many things that many adults lack the cognitive capacity to understand as well. It in no way follows that we are justified in deceiving them about them. Most adults can't explain the workings of an internal combustion engine, but that doesn't give mechanics the right to put "imp-wrangling" or "horse watering" on a repair bill. Regardless of the client's ability to comprehend the truth, the mechanic has the duty to tell it. Similar logic holds for children.

Noble Lies of the Jennings Family

The argument that children aren't entitled to the truth because they can't understand it has a fatal flaw. It justifies virtually all lies that anyone could tell a child. Kidnappers are just as justified in lying to the children they take as parents are in lying to their own children. So, another justification must be presented that allows that some lies told to children may be justified while providing us with a way to distinguish which ones are and which aren't justified.

Fortunately, we have two possible standards by which to distinguish justified and unjustified lies to children: the intention of the lie and the results. These justifications are both variations on one of the oldest defenses of lying. In his *Republic*, Plato (428–348 B.C.E.) presents a defense of a certain kind of lie, one told for the benefit of the person lied to— a noble lie.

A lie can be defined as noble either because of its intentions or its results, but it's wiser to focus on its intentions. The reasons we lie—our intentions—are under our control. The results of a lie, however, are unpredictable. When you lie there is no telling whether the person will actually be deceived, or will later on discover the deception, or how they will respond in either case.

Philip and Elizabeth may have had the best of intentions in concealing their true identities from their children. On the one hand, they were protecting the kids. On the other hand, by concealing their identities, they believed, or at least Elizabeth believed, that they were serving the greater good. Only by lying could they help the noble forces of Communism overcome the exploitive and imperialistic system of capitalism. But in spite of their good intentions, they had no way of knowing when Paige would catch them out in their lies. They couldn't have foreseen that Paige would betray them almost immediately when she discovered the truth. And they couldn't have known that Pastor Tim would keep Paige's confidence. They got lucky. So, whether a lie is noble or not becomes a matter of accident if nobility comes from its results. So, the nobility of lies should be found in the intentions that motivate their telling.

When it comes to lying to children, the intentions that justify such lies must be defined in terms of the two goals of parenting: protecting the child and encouraging its growth into an independent, autonomous being. Once again the conflict between these goals presents a problem, because lies that serve the one will tend to undermine the other. The Jennings's lies to their children are usually intended to protect them, either from the usual everyday dangers of childhood or from the more severe threats posed by a life of espionage.

A Bodyguard of Lies

Lies of protection are complicated, however, by what threats the children are being protected from. We can distinguish three ways the Jenningses lie to protect their children by the types of threats they are intended to shield the children from. First, the Jenningses, like most parents, lie to protect the children from themselves. The Jenningses lie to protect Paige and Henry from everyday dangers, as all parents do.

They exaggerate the threats posed by drugs and sex and other risky behaviors parents want to discourage. These lies and exaggerations in turn encourage sorts of behaviors parents want to encourage, such as refraining from sex and drugs and making self-protective choices.

The Jenningses also lie to protect their children from truths they would find upsetting. When, for example, they were experiencing marital difficulties, they put on a united front for the kids. Most parents do this. Notoriously, many parents send pets to a "farm upstate" rather than admit that pets are mortal and have their children confront the grim specter of death. When Elizabeth was injured in the line of duty, she and Philip invented a fiction about her being sick to explain her absence during her recuperation.

But the Jenningses also lie to protect their children from learning the truth about themselves. Even after they reveal who they are to Paige, they keep on lying to her about what they do in the service of the cause. Elizabeth, for instance, insists repeatedly that she—a multiple and largely remorseless murderer—has never hurt anyone in performing her duties as a spy. That particular lie becomes far more tenuous after Paige watches her mother kill a would-be mugger with little effort and less thought.

Lies of Encouragement

There seems to be a contradiction on the face of the other sorts of lies parents can tell—those intended to encourage independence and autonomy in their children. The problem with lies, morally speaking, is that they interfere with the deceived person's ability to make her own decision. It seems odd, therefore, to lie to someone to help them be autonomous.

But we can lie to people to help them carry out or stick to choices they've already made. Suppose, for example, that Elizabeth wants to quit smoking completely. To help her out, Philip agrees to hold her cigarettes. The two of them agree how many cigarettes she can get and when. In a moment of weakness, Elizabeth demands a cigarette beyond her allotted ration. Philip might, rather than simply tell her no (which might lead to a fight), simply lie and say that he had no more of her cigarettes on him at the moment. In this way, Philip restricts Elizabeth's ability to make a particular choice at this moment, but he does so in the name of carrying out her previous choice.

Philosopher Harry Frankfurt calls this the distinction between first-order and second-order desires. First-order desires are those that regard only their immediate objects—our desires for cigarettes, food, drink, possessions, enjoyment, and so on. Second-order desires are regulatory. They are desires about desires. Elizabeth may desire a cigarette, but she also desires not to desire a cigarette. So, Philip's lie interferes with her ability to fulfill her first-order desire, but in the name of her second-order desire.

This distinction does not map easily onto parental lies to children. The problem is that children below a certain age are what Frankfurt calls wantons—human beings with no second-order desires, or no ability to regulate their first-order desires. Part of a parent's job, in making the child an independent, autonomous adult, is instilling second-order desires and reinforcing the ability make choices based on them.

How can lies do that? Although it seems possible that lying could reinforce second-order desires, it's unclear how they could foster a child's ability to have or act on them. Incentives or disincentives offered would eventually have to manifest, and thus couldn't be lies. Take the Santa Claus myth, for instance. We can make the case that part of the point of this myth is to teach children to delay gratification—a key ability for acting on second-order desires. But a child told that bad behavior leads to coal in the stocking who is consistently bad and yet never gets coal isn't learning anything. Or, more specifically, she's learning to be a wanton.

Lying to create second-order desires or the ability to act on them may not be possible, but it's a simple matter to lie to reinforce second-order desires and their ability to regulate first-order desires. Take, for example, a common lie parents tell their children to encourage healthy eating habits.

For generations, parents have been telling their children to eat their vegetables (or particular, especially hateful vegetables, like spinach) if they want to grow up to be big and strong. Most children want to grow up, and many want to be big and strong. It's simply a lie that those outcomes are in anyway connected to eating vegetables. Provided the child survives to adulthood and consumes adequate calories, it will grow up; vegetables are no more essential to that than any other food. Similarly, becoming big and strong is dependent on a wide variety of factors, none of which have anything to do with one's consumption of spinach or broccoli as a child. But the lie that eating vegetables leads to growing up big and strong encourages the child to act on that second-order desire and regulate her first-order desire to feed the hated green substance to the dog. So, a lie can help turn a child into an adult capable of making reasonable and responsible choices. Unfortunately, the Jenningses' lies to Paige and Henry rarely fit this model. In fact, they tend to have the opposite effect.

Living Someone Else's Lie

A person's ability to make choices—to be autonomous—has a particular relationship with that person's ability to form an identity. The two are mutually reinforcing. We make choices based on who we are, and those choices in turn shape who we are. Philip and Elizabeth have chosen to be spies and parents, and their identities as spies and parents dictate many of their subsequent choices.

But unlike Philip and Elizabeth's cover identities, most of our identities are restricted in some ways by facts about ourselves that we cannot change. However much Matthew may dislike and resent his father at times, he cannot change the fact that he is Stan's son. In forming his identity, Matt has to deal with his relationship with Stan. He can do that in a variety of ways, but he can't avoid doing it.

Philip and Elizabeth undermine their children's potential autonomy by forcing them to live a lie. The Jennings children know nothing about their own parents or origins, really. Their surname, Jennings, is based on their parents' alias. They don't know about other relatives they have; the family tree they've been told about is a work of fiction.

Paige discovering the truth when she does makes her attempt to form her identity that much more difficult. Our teen years are when we begin to contrast ourselves against our parents in a variety of ways. Paige is in the process of doing this when she discovers that she knows nothing about her parents. In defining herself, she has no starting point. Her parents, through their lies, have robbed her both of a solid foundation to build on, and of a concrete opponent to contrast herself against. As a result, Paige is even more lost and alone than most teenagers.

The closest parallel to what Philip and Elizabeth have done is kidnapping. Like a pair of kidnappers who raise their victims as their own, the Jenningses have robbed their own children of their birthright. Paige and Henry are children without a past, without history, without anywhere that they belong in the world. As the children of Soviet spies, they can never be fully American; but as children raised in the US, they could never be at home in the USSR, either.

Just as kidnapping victims must come to terms with the fact that their parents aren't their parents, Paige and Henry will have to come to grips with the fact that they owe their existence to their parents' need to maintain their cover.

The Final Lie

Lying is generally frowned upon, but lying to children is often thought to be acceptable, at least for the parents. The case of the Jenningses, with their lies upon lies, shows clearly that even here lies are at best temporary solutions. The long-term interests of parenting are ultimately best served by honesty. This doesn't mean telling the truth all the time or telling children everything—it simply means not lying. There is an important and often underestimated difference between lying and not telling the truth.

You don't need to lie in order to avoid telling the truth. Certainly there are things you shouldn't tell children. So don't tell them—simply tell them that you won't tell them. Don't make up fairy tales to tell them instead. They help no one.

10
Decisions that Change Who We Are

KEVIN MEEKER

Juggling work and family is difficult, especially if you're a spy.

For Philip and Elizabeth Jennings, Soviet spies posing as an ordinary American married couple in the United States, having children who don't know about their undercover work complicates their lives immensely. From the beginning of the series, Philip and Elizabeth express concern about how their lives as spies might affect their children, Paige and Henry.

In the second episode ("The Clock"), Elizabeth frets particularly about the consequences for the "delicate" Paige if something were to happen to her and Philip. Ironically, the last scene of Season One shows the "delicate" Paige secretly sneaking into the basement to try to figure out why her parents suspiciously spend so much time down there. This snooping scene sets up the conflict to come and casts new light on the relationship between the Jenningses and their children.

Given the difficulty of raising children while spying, one might wonder why Philip and Elizabeth decided to have children at all. One of the most important episodes for understanding this decision is "The Walk-In." Through a series of flashbacks, we catch a glimpse of some of the issues that confront them, and Elizabeth in particular, as they struggle with their decision to have children.

Did they make the right choice? How can we tell? Academics such as economists, statisticians, and philosophers often suggest that people should rely on decision theory to help them make correct choices in an almost mathematical way.

Consider a familiar example. After eating a large Thanksgiving meal, you're trying to decide whether you should eat one last piece of pumpkin pie. On the one hand, you know that you'll enjoy it because you've already tasted it. On the other hand, you also remember that when you've overstuffed before, you've become incredibly sick to your stomach and not enjoyed that last piece of pie. If you have a fifty-fifty chance of becoming sick, then it's best to decline the pie because the ill feeling is much more intense and endures much longer than the brief delight you derive from consuming one more piece of tasty pie.

But what if it's unlikely that you'll become ill? Here it depends partly on how unlikely. If you have, say, a 33-percent chance of getting sick, then it still seems that the intense unpleasantness of becoming ill outweighs the momentary pleasure of the last piece of pie. But what if there's only a ten percent chance? Or two percent? Here many decision theorists would counsel us to assign numerical values to the positive experience of enjoying the pie and the negative experience of becoming ill so that we can then use the probability that one will occur to calculate which choice is the best. Though we may not be able to confidently assign precise numbers to these variables, it seems that a general approximation of these values is enough to be helpful in many circumstances.

A Problem?

The philosopher Laurie Paul has recently argued that from one point of view decision theory is unhelpful. For in making certain choices in life, such as having children, we're deciding whether to have experiences that radically and fundamentally transform what we care about. One of her favorite examples is the fanciful possibility of choosing to permanently become a vampire.

Given that being a vampire is so different from being a human, how can we imaginatively consider the value, numeric or otherwise, of such an experience? How can we even know whether we would value such vampire experiences at all? It seems that we can't answer such questions because we can't know what it's like to be a vampire. Without such knowledge, decision theory can't help us to choose. When making a decision about the pumpkin pie, our past provides us with a relatively firm grasp on how to rate the various experiences (tasting pie versus feeling ill). But the past is not helpful when we must choose new experiences that might change how we estimate what's important in life.

How exactly these prospective changes affect our ability to make such decisions rationally is a matter of dispute. Does the inability stem from the prospect that our deepest values will simply change? Or is the problem that we don't have sufficient knowledge of what it's like to experience such a transformed life? This essay will first recount how the Jenningses' decision to have children seems to radically transform their lives and deepest values. After considering some possible problems with understanding the narrative in this way, we will then consider one way that the story suggests the transformation allows them to have a type of *knowledge* that is difficult to quantify with decision theory.

Of course, we can evaluate the decision to have children from many perspectives. In "Walk-In," Elizabeth clearly struggles with the expectations of her Soviet espionage handlers. They believe that having children can help the Jenningses blend into American society and avoid unnecessary suspicion. Because Elizabeth believes that her espionage activities for the Soviet Union are for "the greater good," having children can be morally good because it helps them achieve this "greater good." From her perspective, we can make the case that the choice to have children is morally rational at the very least.

So why does she hesitate? It's difficult to say. She suggests that she never wanted children. But part of the problem might be that she realizes the transformative nature of having children. Why exactly she and Philip eventually chose to have children isn't entirely clear (to me anyway). Most likely they had many motives or reasons. But their lives seem to be transformed.

The Terrible Trauma

Although Philip and Elizabeth chose to have children, perhaps partly to enhance their espionage cover, they keep their true identities hidden from the children. And this deception was expected by their bosses. Moreover, in the first episode of Season Two ("Comrades") we meet Emmett and Leanne Connors, friends of the Jenningses who face similar issues because they're also spies with children. Unfortunately, Emmett draws Philip into an unexpected situation in which Philip needs to use Henry as a cover in a public place to pick up some information.

The objective is achieved, but Philip's spur-of-the-moment decision to use Henry in a spy mission causes great consternation. For up until that point, the Jenningses had vowed "not to use our kids" in the nitty gritty of the work they do. Toward the end of the episode, Philip regrets involving Henry and tells Elizabeth: "I should have done it without Henry, even if I was more exposed." Although Elizabeth isn't happy about the involvement, she consoles Philip with the idea that the split-second decision was thrust upon him. "You didn't have time to think," she says. Obviously this doesn't satisfy Philip because he once again laments the choice that he made at the end of the next episode ("Cardinal").

The worry that using their children could jeopardize everyone's safety is particularly vivid at this point. For "Comrades" also confronts us with the horrific death of Emmett and Leanne Connors and their daughter Amelia. The Jenningses discover them murdered in a hotel room and immediately think of their own children, with Elizabeth hurrying off to find them. When Philip eventually leaves the room he sees the Connorses' son, Jared, returning from the pool.

Although Elizabeth and Philip reunite with their kids, during much of the second season the Jenningses are looking over their shoulders in fear for their own safety and the safety of their children. For they are unsure who killed the Connorses, and whether the murderers might also come after them. The fear for their children is palpable and poignant as Elizabeth confides that: "All these years, I . . . I never really worried about Paige and Henry being safe" ("Cardinal").

How could Elizabeth reasonably voice such surprise? Surely as a spy she knew (or should have known) that *anyone* associated with them could be in danger at some any point. And surely she realizes that from a certain point of view, just having the children means that they have already "used their kids" in an operation—as a cover to deflect suspicion. Perhaps they don't "use" them when picking up information or engaging directly in other espionage. But given that their whole espionage purpose as agents revolves around promoting the Soviet vision of the greater good at any cost, Elizabeth's surprise suggests that perhaps her priorities have changed in ways that even she had not anticipated. Maybe she's been transformed.

The Total Transformation

It turns out that Jared had killed his own family. In "Echo," the last episode of Season Two, an upset informant, Larrick, shoots Jared in the throat before being killed. As he lies dying, Jared tells Elizabeth the story of how the Soviets had attempted to recruit him, unbeknownst to his parents. After falling in love with his Soviet handler, Kate, he tells his parents that he wanted to be a Soviet spy too.

Jared tells Elizabeth that he and Kate ". . . were going to work together. They didn't understand. My whole life was a lie. Kate told me who I am." He then confesses that he killed his parents when they reacted poorly, hauntingly justifying his actions with the following words: "I had to protect my cover. What we do, it's for something greater than ourselves."

Jared's last words echo what Elizabeth told him before she realized that he had killed his parents: "I never met anyone who loved their kids as much as your parents did." Elizabeth tells Jared just prior to the stunning revelation: "I mean, the risks that they took, it was because they believed in something greater than themselves. You have to understand that. They wanted the world to be better. For everyone. For you." Of course Jared's words are harrowing for the Jenningses. Because Paige and Henry also don't know who they are—children of Soviet spies.

Surely at this point they are considering various chilling questions: how would their kids react to the information that their parents are undercover spies? Jared had heartbreakingly rejected the idea that his parents loved him. Would Paige and Henry doubt Philip and Elizabeth's love if they knew? And perhaps most terrifying of all: "What if the Soviets want to recruit *our* kids?"

They don't have to wonder long. They soon discover through their former supervisor, Claudia, that their Soviet bosses want them to tell Paige about their covert operations. Further, the Jenningses are to entice Paige to become the first building block of the "second-generation illegals" who, being born in the United States, can pass the background checks necessary to move into sensitive government positions. In other words, the Jenningses learn of their government's plan for them to actively recruit their daughter Paige as a future spy.

Elizabeth's reaction is swift and firm: "That's not an option." Claudia is sympathetic to Elizabeth's emotions, but equally firm in reiterating their orders. Although she says that she disagrees with the Soviets' attempt to recruit Jared behind his parents' backs, Claudia agrees with the importance of having such well-placed spies. She tries to undermine any resistance the Jenningses might have to this plan by telling them: "Paige is your daughter, but she's not just yours. She belongs to the cause and to the world. We all do. You haven't forgotten that, have you?" Having received their orders and this pep talk, Philip and Elizabeth stand in stunned silence ("Echo").

But they soon fire a proverbial shot across the Soviet bow. Philip approaches a Soviet official, Arkady, in a public place despite the possibility that Arkady might be under US surveillance. In no uncertain terms he informs him: "If our organization ever gets anywhere near our daughter without our permission, my wife and I are finished." Clearly this defiant statement delivered in such a risky place indicates that having children has, at least temporarily, fundamentally changed their dedication to spying as their primary objective in life.

Family now comes first. Their parenthood pre-empts their spying. Children are no longer simply a cover for their spying. Paige and Henry don't belong to the cause or the world. They are Philip and Elizabeth's kids, the most important things in their lives. This perspective is a far cry from viewing everything in their life as subordinate to the purpose of spying.

Perhaps they had originally calculated that the benefit of deflecting suspicion by having children outweighed the cost of the time such children might take from their spying duties. A decision theorist can presumably model such a choice. But what may be difficult for decision theorists is accounting for the possibility that having the children can fundamentally alter the values and shift the focus *from* total devotion to spying *to* total devotion to the safety of their children. From this perspective, skip ahead in the series and consider "One Day in the Life of Anton Baklanov." After having just found out about her parents' true Soviet identity, Paige is asking many heart-wrenching yet logical questions; she even wonders whether they are her true biological parents. The implication is that even Paige recognizes that children would be a great cover for spies.

Later Elizabeth tells Paige that she is their daughter and that Henry is their son; Elizabeth also seems to disingenuously revise history and insist that they "really wanted them more than you can know." But Paige asks: "How can I believe anything you say?" The look on Elizabeth's face reveals that she is deeply hurt by this understandable reaction, once again indicating that her priorities are now not just espionage—even if they were when they decided to have children. How can one take into account such unforeseen priority shifts before deciding to have children?

The Tale of One or Two Transformations?

But let's return to the point at which the Jenningses are confronted with the request to turn Paige into a spy. To find favor with the Jenningses, and probably to make a more persuasive attempt to persuade them to recruit Paige, the Soviets make a bold move. With a threatening line drawn in the sand, they un-retire Gabriel, the Jenningses' favorite handler. Given their trust of Gabriel, the Soviets believe that he can put them at ease about the plan.

Elizabeth begins to warm to the idea even before Gabriel comes on the scene. Over the course of several episodes, she lets Philip know that she is softening her stance about Paige becoming a spy. She tells Philip that she now sees some of her fire in Paige; she believes that Paige is looking for a cause. Elizabeth thinks that she can channel Paige's newfound religious enthusiasm about the meaningfulness of sacrifice into a more Soviet-inspired view of the common good. After all, some of Paige's church activities, such as protesting at a military facility, share ideological similarities with socialism.

Philip fights back. He points out that they swore to never bring their kids into the spy "business." Such a life would "destroy" Paige. In "Open House" Philip argues with Elizabeth about the life he wants for Paige: "A guarantee that life's going to be easy? For my daughter, yeah." But he's unable to convince her. Finally, in a moment fraught with tension, Elizabeth informs Philip that she's going to recruit Paige with or without his help.

Philip is less than pleased. But Elizabeth moves ahead, with Gabriel egging her on. First, Paige has to learn the truth about her parents. Elizabeth softens the ground by telling Paige about their "activist" background. Eventually,

Paige looks her parents in the eyes and demands to know who they are. They tell her, but insist that she tell no one. Now that Paige knows, Philip still doesn't want her to become like them. Between Elizabeth and Gabriel, though, Philip is feeling squeezed from every direction. In the ninth episode of Season Three, Philip tells Gabriel: "My job is to look after my family because no one else will." No one, not even Elizabeth. Perhaps we see his recognition of this duty in the very first episode when he tracks down a man who made wildly inappropriate comments to Paige in a store, punishing him by stabbing a barbecue tool into various parts of his body.

Although it seemed at one point that Philip and Elizabeth had been transformed by having children, some might question that assessment. Given that Elizabeth so quickly jumped on board with this project, one could ask: has Elizabeth really been transformed? Has Philip?

We've known from the beginning of the series that Philip and Elizabeth are different. Philip doesn't see the same softness or evil in America that Elizabeth does. In the very first episode, he is openly discussing the positive possibility of defecting. Elizabeth is horrified. She even tells her superiors that Philip likes it in the United States too much. This information leads to an excruciating encounter during which the Soviet authorities kidnap and torture Philip and Elizabeth to see if they have been leaking information.

Philip's liking of America could be attributed in part to having kids in the United States. But consider the possibility that Philip is "softer" than Elizabeth and is merely using his kids as an excuse. In the tenth episode of Season Three ("Stingers"), Philip asks Paige's pastor, Tim, whether he has any kids. Pastor Tim replies: "I have a flock." Philip is unimpressed: "It's not the same." Philip seems to be suggesting that because Pastor Tim does not have children of his own, he lacks the requisite knowledge to understand Philip's situation and the decisions that he faces with his children.

Now he could just be saying this because he's trying to avoid a discussion that he can't win. But consider the following scene. At the end of the emotionally draining episode "Comrades," Philip is talking to Martha, the FBI employee whom he has also married but who does not know he is a spy. She thinks that he's talking about working in intelligence for the US when he confides to her: "It's just hard. This job, this life. It gets to you in ways that you didn't think it would." Then he confesses that he does not know if he is cut out for the job, which we know means his Soviet spy gig. Given what's happened to the Connorses in this episode, and the conversation he's already had with Elizabeth, this comment suggests that having children while being a spy has changed him in ways that can't be anticipated.

If having children has changed Philip, then how can we account for Elizabeth's actions given that she's also a parent of the same child? Looking closely at some more details of the story reveals that Elizabeth's transformation is deeper and could help us to understand the problem that transformative experiences present to decision theory.

Elizabeth's Transformation

After some initial resistance, Elizabeth is on board with turning Paige into a Soviet spy. But recall again her revealing comment at the end of "Comrades": "All these years, I . . . I never really worried about Paige and Henry being safe." Now she is afraid. Her fear for her children appears to be greater than her fear for her own life—or even for Philip's. Indeed, the series seems to suggest that fear for children is perhaps the greatest fear of all. So the decision to have children could potentially transform your knowledge: it helps you to understand fear at a deeper level that cannot be understood in any other way.

Perhaps I'm reading too much into this scene from "Comrades." But consider the episode "Pastor Tim": Elizabeth dreams of Paige going to a cabin that Pastor Tim often visits and finding his dead body there. Suddenly the body transforms into Nikolai Timoshev, the KGB colonel who horrifically abused Elizabeth during her training. Elizabeth awakens in fear just as Timoshev grabs Paige. This scene strongly suggests that deep down, on some level, Elizabeth really is fearful of what will happen to Paige if she follows in her footsteps—much more fearful than she has been admitting. Once again, perhaps we could say that her true fear is not for herself, but for her children: a fear that dwarfs all other fears. If having children had not transformed her priorities, then she would be as willing to let Paige die for the cause as she was to let Lucia be killed by Larrick in "New Car."

This fear for her children, and Paige in particular, is at least partially what helps break Elizabeth down. She admits it somewhat, as we have seen. And her dream shows that this fear is constantly eating away at her. Along with other gory and gut-wrenching incidents, Elizabeth's cold exterior melts away. It becomes so obvious that, at the end of the fourth season, even Gabriel recognizes it. Because of Elizabeth's transformation, and Philip's "heart not being in it" (among other reasons), Gabriel recommends that the Jennings family be removed from service. Such a suggestion is surprising because of how vital the Jenningses' work has been and how much the Soviets are salivating over the prospect of having a "second generation illegal" such as Paige.

If I'm right about Elizabeth, then in some ways her transformation is more radical than Philip's. Considering this way of understanding the narrative provides a helpful way to think about the importance and difficulty of making decisions about important matters such as having children. In "Chloramphenicol," Oleg is talking to his father about the death of Oleg's brother. His father claims that, "losing a child is like nothing else." Losing a friend or parent is incredibly heart-wrenching. But those who have suffered the loss of a child often make claims like Oleg's father. To lose a child is to have a deeper understanding of loss. Not everyone who has children lives to see their deaths. And not everyone who has children faces choices such as the Jenningses face and the types of fears associated with these choices. The issue isn't so much that our deepest values change. The possibility that *The Americans* raises is that while everyone can understand fear and grief, you can't know the distinctive dimension of what it's like to fear for your child or grieve for your child unless you're a parent.

Granted, *The Americans* is just a story—a story, however, that requires quite a bit of interpretation and reading between the lines. Even if it does rest on the idea that having children is transformative in an important way, that idea could be wrong. We're dealing with fiction after all. Further, a definitive discussion of how transformative experiences might affect decision theory would require a more complicated consideration of the details of decision theory itself.

While *The Americans* does not prove that the choice to have a child presents an insuperable problem for decision theory's desire to quantify the rationality of choices, it is still instructive. With its vivid story-telling, memorable lines, and revealing facial expressions of its characters, it can put us in a position to wonder: how can I make a rational choice when my future experiences will transform me and potentially make me understand fear and loss in a way I never could have imagined? *The Americans* alerts us to this possibility in a way that is incredibly poignant and powerful.

11
We're Only What We Remember

ANDREA ZANIN

Elizabeth and Philip Jennings; the couple next door, with their homemade brownies, ready smiles, and picture-perfect garden—they keep some weird hours but nothing unusual for travel agents with a couple of kids.

Place this semblance of normality into suburban Washington DC, circa 1981, and you've got *The Americans*, an espionage drama produced by former CIA officer Joe Weisberg (street cred alert!) that tells the story of two Soviet KGB officers posing as an American married couple who quietly sabotage government operations and neutralize targets whilst raising two teenagers, with an FBI counterintelligence agent as a neighbor (and you thought *your* life was stressful?).

Eighties America was a time of paranoia; the threat of nuclear war was imminent and Communists lurked behind every bush. Sort of like now, only it's jihadists doing the lurking. Cold War espionage was a deadly serious game. Elizabeth is a force to be reckoned with; utilitarian and pragmatic to the max, this is a gal who will *put you down* one time. Philip equally lethal, is the more demonstrative of the pair, functioning as the emotional glue between Elizabeth and their children (Paige and Henry), but he's a killer; make no mistake. Together, they're like Captain America, only Russian.

Their marriage is one of necessity. Recruited into the KGB at a young age; trained and then sent on assignment to America, Elizabeth and Philip buy into an existence enveloped in solitude and dominated by professional purpose. In spite of the indifference that typically defines an arranged marriage, the operatives do eventually fall in love and actually, they're a pretty steamy item. But killer sex (pardon the spy pun) does not preclude team Jennings from having to navigate the complications of wedlock and work out the same old awkward existential relationship stuff that defines the interactions between 'regular' couples.

One of the show's most poignant themes is that of identity. *The Americans* plays with the philosophy of self, which is particularly complex in the case of Elizabeth and Phillip, who mask their Russian birthright with an American hashtag, so to speak. In order to fulfill their function as *spy*, they are required to give up their culture, their names and families; all the ingredients for identity. They're asked to live an assumed personality and to do so effectively, they must *forget*. FBI operative Chris Amador describes undercover agents, to his partner Stan Beeman: "They look like us, they speak better English than we do . . . they're not allowed to say a single word of Russian when they get here" ("Pilot"). It's a tough task—to forget—because memory is innate; like blinking or breathing, it's a function of being. Philosopher John Locke (1632–1704) articulates memory as a necessary and sufficient condition of self, and, therein, personal identity.

One of the Enlightenment era's foremost thinkers, Locke understood the correlation between memory and self, which in turn informs identity. Locke defines the 'self' as "a thinking intelligent being, that has reason and reflection, and can consider itself as itself, the same thinking thing, in different times and places. Locke argues that consciousness always accompanies thinking and that personal identity extends only so far as one's consciousness. He goes on to equate consciousness with memory when he says that as far as consciousness can be extended backwards to any past action or thought, so far reaches the identity of that person; it's the same self now as it was then. In other words, the 'self' is not limited to the present, it is equally defined by the past—or, "different times and places."

The flashbacks that interrupt Elizabeth and Philip's lives at regular intervals establish the importance of memory as an influence on self. It is through these "extensions backwards to past action of thought" that team Jennings enacts consciousness and asserts identity. Yet *The Americans* not only shows how Philip and Elizabeth's memories serve their respective identities or inform their sense of self but questions the reliability of those memories.

I Don't Know if You Know Who I Am

Our initial impression of Elizabeth and Philip is forged through the context of memory. We first meet Elizabeth in a bar, but not *as Elizabeth*; rather a blonde hooker on a mission to gain information from a federal agent. The mystery of her identity is emphasized through a mirror image frame; multiple Elizabeths—which is the real one? It's a motif repeated.

Elizabeth takes the agent to bed, as hookers do, and as she seduces her target, her image reflects in a mirror opposite the bed—kinky, yes, but also thematic. Not much later, the 'real' Elizabeth is mirrored in a car window and as she pauses to look at her reflection, her mind takes her back to 1960, Russia, where her younger self is practicing fighting moves with her trainer. Elizabeth's trainer gives way to Captain Nikolai Timoshev, a high-ranking official who beats Elizabeth, eventually raping her. This is the same Timoshev who has been captured as a consequence of defecting and waits bound and gagged in the trunk of the Jenningses' car. It's no surprise that Elizabeth next catches her reflection in the blade of a ready-to-slice, dice, or kill kitchen knife—contemplating violence against the man who hurt her; a figment of memory that has emerged across time, continent, and culture.

Locke suggests the ideas that make the deepest and most lasting impressions, are those which are accompanied with pleasure or pain; making us avoid painful subjects with the aim of self-preservation, settling in the memory a caution for the future. Just as Elizabeth did not report the rape, she does not use the knife—perhaps to avoid the resurgence of the pain wrought by this particular memory; a measure of self protection, as suggested by Locke. And ultimately, it is Philip who offs Timoshev.

Elizabeth's reaction to this particular memory offers insight into the stoicism and heightened sense of control that pervades her character. Elizabeth's icy exterior is shown to be something nurtured by her training. Although anger takes over when confronting Timoshev, Elizabeth "wins" by gaining control of her emotions, as she was taught; to submit to the demands of the Cause, however painful they might be. Through this memory, we glimpse the "self" that underlies Elizabeth's American identity, and interestingly it's only after her confrontation with Timoshev, where she relives the violence of rape, that she is able to open up to Philip about her past—who she is, *or was*. It takes fifteen years of marriage for Elizabeth to tell Philip her name, *Nadezhda*.

Elizabeth remembers *Nadezhda*; a Russian girl, born in Smolensk, raised by her mother (after her father—who was pale, with bushy eyebrows—was killed by the Nazis in Stalingrad when she was two) and grew up with three other families in a single apartment. This is not the childhood of Elizabeth Jennings—who likely grew up as an only child in suburban America with loving parents and nice friends . . . so we muse. But the memory of the cold, the poverty . . . *of Russia*, exists in Elizabeth's consciousness and as such, informs her identity. There is, however, a conundrum: Nadezhda and Elizabeth are physically the same person but they are also, confusingly, opposing identities and so *not* literally the same person. And to complicate matters further, Elizabeth's identity is confounded by the characters she assumes for the mission's sake—whether it's CIA security officer Laura Gering, recovering alcoholic Michelle, or social worker Ann Chadwick. What happens when the self you remember is not the same as your identity at the moment of memory?

To understand this, you have to look at the difference between "identity" and "self" in their most precise contexts. Applied as nouns, "self" is the subject of your own experience of phenomena—and the perceptions, emotions and thoughts that emanate, while "identity" is *sameness*, identicalness; the quality or fact of (several specified things) being the same. So, when we're talking *people*; "identity" is that which is identical to the "self" or the subject of the identity.

Locke, too, speaks of "sameness"; defining identity as the sameness of a rational being—an identity that agrees with the character of "self." Given this assertion, any change in the self reflects a change in personal identity, and any change in personal identity therefore implies that the self has changed. As it's Nadezhda's memories that pervade the consciousness which inhabits the physical being of Elizabeth, Elizabeth's defining self has to be that of Nadezhda; the self that was born into the world and who "perceived" and "experienced" whilst growing up. Nadezhda is the subject, and Elizabeth—or blonde hooker, *or* Laura, Ann, and Michelle—are the identities that are all informed by the "self" that is subject to the perceived memories.

The problem with this is that when Nadezhda dons her Elizabeth mask, or any of her varying identities, they are not the "same" as the self that informs them. Does this make Elizabeth an irrational being, from Locke's perspective?

Dumb Stuff

The relationship between identity and self is equally incongruous for Philip, whose most poignant memory is of Mischa, his Russian alter ego. In a repeated flashback sequence, Philip sees his younger self as an adolescent evading bullies, one of whom he bludgeons to death with a rock. Even though the memory is eating at his thoughts, Philip doesn't tell Elizabeth about it. He does, however, confide in fake wife Martha as well as the peeps at the *est* sessions he attends (well, as much as he can without blowing his cover). It's complicated, with Elizabeth—she is privy to all of his identities and even she struggles to relate to Philip as himself (whoever that may be). On one occasion she gets jiggy with her husband in his Clark costume; he immediately reverts to "Philip mode," kissing Elizabeth with characteristic sensuality but she wants to see Clark "the animal"—as Martha has described him. He relents by having vicious "Is this what you want?" sex with Elizabeth—from behind—an obvious allusion to the rape flashback from our first rendezvous with Elizabeth.

After the horrible sex, Philip disappears to the bathroom; disgusted with himself he rips off his Clark-wig and disguise, while Elizabeth sobs on the bed. He's pissed that the woman he loves wants him to be a man that he is not but also, his aggression could easily be linked to the submerged memory of his first murder. It's a formative moment that he wonders about to fake-wife Martha; "I keep having these memories from when I was a kid . . . dumb stuff. But you know how some of it makes you think, 'I wonder if this is why I act this way, or why I'm so angry about that'" ("Glanders").

In "Do Mail Robots Dream of Electric Sheep?" we meet Betty, who is in the wrong place at the wrong time and is about to be killed by Elizabeth. Betty gets talking, *remembering*, and tells Elizabeth about her dead husband Gil, who fought in World War II and liberated concentration camps. Gil went off to war a Christian Scientist, and then came back four years later believing in nothing at all; "What he saw, it stayed with him," Betty says. Trauma can change people; alter the self—which is never the same again; it copes by learning to be something different.

It's as if Philip has dealt with the trauma of taking a human life at such a young age by hiding in the identity of Philip but as the violence escalates in his job as spy, so too does his emotional discontent. Philip is forced to disfigure one of his closest informants (who was mistakenly murdered by target Yousaf Rana in the game of espionage). He folds her like a piece of origami so that she can fit in a suitcase and be disposed of ("Baggage"). He is also tasked with killing Gene, whose innocence is reflected in the school-boy action figures that guiltlessly impose presence on his house, in an effort to throw suspicion off Martha at the FBI ("Glanders"). These particular actions push Philip onto a precipice of self-reckoning. He bumps into Stan's ex, Sandra, at an *est* meeting, and she tells him; "I'm not sure if anyone in my life has ever really known me" ("March 8, 1983"). Philip offers no response but perhaps Sandra articulates what Philip cannot; that the crux of his pain and anger, brought to the fore by the "murder memory," is that no one has really known him either. Perhaps he does not even know himself?

Elizabeth seems to have found a way for *Elizabeth* and *Nadezdha* to co-exist whilst Mischa is at odds with Philip; personifying the Cold War in an all-out "Russia verses America" battle of the mind. Mischa connects to America—to Philip; in the pilot we see Philip trying on cowboy boots, the ultimate symbol of American machismo. Later he suggests defecting to America, *for real*—taking the good life, which isn't "so bad" ("Pilot"). We also know that Elizabeth has, on more than one occasion, reported concerns about his allegiance to Center. In contrast to Philip's skepticism over the bigwigs that call the shots over in Russia, Elizabeth is fiercely loyal to the Cause. When Philip presses Elizabeth about her seeming enjoyment of American life, she responds by saying that she is here to do a job and life in America is easier not better ("New Car"). It's an attitude that comes up repeatedly and *est* becomes a catalyst for Elizabeth's animosity: "I just think it's very *American*, the whole thing ("The Magic of David Copperfield V: The Statue of Liberty Disappears"). Elizabeth doesn't appreciate the over-sentimentality that Americans attach to their emotions; she's *Russian*, dammit.

Elizabeth's memories fuel her Russianness whereas Philip's seem to estrange him from the Motherland. In "Baggage", Elizabeth remembers the day she told her mother she had been recruited by the KGB; her mother did not blink an eye before telling her to serve her country—"When I was called, my mother didn't hesitate." It is this memory that drives her desire for Paige to serve, or at least; to have the opportunity to be part of the fight to make the world a better place. Philip is over being a spy. He wants a better life for Paige and Henry, in a place where "electricity works all the time, food's pretty great, there's closet space" ("Pilot"). In talking about his 'job' with the folk at *est*, Philip mentions not wanting to go into the office and make arrangements for people he doesn't know and don't give a shit about him; "Every morning I wake up with this sick feeling in the pit of my stomach." The *est* coach asks Philip why he doesn't quit, and Philip answers "I can't. Because I have commitments to people who trust me and people I love" ("Persona Non Grata").

Forget Me Not

Perhaps the character who best encapsulates the notion of misplaced identity is Paige Jennings—daughter to Elizabeth and Philip. One of the biggest moments in Paige's life, and indeed the series itself, is when her parents reveal the truth about who they are. Articulating their Russian identities in the American context of their lives seems to reinforce the gravitas of *Nadezhda* and even *Mischa* as the authentic selves of Elizabeth and Philip, respectively. Elizabeth speaks in Russian (as per Paige's request); a language she hasn't spoken in years, further enforcing Nadezhda as identity of heart. They lay it all out for Paige in "Stingers"; that they were born in a different country, in the Soviet Union, and they're in America to gather information for their country.

Paige finally says it: "You're spies?" Forget the penny, it's more like a giant concrete slab that drops. As she contemplates this newfound truth, Paige is forced to question her own identity because everything on which it is based—*her life*—is called into question; the reliability of her memories is thrown into disarray. In "I am Abassin Zadran" Paige introduces her parents to a new, fun game, called "Which Family Member *Not* Pretend?": it requires a family photo album, a memory and a good imagination. As it so happens, the game is not *all that fun* when your parents are spies and your life is a farce. Philip tries to soften the 'I don't know who I am' blow with a couple of pictures; one from the night Henry was born, and one from a family camping trip, saying to Paige "It's not all a lie." Thanks, Dad, but no cigar.

Soon after the great revelation, Elizabeth and Paige jet off to visit Elizabeth's dying mother—Paige's grandmother. They have a tearful reunion in a hotel room and in spite of the culture barrier, they all clasp hands and connect. *It's lovely* . . . but tainted by time the minute it's over. Back on American soil, Paige says, "It's weird . . . being there and being here now" ("Everyone Lies"). The self that met her Russian grandmother is not the same as the all-American girl who is now in possession of the memory—just as Elizabeth and Philip's memories of childhood to do not reflect the "sameness" required for the semblance of a rational identity.

Paige is *American*, with an *American* family—right? Apparently not. In "One Day in the Life of Anton Baklanov" Elizabeth offers Paige a history lesson in an effort to help her re-claim her identity; she tells Paige about her mother and their lifestyle in Russia. She says of her father, "We had this picture of him in his uniform; we used to look at it all the time. I don't remember him." It's this comment, when looking at memory and identity through a Lockean lens, which brings to the fore one of the philosopher's most controversial ideas. Locke claims that if we lose sight of our past selves, doubts are raised whether we are the same thinking thing. In other words, the memory of our experiences is what makes them real; if we remember something, it must have happened.

With this reasoning, Locke concludes that the converse of the previous argument is true: if you cannot remember an experience, then one did not have that experience. So, Elizabeth cannot remember her father—she has lost sight of this past self—does her dad then *not* exist? Obviously, this cannot be true. Locke's reasoning is refuted by later memory theorists including H.P. Grice, Thomas Reid, and John Perry, all of whom have amended Locke's theory to include forgotten memories as relevant to personal identity. Of the three theorists, Grice offers the most comprehensive adaptation. He introduces a new term, total temporary state (t.t.s.), which he explains is composed of all the experiences any one person is having at a given time. Grice argues that each total temporary state of a single self or person contains some element, a remembered experience or impression, shared by the t.t.s. preceding it in time also belonging to that person.

As much as Grice's interpretation of Lockean Memory Theory brings Elizabeth's father back to life, *The Americans* emits a pervading sense that without memory, we are nothing. The relationship that Philip and Elizabeth have with their memories attests to the importance of memory as in integral influence on the self, and there are more subtle supporting references throughout the show that serve to enhance this importance. In one of the taped "letters" from Elizabeth's mom, she says "My darling Nadezhda, . . . This year has been hard. Your uncle, Antoli—in the fall, I noticed he was starting to forget things. Now he's . . . it's like he's not there anymore" ("The Colonel").

The idea that with no memories, we are *nothing* comes up again in the show when Anton Baklanov, the guy Nina Krilova (double, no—*triple* agent) investigates in the Soviet laboratory opens up to her about the son who he was taken away from; who doesn't know him. He talks about being a memory to his son; perhaps not a good one—a father who left him without a word, never called or sent a letter.

Baklanov, who knows his future is precarious, says that if he is sent to a camp, never to see his son again, he pictures himself as dust . . . just ground up into the dirt. With no contact Baklanov will fade in his son's memory, to nothing—which he equates with death.

The Americans doesn't necessarily offer any solution to the identity crises experienced by the characters in the show but it does offer a poignant truth; that the malleability of memory forces the self into a constant state of flux, which makes identity, by and large, an enigma.

12
Better Never to Have Been?

Frauke Albersmeier

What motivates parents to put the loaded gun of life to their future children's heads?

For Philip and Elizabeth Jennings, the answer is clear: They need their kids as part of their cover. Paige and Henry Jennings are living props in the play their spy parents perform for their neighborhood and for the American government. The children's use by their own parents is blatant and—you probably think—repugnant.

On the other hand, as the offspring of white, middle-class "Americans" living in a 1980s suburb, those kids don't seem to be suffering a particularly terrible fate. We might feel unease witnessing their outright utilization, but the kids' pretty decent living standard might just let us shrug off our irritation. These reactions mirror the verdicts that two major types of ethical theory should produce about the Jenningses.

A *consequentialist* would focus on the overall outcome for Paige and Henry and might come to the conclusion that since Elizabeth and Philip manage to make their kids' lives worth living, they've done nothing wrong in creating them. For a *Kantian*, the fact that the Jenningses treat their children as means to their secret ends, rather than as "ends in themselves," would be a prize example of a morally bad act. Bringing children into existence in order to furnish a credible fake life with them violates their nature as autonomous human beings.

But even the consequentialist might have an accusation to make against Philip and Elizabeth. Paige's and Henry's lives are going well enough to make them worth living, but does this make it right that they were born in the first place?

Believe it or not, there is a philosophical theory known as *antinatalism*—the view that it is always morally wrong to have kids, because coming into existence is always a bad thing. According to antinatalism, it would be best if all humans, and any other sentient beings, stopped reproducing. One of the main proponents of this idea is David Benatar, who thinks that none of the good things in life can outweigh any of the inevitable bad stuff that happens to all of us and that, therefore, coming into existence is always bad. According to this way of looking at it, the Jenningses are just as wrong as anyone else who thinks that it's morally okay for people to have children.

Merely Breeding Socialists?

It's obvious that the Jenningses use their children as part of their cover. In fact, they may have never had any other motive for having children in the first place. At least for Elizabeth, the decision to have children was difficult. Flashbacks to her conversations with Zhukov and Leanne show her emotional turmoil ("Covert War," "The Walk-In"). We know that becoming a parent was one of the many sacrifices Elizabeth made as a devoted KGB agent. But, like some of her other sacrifices, this one involves other people—victims who never gave their consent. This situation would worry different moral philosophers in different ways.

For someone in the Kantian tradition of ethics, what makes an act right or wrong is the agent's motive for acting. Kant famously proposed a principle he thought all morally defensible intentions needed to conform to: the categorical imperative. One version of the categorical imperative states that we should never treat humans, ourselves as well as others, "merely as a means to an end, but always at the same time as an end." We shouldn't use people in a way that disregards the fact that they're autonomous beings. To act counter to the categorical imperative would not only be immoral, but irrational. All morality is based on respect for autonomy. In treating others as "mere means" we deny the basis of all morality.

Now, do Philip and Elizabeth treat their children as "mere means"? When we zoom into particular scenes, the issue becomes ambiguous. When Philip and Elizabeth have an argument over defecting to America, they say this about their children:

> ELIZABETH: We swore we would never tell them. Let them grow up and live their own life. They're not to be a part of this.
>
> PHILIP: If they're not to be a part of this, they will be American. You can't stand that. I see that every day.
>
> ELIZABETH: I'm not finished with them yet. They don't have to be regular Americans. They can be socialists.
>
> PHILIP: They're not gonna be socialists. This place doesn't turn out socialists. ("Pilot")

It's obvious that Philip has provoked Elizabeth to contradict her initial avowal of liberty: she admits that the only acceptable outcome of Paige and Henry growing up to "live their own life" would be for them to become socialists. Philip's Marxist retort is probably correct. The material conditions in the US wouldn't allow for this outcome.

But even if they did: Elizabeth's reaction does not give her away as a reckless ideologue. Her role as a mother is more than just producing new socialists. The fact that she's working to turn her kids into socialists doesn't mean she's disrespectfully treating them as mere means to further some ideological end. She believes in the moral superiority of socialism, which could create "a world without exploitation and dignity for all" ("Behind the Red Door"). Her concern for her children just has to be consistent with this political agenda. It can still be genuine concern for them in their own right.

But what about the initial act of creating the children? All the hints we have been given so far provide reason to believe that Philip and Elizabeth were convinced that Center expected them to have children as part of their fake identity. The Jenningses did what was expected of them. We have no reason whatsoever to believe that either parent had any other intention when creating these children. In "The Walk-In," we're taken back to the day when Elizabeth made up her mind about starting a family and we learn that for her the final incentive to go along with Center's directive was news that the socialist cause was losing in Vietnam. If Center had wanted them to join the Vietcong, they would instead have caught a plane to Vietnam that night.

Video Games and Guilt

Bringing a child into existence for the sake of some political or personal agenda may be pretty bad. But in the eyes of an antinatalist, that just adds to the negative consequence of being alive in the first place. From the moment they're born, sentient beings are exposed to lives where good and bad stuff will happen to them, but unfortunately, the good can never outweigh the bad. The Jenningses may be wrong to have children for political reasons—but the antinatalist philosopher Benatar's point is that it's not just wrong to have children for the wrong reasons, it's always wrong to have children—period.

According to Benatar, we not only overestimate people's average quality of life, we also confuse two senses of how a life can be worthwhile. Looking at Paige's and Henry's lives, they seem pretty good. It's hard to think that anyone would say these lives are so bad as to make them not "worth living." Even though Paige is increasingly burdened by the family's secret, she clearly doesn't need to be put out of her misery by ending her life.

The same is true for Henry. He suffers when his parents temporarily split up. But his worst misery is his lack of an

Atari system. Things aren't going terribly badly for Henry. He grows close to Stan, even though not his own father, he takes it well when he's told that there's no way his hot teacher would ever fall for him, and he experiences many pleasurable moments being supplied with illegal copies of movies, playing games with Stan, and spending more and more time in front of his C64.

But this is the wrong way to look at it, says Benatar. We should distinguish between what makes a life "worth continuing"—which Paige's and Henry's lives surely are—and what can make a life "worth starting." The bad stuff in their lives may not be enough to make their live not *worth continuing*. But as the antinatalist would have it, any one of the bad things that were going to happen to them is enough to make their lives *not worth starting*.

This is due to a "basic asymmetry" that holds between the good and the bad things in a future life. Benatar focuses on "pleasure" versus "pain"—things a future child would *experience* as good and bad. Let's take Henry's breaking and entering-experience ("New Car"). The pleasure Henry took from playing video games in the neighbor's house was, of course, *good* for him, while the crushing feeling of guilt he experiences after being caught there was *bad*.

The story is different if Henry never exists. It is good when we prevent something bad from happening. So, if Henry had never come into existence, it would be good because his painful feelings of guilt would never have happened. Sure, Henry would never have enjoyed the video game, but this lack of a pleasurable experience is not bad. The lack of an extra pleasure does not harm a person, but the avoidance of a genuine pain is always good for them.

Had Henry never been born, he wouldn't have experienced a painful humiliation, the no-Henry-no-guilt-option is preferable with Henry's best interests in mind. We shouldn't assume the converse is true of the time he spent playing: had he not existed and never gotten to enjoy the game, the lack of potential joy wouldn't have been a deprivation for Henry, because there would have been no Henry to be deprived of joy.

An existing child who suffers pain is a terrible thing. A non-existing child who does not get to play a video game is not.

Future Spies

There's a well-known problem for the claim that coming into existence can be harmful *at all*, made famous by Derek Parfit as the "non-identity problem," and also known as the "paradox of future individuals." Normally, when we say someone is being harmed, we mean they have been made worse off. In cases where people are exposed to something bad by being brought into existence, this doesn't seem to work. Being born into the horrors of World War II and the hardships that it entailed didn't make Nadezhda and Mischa worse off, because they didn't exist before. Moreover, they wouldn't have been born the same persons (so it's a "non-identity problem") had their parents postponed procreation to some other time. We can even say that Paige and Henry couldn't have been born to the same parents at the same time without being born the children of spies with all the risks and hardships that come with that. Our ordinary sense of "harming" doesn't capture what goes wrong when someone is being born into a bad condition. At least that's what the non-identity problem states.

But Benatar insists that "harming" doesn't require this kind of comparison, because existing and never existing are comparable after all. The idea behind the basic asymmetry is that we can compare a person's interests when they exist to when they don't. Of course, in the no-Henry-no-guilt-scenario there is not some *potential* Henry who is better off for not existing. It is just that when comparing the two scenarios, or "possible worlds," we have a reason to say that the world where Henry is never born (and never feels either pain nor pleasure) is better than the one where he comes into existence (and gets to experience both pleasure and pain).

If someone does not exist they cannot be harmed at all. If they do exist they can be. The Jennings children experience some joy. But we are not morally required to promote joy. The

Jennings children also experience some misery. Philip and Elizabeth are a necessary cause of their children's existence and so also a cause of their suffering. This is where the basic asymmetry kicks in. It's good to cause an existing person joy but we are *not* required to create happy people. It's bad to cause someone's suffering, and we *are* required to avoid causing suffering. All parents cause the suffering of their children.

Parental Russian Roulette

Elizabeth notes again and again how easy everything is for American children. She hasn't forgotten her own destitution growing up with a widowed mother in post-war Smolensk. Compared to her life, Paige and Henry have nothing to complain about. The antinatalist can agree with all of this and still claim that even the relatively luxurious lives of Paige and Henry Jennings are still bad lives. The best of lives are actually much worse than we typically assume. We tend to overlook the many big and small negative experiences, everything from hunger to tiredness, boredom to stress, grief and loneliness to disappointment, having to do homework to lacking access to video games or even the frustration over being denied an additional pair of leg warmers ("Duty and Honor"). Our tendency to disregard these everyday evils may help us to rate our lives as "worth continuing," but it may disqualify us as judges about whether lives like these are actually "worth starting."

Apart from these minor discomforts, there are more serious, sometimes truly horrible, things that could happen to anyone. Elizabeth is raped ("Pilot"). Paige and Henry are almost molested, raped, or killed hitchhiking home from the mall ("Trust Me"). The three daughters of an FBI agent lose their father in the safe house bombing ("Mutually Assured Destruction"). Annelise is slowly strangled after confessing her true feelings, and her true identity to her lover ("EST Men"). The South African racist gets burned alive ("Divestment"; this is bad for him at least). And even though the risks of horrible things happening to them is bound to be high for the children of spies, until what happened to Leanne and Emmett happened, Elizabeth says she had "never worried about Paige and Henry being safe" ("Cardinal"). So, even spies can be dangerously naive.

Parents are playing Russian Roulette with their children—this is the image Benatar chooses to illustrate how procreation exposes the created individuals to severe risks and, ultimately harms. As he sees it, there is no point in hoping that even one of the bullets is missing in the gun—there is no escaping harm. But maybe you're not sold on the basic asymmetry. Well, Benatar thinks, that even if we start weighing the good and the bad things in our lives to prove that our lives are worth living, the outcome is bound to be negative. If we are doing the math right, we have to admit that the quality of our life is actually so poor that it was never worth starting. Even if our parents don't deceive us and subject us to horrible risks, because they're spies, we are all actually doing much worse than we think we are.

Use and Abuse

People do not typically cite their future child's well-being as a reason to create that child. Their motivation is typically much more egoistic—and therefore maybe even worse than the Jenningses'. Unlike other couples who deliberately procreate, Elizabeth and Philip don't have their children out of a personal lifestyle choice, but for the sake of a higher cause: socialism, and thereby for the sake of a better world for all mankind.

Compare this with Martha's motivation for starting a family with Clark. When she takes him to look at children in foster care, it looks as if they were window shopping, looking for a cute kid. Clark is very aware of that, saying: "We're not buying one today." Next, Martha tries to sell the idea of having a child: "This isn't just me. Think about what it would be like to come home and have that little girl running towards you and throwing your arms around you. We have a lot of love now, but there are other kinds of love" ("Salang Pass").

Martha wants a kid because she wants to be unconditionally loved and welcomed with joy and excitement when she's coming home from a long day at work. The kid's need for unconditional love, and for care and protection—things that can be very demanding to provide—only occurs to her as an additional strategic argument to win over Clark, on a par with the fact that foster kids can be returned if things don't work out ("Open House"). Of course, in the eyes of an antinatalist, she fares better than an actual—biological—parent, since she's ready to settle for an already existing child instead of bringing one into the world in order to fulfill her emotional needs. But otherwise, her state of mind probably isn't so different from that of a typical prospective parent.

Having a somehow nobler motive for wanting to be parents doesn't yet make Philip and Elizabeth better overall. What can be upsetting about their take on their role as parents is the overall way of prioritizing their several duties (as secret agents and parents). In the pilot, Philip claims: "Our family comes first." In fact, the kids almost always come second, their well-being is their parents' priority to the extent it's consistent with the success of the mission. This is obvious from the way they both keep taking risks that affect the children.

Elizabeth is unlike Philip and other parents, in that she stays true to her initial motive behind having children: she's more consistent in using her children according to the plan for the mission and to new instructions from Center. While for Philip, whether his daughter's life goes well is a matter of whether it goes well for *her*, for Elizabeth the question is whether it is spent furthering a good cause—whether it goes well for everyone. That's not necessarily a bad attitude, but that she doesn't always consider her daughter as an end in herself at the same time, shows in this exchange:

ELIZABETH: I like spending time with her. Do I want certain things for her? Yeah! All parents do!

PHILIP: Do you know what most parents want? Good college, good marriage, good job.

ELIZABETH: Well, that's a fine list ("Dimebag").

Her sarcasm about other parents' good intentions makes it obvious that she differs from them in *what* she wants "for" her child. Most other parents, at least once their children are born, replace egoistic motives for procreation by genuine concern for the children's needs. Elizabeth may never have been egoistic, but she sure isn't focused primarily on her kids' needs and desires. And although Philip often disagrees with her in that respect, his actions do not always match his words. For example, in the amusement park, he initially refuses to, but eventually uses Henry for the job Emmett assigns him ("Comrades"). In keeping with her role as the dutiful agent, Elizabeth reassures him when he feels regret about dragging Henry into this ("Cardinal").

Both of them are conflicted when they're pushed—first by Center, then by events—to involve Paige in their mission as more than just their cover. When Claudia reminds them: "Paige is your daughter. But she's not just yours. She belongs to the cause," Philip and Elizabeth seem irritated ("Echo"). It is so normal to think that parents have some kind of claim to their children, that it doesn't occur to anyone that Paige might belong to no one but herself.

Bad Things Happen

"Do you have children?" On several occasions this question makes childless people react like they're admitting a flaw: Pastor Tim when asked by Philip ("Stingers") or Nina when asked by Baklanov ("One Day in the Life of Anton Baklanov"). More than the people who ask the question, the ones who answer it demonstrate that having kids is widely seen as something of an accomplishment, a desirable, even praiseworthy part of life. The antinatalist view suggests otherwise.

Claudia is right ("Duty and Honor"): Bad things really do happen—to all sorts of people, not just spies. The Jennings aren't just condemned for the innocent people they kill. They should be condemned for the innocent people they create.

IV

Beyond Good
and Evil

13
Good Arguments for Doing Bad Things

NILS RAUHUT

The Americans depicts the actions of undercover agents that run the gamut from the morally odious to the morally horrific. As an undercover agent, you have to be willing to kill innocent busboys ("Comrades"), blackmail decent people (like Viola Johnson in "The Clock") and indecent people (like Andrew Larrick in "Martial Eagle")—even desecrate the corpse of a friend ("Baggage"). The list goes on.

These are actions, which no sane, rational person would enjoy performing, but which are standard fare for undercover spies. It's obvious, therefore, that the life of undercover espionage requires agents to sacrifice part of their humanity and moral integrity in order to complete their missions. Are these sacrifices justifiable? Are they reasonable? Would a fully rational person, a person who understands what is entailed by a life of espionage ever voluntarily and freely sign up for undercover assignments or would a rational person always have reasons to reject such a life and all that it entails?

A careful analysis of this question is closely connected to one of the central overall plotlines in *The Americans*. As Paige, gradually finds out who her parents really are, she must decide whether the secret life of her parents and all that it entails can be justified. Her relationship to her parents depends on the way she answers this question. If it turns out that her parents are trapped in a life of senseless violence which no sane rational person would ever voluntarily pursue, then she has little choice but to turn away from them and seek shelter in her relationship to Pastor Tim and the church. If, on the other hand, it's possible to make sense of the horrific things her parents do, she might be able to accept her parents for what they truly are and start building a lasting relationship with them.

There are three types of arguments that attempt to justify the life and actions of undercover agents like Philip and Elizabeth Jenkins.

Patriotism: Not Just a Refuge for Scoundrels

At several points in the series Elizabeth and other protagonists appeal to patriotism as an ultimate rational for their grisly actions. In a conversation with Philip, Elizabeth recalls, for example, that when the opportunity arose for her to be trained as an undercover agent, her mother did not hesitate. She encouraged her to serve her country even if that meant that she could not see her daughter again. The idea that patriotism can justify death, pain, and suffering has a long tradition in Western philosophy. For example, in Plato's dialogue *Crito*, Socrates characterizes the laws of Athens as making the following demand:

> You must . . . obey the laws' orders and endure in silence whatever they instruct you to endure, whether blows or bonds, and if they lead you into war to be wounded or killed, you must obey. To do so is right, and you must not give way or retreat or leave your post, but . . . you must obey the commands of your city and country.

The basic line of reasoning behind the patriotism defense can be reconstructed as follows:

1. Serving your country and obeying its orders is a morally good thing.

2. For undercover agents, serving your country requires the killing of innocent people (and performing other gruesome acts).

Therefore: For undercover agents, killing innocent people (and performing other gruesome acts) is a morally good thing.

This line of thought provides an especially fitting moral defense for Elizabeth and Philip since they do not kill or torture for personal reasons. They do it to complete their mission and serve their country. There are numerous instances where both Philip and Elizabeth take on extra risks in order to minimize human pain and suffering. For example, in "New Car" they try to spare the life of the truck driver who allows them to enter the contra training base and in "Divestment" Elizabeth and Philip convince Reuben to spare the life of South African student Todd. This shows that in the middle of all the horrible acts they have to perform both Elizabeth and Philip try to preserve their humanity. Unlike US Navy SEAL Andrew Larrick, for example, who seems to kill without regret and remorse, Elizabeth and Philip have not lost their moral sensibilities. The gruesome things they do, they do because they have to—for the sake of the mission; for the sake of Center and Mother Russia.

Is this appeal to patriotism plausible? Should a rational person accept this as a cogent argument? To answer this question, let's consider the case of the German officer Count Claus von Stauffenberg. Stauffenberg was a fully committed patriot. He served in the German Wehrmacht with distinction. During the Africa Campaign he lost his left eye, right hand and two fingers on his left hand. Nevertheless, Stauffenberg played a crucial part in the German resistance to Hitler and was the central figure in the attempt to assassinate Hitler on July 20th, 1944.

The case of Stauffenberg points to an interesting ambiguity in the patriotism defense. If it's true that serving your country is a morally good thing, then it becomes absolutely crucial that you must have no doubts about who speaks for your country. In the case of Stauffenberg, he became increasingly convinced that following Hitler's orders was not in the interest of his country. A similar problem seems to emerge for Elizabeth and Philip. As long as Philip and Elizabeth are convinced that Center, through their handlers Claudia and Gabriel, speak for Mother Russia the patriotism defense is viable. However, as soon as they start to doubt that Center's commands are right, the patriotism defense becomes subject to doubt.

This tension is illustrated in "Echo" where Philip makes contact with Arkady, the head of the Russian Rezidentura, and tells him that if Center ever made contact with Paige and tried to recruit her, both he and Elizabeth would leave the KGB. Philip seems to suggest here that recruiting Paige for the KGB without her parents' permission is unacceptable and morally wrong even if Center were to order that it should be done. The patriotism defense works smoothly only as long as Philip and Elizabeth have faith that Center will get it right. If that faith is broken or severely undermined, it becomes increasingly difficult to appeal to patriotism as a viable justification for the gruesome acts both of them are asked to perform.

The patriotism defense, therefore, offers at best a somewhat tenuous justification. It works only as long as you have no doubt that the political authorities who claim to speak for your country are indeed ordering what is morally right and in the interest of your country. Moreover, it's far from clear whether the patriotism defense has any appeal to Paige. Paige has no connection to Mother Russia and she's also not a very patriotic American. It thus seems unlikely that the appeal to patriotism would allow her to look at her parents' life as justified.

Making a Difference

A second type of justification for the life of undercover agents is connected to the desire "to make a difference." The person who best illustrates this type of justification in *The Americans* is Fred, the spy who was originally recruited by Emmet and Leanne Connors, but who, after the untimely deaths of Emmet and Leanne in the episode "Comrades," is handled by Philip. Fred lives a lonely life. He has no kids, no wife, and apparently no vices. He spends none of the money he received from the KGB. Fred's life appears empty and it seems that he became a spy in order to find some meaning and purpose.

In a conversation with Philip, Fred reveals that he was not satisfied with an ordinary quiet 8:00 A.M. to 5:00 P.M. accountant's job. He says to Philip: "Emmet saw something in me, he saw that I was special and that I could make a difference." Philip picks up on Fred's motivation and in the episode "Operation Chronicle," he convinces Fred to take on the dangerous mission to wander into a secure factory area so that his shoes can pick up samples of radar absorbing paint with the following words: "Stealth technology is the thing that will make the difference." Fred, who's somewhat reluctant to take on this dangerous mission, seems moved by these words and takes on the mission. Making a difference is what he is all about. In this situation, Philip manipulates Fred by exploiting his quest for meaning. However, the fact that Philip and Emmet manipulate Fred does not automatically undermine the authenticity of Fred's desire to make a difference.

This opens up a new line of justification for the life of undercover espionage.

I think the basic line of thinking can be captured by the following argument.

1. Living an empty life—a life without meaning—is the worst possible life.

2. A life that makes a difference has meaning.

3. The life of undercover agents even if it entails killing innocent people (and performing other gruesome acts) makes a difference.

Therefore: The life of undercover agents has meaning and is better than an empty life.

The conclusion of this argument is significantly weaker than the conclusion of the patriotism defense. The argument does not claim that a life of undercover activities is morally good or morally praiseworthy. What it claims instead is that the life of undercover spying has meaning in a way that many ordinary lives don't. The crucial premise, therefore, is premise #2. Is it plausible to accept this premise? Does it make sense to think that Fred manages to create and find meaning by making a difference as an undercover spy?

There are reasons to be skeptical about this claim. In one of his missions, Fred helps the KGB to obtain plans for a new submarine propeller. However, it turns out that the plans were a trap. The propeller had an intentional design flaw and when the Russian Navy in an attempt to catch up with the Americans tests the new propeller on a new submarine, 160 sailors die a horrible death deep underwater.

In this case Fred's actions make a difference, but it looks problematic to say that Fred's actions have meaning. Making a difference, it seems, is not always sufficient for making an action or a life meaningful. In order to create meaning, it seems, it's not enough to simply do things that are consequential. What's required in addition is that your actions lead to positive consequences. But how is Fred supposed to know whether his spying activities will lead to more well-being and happiness? His inability to know whether he makes a positive difference threatens to undermine his hopes of finding purpose and meaning. Spying for the KGB threatens to trap him in the same kind of absurd life he was trying to escape from. This appears to undermine the plausibility of premise #2 and thus threatens to undermine the persuasiveness of the entire line of thought.

Before we give up on the argument, it will be useful to take a quick look at the French philosopher Albert Camus. In his famous essay "The Myth of Sisyphus," Camus describes the fate of Sisyphus as a metaphor for the human condition. Sisyphus is using all his strength to push a rock up a mountain although he knows that his effort will not succeed and that he will have to begin the task anew after the rock has rolled down the mountain.

In this situation, we might be tempted to say that Sisyphus is trapped in an absurd situation, but Camus came to a different conclusion. For Camus, Sisyphus is not necessarily trapped. By openly acknowledging the absurdity of his efforts and by consciously deciding to keep on pushing, it's possible for Sisyphus to reach a state of contented acceptance. Courageously acting in the face of ultimate absurdity is, according to Camus, the only way humans can create meaning. If we follow Camus's thought here, Fred emerges as the prototypical anti-hero.

During his last mission ("Operation Chronicle"), Fred seems aware that Philip is manipulating him and that this mission might kill him. Nevertheless, he courageously completes the mission and dies without complaint. He does so, I think, because working and dying as an undercover agent allows him to defy the ultimate meaninglessness of ordinary existence. The crucial thing to notice is that Fred's ability to find meaning is the reason why his life makes a difference rather than the other way. We, therefore, have to reformulate the argument as follows:

1. Acknowledging the inherent absurdity of life and acting heroically in the face of this meaninglessness is the only way humans can create meaning.

2. The life of undercover agents even if it entails killing innocent people (and performing other gruesome acts) forces agents to acknowledge the inherent absurdity of life and allows them to act heroically.

3. Any life that creates meaning makes a difference and is better than an ordinary life.

Therefore: The life of undercover agents makes a difference and is better than an ordinary life.

This version of the argument captures the reason why Fred became a spy and it's also the strongest version of the meaning argument. However, is this argument strong enough to convince Paige that a life of espionage might be the path to finding purpose and meaning? I think the answer to this question depends on the way Paige comes to perceive her own existence. If she develops into a person who resembles Fred or FBI agent Stan Beeman, who both struggle to find meaning in their personal lives, the argument might have considerable appeal. In this case, making a difference and finding meaning might become the central project of her life and she might be tempted to see a life of undercover agency as heroic way to defy the emptiness of ordinary existence. If, on the other hand, she develops into a person like Pastor Tom who has found meaning and purpose in his relationship to God, the argument will have little or no appeal to her.

Making the World a Better Place

Let's now turn to the final justification for the life of secret agents that's presented to us in *The Americans*. This justification is most vividly illustrated in the episode "Do Mail Robots Dream of Electric Sheep?" Elizabeth and Philip break into a repair facility in order to install a recording device into a mail robot that's used by the FBI. While doing this, they are surprised by Betty, an older woman, who has the habit of doing the accounting for the repair shop late at night. Since Betty's testimony would undermine the operation as well as the cover of Elizabeth and Philip, it's necessary for Elizabeth to kill her. She does so by forcing Betty to take an overdose of her heart medication. As Betty takes pill after pill, the following conversation between Betty and Elizabeth takes place.

BETTY: Do you have children?

ELIZABETH: Yes.

BETTY: And this is what you do?

ELIZABETH: Sometimes.

BETTY: Why?

ELIZABETH: To make the world a better place!

BETTY: You think that doing this to me will make the world a better place?

ELIZABETH: I am sorry, but it will.

Betty is not impressed by this justification. She tells Elizabeth: "This is what evil people tell themselves when they do evil things." However, it seems that Elizabeth is convinced. She seems to believe that all the gruesome acts she performs bring about a better world.

Unfortunately, the conversation between Betty and Elizabeth is incomplete. Elizabeth never explains more fully what she has in mind here. So, in order to make sense of her convictions we need to supply some additional background beliefs that supplement Elizabeth's reasoning in this context.

As far as I can see, there are two possible background assumptions that would complete Elizabeth's argument. First, when Elizabeth takes first steps to recruit Paige for the KGB, she takes Paige to a ghetto and encourages her to read about racial discrimination in the US. This suggests that Elizabeth is inclined to see the US as well as capitalism as a political system that marginalizes and oppresses people not only in the US but also all over the world. By taking actions that weaken and destroy the US, Elizabeth hopes to create a better world, a world that's free of oppression and discrimination.

Sure, in order to bring about this world she has to kill innocent people like Betty, but that suffering is far less than the suffering she helps to eliminate by liberating people from the political oppression imposed by American-style capitalism all over the globe. The second possibility here is that Elizabeth believes in some kind of historical determinism that's often an essential component of Communist orthodoxy. If Elizabeth believes that history invariably must develop towards a classless and free society then it's quite reasonable to perform actions that bring about this blissful state more quickly. Both of these background assumptions would explain why Elizabeth is convinced that she's justified in killing Betty and other innocent beings.

Should a rational person be convinced by this reasoning or should a rational person agree with Betty and think that "This is just a tale evil people tell each other when they do evil things"? The answer to this question depends on what we think about political ideology. If the inevitable emergence of a classless society is plausible, so is Elizabeth's justification. It's, however, no surprise that an average American like Betty is not convinced at this point. Americans like Betty are inclined to think that Elizabeth has been brainwashed to subscribe to a Communist political ideology. What Betty doesn't realize is that in the eyes of Elizabeth, Betty has been brainwashed to be blind to the oppression caused by the US and capitalism.

This suggests that there might be no neutral, ideology-free vantage point available for us to settle the question. However, if we have to pick our political ideological poison, so to speak, no matter what we believe, it's not irrational to prefer Communism to free-market capitalist ideology. This shows that Elizabeth's hope to make the world a better place through her undercover work cannot be shown to be irrational. On the other hand, it's also clear that it cannot be shown be rational either. It follows, therefore, that the idea that undercover operations bring about a better world—just like the other justifications—is somewhat incomplete.

Paige?

We have seen that each of the three justifications for the gruesome activities of undercover agents can be challenged. Where does this leave us? What does this mean for Paige? Does she have any chance to accept her parents' undercover activities? Although each of the three justifications taken in isolation is incomplete, the possibility arises that the three justifications can be combined into a comprehensive defense. This is exactly what Elizabeth seems to do. Elizabeth is a patriot; she wants to make a difference; and she is convinced that she is making the world a better place. Elizabeth draws strength from all three possible justifications. Although each argument considered in isolation is incomplete, the arguments mutually support each other in Elizabeth's mind and life. Is this also a possibility for Paige?

In order to answer this question it's helpful to reflect on Philip. Philip is in the same position as Elizabeth but he, unlike Elizabeth, seems to have doubts about each of these justifications. Philip is clearly not a fully committed patriot. In the very first episode, he seriously contemplates turning himself in to the FBI, in order to enter a witness protection program and start a new life with his family. For a full-blown patriot like Elizabeth this is, of course, not an option. Philip is also far from sure whether he is making a difference. In many instances, he seems to question the meaning behind his killings. This is one of the reasons why he is attracted to going to the *est* program where he can come to terms with his feelings of guilt and regret.

Finally, Philip seems also not committed to the Communist political ideology. There are numerous times when he points out to Elizabeth that life in the US has its blessings. It seems then that he is open to the idea that US-style capitalism might bring as much joy as pain. Philip, therefore, seems to draw a very different overall conclusion than Elizabeth. He seems to conclude that the weaknesses of each justification reinforce each other and that the morality of his undercover life is in doubt.

So, how will Paige react? What conclusion will she embrace? I think this depends fundamentally on whether Paige follows in the footsteps of her mother or father. Both paths are from a reasonable point of view open to her.

14
Spies Like U.S.

MASSIMO RONDOLINO

The mission is at risk! Elizabeth and Philip have not been able to coerce Viola, Defense Secretary Casper Weinberger's maid, to plant a bug in his study. Time is short. Desperate measures are warranted: it's now, or never . . .

"I don't believe anything you say," Viola says to Elizabeth. "Your son is dying, you know that is the truth," she replies. As Philip walks in the room, Viola appeals to her faith: "I know the Devil . . . I listen to my Lord, he protects me. He guides me." Philip's reaction is swift: he grabs a pillow and begins to smother Viola's son. Viola screams and tries to fight him off her only child. "No! No! No! What people are you? Who are you?" ("The Clock").

What people are they, *really*? Viola is traumatized by what she is experiencing, and what her life has been turned into. Her world has been twisted and transformed into a living hell. Yet, even in the face of the evidence, the truth that her son is dying, she defends her picture of reality, grounded in the narrative that a loving almighty God will shield her (and her son) from evil.

Philip's brutal act shakes Viola to her core. The Devil is suddenly very real and present; God . . . possibly not so much. What human being would impose such horror on another? For what reason? Eventually, Viola succumbs to their pressures, and places the bug in Weinberger's home.

Nothing But the Truth

Viola's question about what kind of people her tormentors are, is, in fact, a fundamental tear into the assumptions on which we build our existence. It is a question that asks us to directly address our implicit, and yet fundamental, relationship with truth.

Generally, truth can either be seen as absolute, or relative. If truth is absolute, whoever has access to truth is right. Everyone who does not is wrong. If truth is relative, your truth is as good as mine, and vice versa, and neither can trump the other. So, in a sense, we are all right and yet we are also all wrong, depending on who you ask. But what actually is *truth*?

One way of understanding truth is to see it as what is in accordance with the facts of the world. There are, undeniably, things in the world that are obvious, such as the fact that without air we die. Viola is aware of this truth when Philip presses a pillow into her son's face. These, so called, matter-of-fact things speak for themselves and it is enough to experience them to know that they are true. The fact that air is vital to our survival will always be true to anyone, whether they have had to gasp for it or not.

Our lives are not merely bundles of such obvious facts. Most of the things that make up our lives are not manifestly evident. They require interpretation. Viola may suddenly realize that air is not flowing into her son's chest and that he is dying. But what does this mean? Is it a simple fact of his mortality? Is it a sign of the existence of evil? Is it a test from God? Or . . . is she having a bad dream?

In this instance, Viola needs more information to determine the context within which she can make sense of the fact that her son is deprived of air and is dying. She also needs a framework of pre-existing knowledge with which to interpret this triangulation of fact and context. What Viola ends up with, then, is a story that will allow her to discern a truth behind her experience. For Viola, the truth of her hellish experience is that there is evil in the world, and that an all-loving and caring God will provide for her and her son as long as she puts her faith in him.

But what if, like Elizabeth and Philip, we do not believe in God or the Devil? Would Viola's interpretation of reality still be true? This is what we mean when we ponder whether truth is absolute or relative. If absolute, Viola's God exists and Elizabeth and Philip are wrong. Truth is then something that is objectively in the world that we must carefully and accurately uncover, lest we cannot have it.

If truth is relative Viola, and Elizabeth and Philip are correct, relatively to their respective experiences of reality: God exists and there is no God. If truth is relative it is a sophisticated structure that allows us to make sense of the world.

What is interesting about relative truth is that Viola's truth is *the* truth for her. She acts as if *her* truth were *the* truth. So do the Jenningses. Consequently, Viola would not recognize their truth as *truth*, even in the face of clear evidence, such as her dying son. For Viola Philip's violence is proof that the Devil exists. So must God also, to right his wrongs. Crucially, then, even if truth is relative, we all, like Viola, individually act as if it was absolute.

This tension is at the heart of how we create our identity, and shape our understanding of the world. Our beliefs shape *the* truth for us. This truth is a compass, plotting the path of our existence. Our sense of *the* truth shapes our values, our sense of our own history and of our purpose. It gives meaning to our past, purpose to our present, and a guide to our future.

Nothin' But a Lotta Talk and a Badge

Let's take Stan, for example. Prior to his assignment in counter-intelligence, he worked three years, infiltrating a white-supremacist group in Arkansas. We know that he is a very good detective. Shortly after moving next door to Elizabeth and Philip, for example, and having just barely had enough time to form an impression about his new neighbors, he rightly suspects them to be the Russian spies his unit is seeking.

Stan reflects on the high cost of being a good detective. He wonders whether all that time undercover may have shaped him into a great FBI agent, but also left him damaged and unable to live a meaningful civilian life. Stan has clear and compelling evidence. The relationship with his son and wife is deteriorating: Matthew is increasingly dismissive and confrontational. Sandra has left him for a man she met at an *est* seminar.

Despite such doubts we know that Stan is a good guy. So does he. But even Stan cannot deny that some facts in his life may speak to the contrary. What do we make of the risks he takes, the suffering he imposes, the lying, the cheating, and the killing. What person is he, *really*? What is *the* truth: is Stan a good agent and a *good* guy, whose hard work makes the world a better place? Or is he a liar, a cheater and a killer, like any one of the *bad* guys that he strives to find. Are "good guy" and "bad guy" just the names of players on opposite teams?

Stan's self-conception is as the person that catches bad people. If you and the bad guys are enemies, than it means that you are in opposition. Stan must be the opposite of bad. He must be good.

Such simple logic can hardly justify lying, cheating, killing, and destroying family relationships, all in the name of catching the, arguably, *bad guys*. Where simple logic fails, though, a story may succeed, a story that grounds Stan's set of beliefs and values in a past and lets him understand his present. This would also be a story that tells him how a brighter future would necessarily arise from the actions that he takes today. Such a story built around a core logical structure, can offer everything Stan needs to make sense of his existence in light of how he perceives the world to be.

Crucially, Stan lives in a nation whose public narrative identifies white supremacists, and Russians as the enemy. According to this public narrative, both seek social domination. (Though, here, one should also ask whose truth this narrative is, thus seeing that whichever group of people holds this narrative to be true, also sees itself as rightfully dominant above all others.)

Whether it is a group of white people who argue for their success at the cost of the lives of others that are not like them, or a group of people that promote global Marxist enlightened dictatorship of the proletariat, both stand at odds with the core values that are seen as emblematic of Stan's world: equality and freedom for all—white and non-white, rich and poor, bourgeoisie and proletariat. So, at least, goes the official discourse of Stan's world.

Fighting white supremacists and Russians means necessarily doing good, because it entails upholding those core values in which Stan's world is grounded and through which its history is written. All Stan's actions contribute to the actualization of *the good* in a universal sense. In Stan's world, Soviet Russia is *evil*. Any action that is directed to stopping it, in any form and to any measure is *supremely good*.

Seen in this perspective, everything else in Stan's life fades into the shadow of triviality, including all lying, cheating, and killing in pursuit of this supreme good. For what does it matter to pursue the happiness of a small family nucleus of three people, or even just the happiness of two individuals joined together in matrimony, when we compare it to ensuring that evil does not prevail? For Stan, catching Russians is a universal moral imperative!

The story that Stan and his colleagues tell each other legitimizes their every action. Stan wears a badge identifying him as an FBI agent. This defines his profession, and informs his thoughts and actions. Yet, it is the all pervading American rhetoric of freedom and equality, and the Russia-is-evil talk that consistently allows Stan to turn every fact into truth, even in the face of seemingly contradictory evidence, like lying, cheating, and killing.

What We've Got Here (Maybe) Is Failure to Communicate

We have seen that for both Viola and Stan the narratives that they use to interpret the world necessarily shape their construction of truth. Looked at from a different perspective this does not seem to be absolute truth. The evil nature of their Russian enemies is simply true relative to Viola and Stan's experiences of reality. Yet, absolute and relative truth are not as opposed as it may seem.

The effects of our possessing *the* truth are identical regardless whether *our* truth is absolute or relative. In other words, *how* we are able to explain to ourselves that we have access to truth is not affected by its being *our* or *the* truth, as Viola and Stan show us. Both tell themselves stories that provide an explanation for why the world is the way they perceive it, and how it will be tomorrow as an effect of what they do and who they are today. They justify, or *legitimize*, their beliefs with narratives (God, for Viola, and equality and liberty, for Stan) that then enable them to see them as true, by virtue of the facts that their stories provide as evidence.

Maybe if Viola were able to communicate more effectively with Elizabeth and Philip, they would all be able to see the same truth. The two Russians could at last recognize the all-loving American God. Then, they could all stop fighting. Viola could demonstrate facts that Elizabeth and Philip are not taking into account such as the monstrous evil that is blackmailing Viola with her son's life, or spying on and stealing state secrets to the endangerment of American citizens' ability to live in a world of equality and freedom. Maybe she only needs to help Elizabeth and Philip see that what they think is truth is not *true* after all. Viola calls on her faith repeatedly, as if to will her truth through words onto the Russians.

Viola acts as if Elizabeth and Philip could be brought to see *the* truth, if only they listened. Stan has a similar attitude to the Russians in general. Viola and Stan's position, though, necessarily assumes that it is possible to distinguish between truths: on the one hand, Elizabeth and Philip's relative (delusional) "truth", and, on the other hand, *the* truth. Thus this view maintains that it is possible to awaken from one's dogmatic slumber, once the one and only truth has been recognized as *the* truth.

Yet our perception of the world-as-it-is cannot be so clearly distinguished from that of the world-as-we-wish-it-to-be. As in the cases of Viola and Stan, the stories that give credibility and truth to their beliefs are so intimately connected with who they are and who they want to be, that it is virtually impossible for them to separate their subjective experience of the world from their representation of its objective reality.

The Jennings Show

What if Viola and Stan, Elizabeth and Philip were all characters in a TV show? Their respective views of reality, their truths, would be nothing more than the product of the creative work of a team of screen writers, directors, and actors. Their worlds would be fiction and entertainment. Yet, as we have seen above, the stories that we tell about the world are a direct reflection of what we hold to be the truth about the world. Thus, the particular way in which a narrative, whether fictional or historical, portrays the world can tell us about what truth the story communicates as a way to legitimize who we are and how we live.

Furthermore, as the reflection on the truths of Viola and Stan have allowed us to see, this is so regardless of whether the story itself is consciously produced to express such a truth or not. In other words, the effectiveness of a narrative to legitimize a given view of the world is independent of the desire (or lack thereof) of its creators to actively promote a given truth.

If this were so, then, what truth would the spy TV show convey? What worldview would *The Americans* implicitly take as *the* truth in its portrayal of the leading characters: Elizabeth and Philip?

We can immediately see that the two leading characters are, in fact, anti-heroes. From the perspective of the American creators and audience of the show, Elizabeth and Philip embody the archetypal modern enemy: Soviet Russia. How could we, the viewers, then, ever sympathize with such characters, whose success and survival automatically and intuitively translate into our loss and demise?

Thankfully, Soviet Russia has long since collapsed, and we can now comfortably root for such an enemy, since any eventual victory for Elizabeth and Philip is safely circumscribed within a historical truth that has them, and any other Russian spy, as the losers. Yet, though this may allow us to feel that we can safely cheer them on, it can hardly warrant our empathy for their struggles, which, in turn, is a necessary process for the fictional narrative to work—for, if we cannot sympathize and empathize with a character, how can we ever care for their adventures? How could the fiction ever enthrall us?

So, what if Viola, Stan, and the Jenningses, though, were all characters in a TV show? As we have seen, the stories that we tell are a direct reflection of what we hold to be the truth. With this in mind, we can then look closely at the particular way in which *The Americans'* narrative portrays the world, and discern what truth the story communicates, and what view of the world it legitimizes, together with who its inhabitants are and how they ought to live.

American Spy

Reading carefully how Elizabeth and Philip are portrayed on the show, we can see that in *The Americans* love is the greatest virtue. Even when their actions on screen present them as cold and ruthless, and definitely un-American, their personality and outlook on the world are justified by their loyalty, first and foremost, to each other and their children, and then, secondly, to the role that they play: Russian spies in the USA.

Most importantly, even when their behavior is the least humane, the fact that both Elizabeth and Philip consistently display loving and caring emotions for each other and their children in reaction to a threat, tells us that, in *The Americans'* narrative, love, in general, and love for one's family, in particular, is a sign of humanity and goodness. This means, therefore, that if you're truly human, then you must value family and emotional connections above all else. Conversely, if, first and foremost, a person values family, their spouse and children, then that person is truly human.

Because of this, we can empathize with Elizabeth and Philip, in spite of their being Russian spies, because they are fundamentally human: they care for those who they love, in an absolute sense.

This narrative of love and family, which legitimizes Elizabeth and Philip, also significantly legitimizes our very own American worldview. *The Americans'* humanizing traits, in fact, are, at their core, the American social values of a traditional family, built on the mutual love and respect of the two spouses and the defense, at all cost, of their children. Thus, in the show's narrative, being human is, in effect, being *truly* American, and vice versa: only if you're American, then, can you be truly human—although, notably, in this perspective you're not American by nationality but by the upholding of American family virtues.

To this end, Stan is a case in point. He is the show's American-born anti-hero who, due to his choice of defending formal American values, such as liberty and equality, over values grounded in the sacredness of love and family, epitomizes the conflicted character on the verge of inhumanity. Here, then, it is Elizabeth and Philip who are true *good* human beings, because their actions conform to our collective American rhetoric of values. Ultimately, we, the viewers, cannot but root for the Jenningses because they are spies who, in the end, are just like us.

15
Spies Finding the Good Life

ALEXANDER CHRISTIAN

On the surface, the Jenningses live the American dream: The family lives in a suburb near Washington, DC, Elizabeth and Philip run a travel agency, daughter Paige shops at the local mall, and Henry talks cars with his dad. Their public life is placid, ordinary—and totally fake.

Elizabeth and Philip are KGB agents. They can kill with their bare hands, they sleep with or torture people to retrieve information—their secret life is full of deception and violence. They're personified opposites to integrity and honesty, virtues many philosophers have considered crucial characteristics of a good life. But their apparent shortcomings are necessary evils. They live in a decadent capitalist society, in which, for them, the good life can't be completely honest.

Theodor W. Adorno reflected on the possibility of an authentic, good life in a dysfunctional society. In *Minima Moralia: Reflections From Damaged Life*, he sums up his pessimism on the issue in the dictum "There is no right life in the wrong one." To Adorno, it's impossible to be authentic and morally good in a society shaped by a fascist or capitalist ideology. Being critical of this ideology won't save you from being corrupted. Adorno illustrates this idea with short reflections and aphorisms, covering small everyday experiences as well as general political considerations. His thoughts oscillate on what's called the human condition, or *conditio humana*: the social, economic and political conditions which shape everyday interactions between people and their way of thinking about themselves and others.

Adorno wrote this book as an exile living in the US. He delivers a pessimistic critique of the "culture industry." Like the Jenningses, he initially had trouble adjusting to the American way of life. Unlike them, he seems pretty hung up on that. Lacking a rigorous argumentation, *Minimal Moralia* is notoriously unclear about its central concepts, like the nature of a good life. It can seem like the sigh of Adorno's world-weariness, but the philosophical points he makes speak to Philip and, especially, Elizabeth.

Adorno maintains that capitalism forces onto humans a life-form which makes the individual blind and deaf to what could possibly constitute a good life. Adorno provides the reader with no positive approach to a good life and rather constantly negates the possibility of a good life in existing societies. He's particularly worried about the omnipresence of consumer products and the surrender of more and more social realms like art or the private life to economic considerations.

In the philosophical tradition, the concepts of "the good life" and a life spent making morally good decisions have often overlapped, but are not one and the same. Adorno isn't really clear about how he understands "living a good life" and "doing morally well," but generally, living a good life is not the sum of morally good decisions, such as refraining from killing an innocent, obliging pastor and his wife. It rather concerns the entirety of an individual's life, comprising honest deep relationships between well-educated friends, the ability to communicate with others, to enjoy music and art together and to participate in political and philosophical debates unobstructed by social, economic and political constraints.

Like Adorno, Elizabeth and Philip struggle with their human condition within American society. But given their devotion to a higher cause, which renders any integration into the wrong society mere strategy to protect their true ideals, they might be said to live a right life in the wrong one after all.

Conditio Suburbia

The Jenningses lead a privileged life. Their reality in America is very different from the reality they left behind in the Soviet Union. They don't need to fear hunger, they can freely express their thoughts, and they have plenty of opportunity to live an easy life—things their fellow proletarians back in the Motherland could only dream of. Elizabeth calls the American way of life easier, but not good. She looks down with disdain on wealthy Americans who have been relatively unaffected by the atrocities of World War II.

A KGB agent and convinced socialist, Elizabeth perceives American society as a source of existential threat to the Soviet Union. It is her priority to help her people catch the American aggressors, who are even leading in the development of appalling biological weapons of mass destruction. Average Americans are oblivious. The American people are distracted from the social inequalities in their own country by consumerism and religion. She tries to explain this to Paige on a walk through the ghetto where Gregory lived, and died. Elizabeth's pessimism about the human condition in a capitalist society even tops Adorno's cultural critique. Philip on the other hand doesn't share his wife's disdain for the American society. He's open to at least some aspects of the American way of life, like the automotive industry and particularly his very own white Chevrolet Camaro Z-28. He doesn't look down on the American people, but even points out that "they aren't all bad" ("Pilot").

Besides the obvious struggle to reconcile a critical socialist mindset with the dictates of consumerism and leisure activities—having to take their kids to yet another mall, arguing about TV-time and video games—there are other circumstances in 1980s suburbia that make it hard to live a meaningful life. Elizabeth has trouble accepting gender roles in America. When the new neighbors move in, it's her job to bake brownies; she's expected to prepare a meat loaf, whereas Philip just brings his winning personality to dinner ("Pilot"). She has to endure chitchat with other wives at a barbecue and is expected to clear the table after dinner at the Beemans' house, whereas Philip can sit back and have a beer or two and has also picked up a new hobby, playing racket ball with his buddy Stan.

Nadezhda and Mischa have to be Elizabeth and Philip for most of the time—unless they have to play yet other roles for an ever-changing audience. They can't deviate much from the value system the Jenningses are expected to enact. This doesn't only affect the big moral issues (like occasionally waiving gender equality or showing acceptance for her daughter's religious ambitions), but goes all the way down to the smallest matters of taste. The all-encompassing challenge of maintaining their cover even intrudes on intimate moments. Because of the ever-present risk of being discovered, no Russian word can ever pass their lips, they can't have borscht and pirozhki, not even on Victory Day (9th May), the holiday that commemorates the victory of the Soviet Union over Nazi Germany in the Great Patriotic War ("Dinner for Seven").

These small everyday experiences aren't minor side-issues when it comes to the good life—they're what should make up the good life. The *conditio suburbia* makes it impossible for Philip and Elizabeth to live out their cultural identity. Like Adorno in his exile in California and New York, the Jenningses miss the small, seemingly unimportant, aspects of their cultural heritage. This shows on the few occasions, when they are free to enjoy Russian food: In "The Clock," Stan Beeman brings a tin of Russian caviar over to the Jenningses' house and combines the delicacy with a six-pack of cheap American beer and some chips. Philip, brought up poor in the city of Tobolsk, has to hide his excitement for the caviar.

But later that night, he prepares a plate with caviar for Nadezshda and they share this treat, remembering their harsh childhood in the Soviet Union, where they had no means to indulge in such delicacies. In this short moment, sitting together during the night, eating caviar from home, Nadezhda and Mischa are able to enjoy a short moment of a

good life, yet fragile given that it has to be enjoyed in secrecy, even shielded from their own children. On another occasion ("Travel Agents"), the communication officer presents
Philip with a bowl of borscht, a traditional Russian soup
made with red beets and root vegetables, garnished with
sour cream and dill. Philip immediately tastes the ginger,
yet he doesn't even have time to reflect on whether he likes
this culinary variation, because he has to take a call from
his fake wife Martha.

Again and again even the small bits of cultural identity
fall prey to the circumstances of either their professional life
as KGB agents or their fake private life as travel agents and
ordinary citizens. Sure, the Jenningses have more serious
problems, but the good life does begin with the small things.
It also spans the decisions that affect the weal and woe of others, and in this regard, the Jenningses have a number of skele-
tons in the cupboard—and sometimes a body in the trunk.

Trust, Honesty, and the Greater Good

Everyone with a spark of decency would agree that Philip
and Elizabeth do horribly bad things—they get their hands
dirty. "The problem of dirty hands" is the topic of a debate in
ethics and political philosophy about the question whether
political leaders can be morally justified in doing things usually considered morally impermissible in service of the
greater good like protecting their country from an existential
threat. The same can be asked of secret agents, who also act
on behalf of their country. It's obvious that the Jenningses
have answered the question affirmatively, because their
hands are, again and again, literally covered in blood.

Philip and Elizabeth not only deceive their informants,
but also leave their children largely unaware about their true
identity. They blackmail innocent people. They order their
field agents to prostitute themselves. They kill innocent people in covert operations and conduct contract killings of the
Soviet Union's enemies. They do all this in service to their
country. Given the circumstances—the economic superiority

of the class enemy, the arms race between the US and the Soviet Union, and an ongoing risk that the Cold War might become hot—every means seems acceptable.

Philip and Elizabeth are painfully aware of the moral problems associated with their methods. When Philip kills an innocent soldier in order to avoid being captured surveilling a US-based Nicaraguan contras training camp ("Martial Eagle"), he is shocked and copes with a strong feeling of remorse. He feels even worse when he discovers that the truck driver they had captured has frozen to death right before Philip is able to release him ("Martial Eagle"). It's hard for Philip to act right, even with good intentions, in a bad world. Likewise, Elizabeth is very reluctant to blackmail Don Seong in order to gain access to Foster Medical Research ("Dinner for Seven"). She's made friends with Young-Hee, Don's wife, and seems to have genuinely enjoyed the time they've spent together, going to the movies, making snarky comments about makeup sales meetings, and cooking Korean food. Elizabeth even cooks hot Korean dishes with tofu for her own family and mentions her new friend to her children. So there are *aspects of a good life*, apart from the morally bad things Philip and Elizabeth have to do in order to uphold their mission.

Sometimes, they even try to set their own limits to what they will do in service of their mission. Philip, for instance, is very reluctant to start a sexual relationship with Kimmy, the underage daughter of a CIA agent. It seems that he succeeds in setting a moral boundary when he manages to maintain the relationship without letting it become physical. But in the end, he's just lucky. Kimmy buys his story about a religious awakening (inspired by his daughter's experiences, which he isn't really able to relate to) and can be handled without Philip responding to her advances. In ethics, these kinds of cases are described as cases of "moral luck": an agent succeeds in doing the morally good thing, but it is rather favorable circumstances than his own ability to control the situation that secure the morally good outcome. Had Kimmy not been open to prayer, Philip would have had to sleep with the teenager. The Jenningses' missions are the top priority. They are not allowed to set their own moral standards. Philip's and Elizabeth's occupation confronts them with extrema ratio decisions on a daily basis. They may want to treat other people in a decent, respectful manner. They may want to establish a good life, with trustful, honest and deep relationships. However, the survival of the Soviet Union comes first, always.

In the personal domain, they can, in very limited ways, occasionally reverse their priorities. When Philip advises Kimmy to keep her father's occupation secret from now on, and that it was a mistake to tell him about it, that certainly doesn't serve his own professional and political mission. But it does satisfy his own need to act towards Kimmy in a benign, helpful way, as a fatherly friend, and to make up for the difficulties in his relationship with his own daughter by at least helping Kimmy to maintain the one with her father. He deliberately puts the quality of these personal relationships before the mission that usually forces him to be dishonest and sometimes even cruel. Contrary to what Adorno claims, it seems that at least pieces of a good life can be preserved even in the most thoroughly fabricated wrong life.

Sometimes it can't be avoided; something real and truthful grows in a relationship between people naturally. The relationship between Martha Hanson and "Clark Westerfeld" is a good example. At first, Philip's intention was clear: In order to gain access to the FBI counterintelligence department, he seduced the department's supervisor's secretary, and convinced her to bug his office. To Philip the relationship was merely a professional issue. For the largest part of their relationship, he is able to keep a professional distance. But over the course of Season Four, a respectful, honest stance towards her shows. In "The Magic of David Copperfield V: The Statue of Liberty Disappears" his feelings and respect towards Martha become obvious. Standing in the Jenningses' kitchen, Elizabeth tells Philip that she feels bad for him, since he lost an important person after Martha left for Moscow.

ELIZABETH: [solicitously] She was a nice woman. She was straight-ahead, uncomplicated. Simple. She was . . .

PHILIP: She wasn't simple.

ELIZABETH: I don t mean *simple*, I meant . . . easy. You know . . . to talk to. You could probably talk to her. You could probably talk to her about those things that you've been talking about.

PHILIP: She was actually very complicated.

ELIZABETH: Of course.

PHILIP: People underestimated her.

ELIZABETH: Apparently.

This short dialog illustrates that Philip isn't willing to accept the slightest derogatory implication toward Martha's character, having a deep and in the recent time even relatively honest relationship with her, having told her his real name and occupation.

Born in the USSR

Philip and Elizabeth, although capable of doing horrible things to other people, have a certain urge—just like everyone—to live a decent life. But just like Adorno, they struggle to find what a good life could be for themselves. Under adverse conditions, Philip and Elizabeth try to fathom the possibilities of a good life, both in their long partnership and in their relationship with their children.

When arriving in America, both needed time to adjust to each other. Especially, Elizabeth struggled with establishing an intimate relationship with Philip. Even though she found him attractive, she was resistant to surrendering even the last bit of privacy to the mission. What stood between both was a lack of biographical knowledge, necessary to being responsive to one another, withheld from them due to strict orders to keep their backgrounds secret. It took Elizabeth sixteen years to finally fall in love with Philip ("Gregory"). They eventually defy their orders and tell each other about their real names. Over time, they share more information about their life in the Soviet Union. These moments of true openness and honesty are often accompanied by physical intimacy ("Salang Pass"), and seem to make their task more bearable. Instead of burdening their conscience due to their disobedience, these glimpses of truth add to their quality of life.

As far as their children are concerned, Philip and Elizabeth disagree about the suitable conception of a good life. Their relationship with Paige provides more explicit insights into their rival ideas about their children's future than the comparatively smooth, almost marginal relationship with Henry. Paige's interest in Christian faith is one of the main topics in Seasons Two and Three. More interested in her church actives, she quits playing volleyball and starts reading the Bible in a church youth group ("Behind the Red Door"). She becomes friends with Pastor Tim and donates her allowance to the church without speaking to her parents.

Philip and Elizabeth are not exactly happy with these developments. Both the parents rather hope for their children to become good socialists with an atheist mindset ("Behind the Red Door"). At the same time, Elizabeth seems to approve of Paige's social activism, letting her participate in activities that conform to her own political ideals, like a demonstration against nuclear weapons ("Stealth"). Eager to install her own cherished values in her daughter, Elizabeth doesn't allow the amount of religious indoctrination a Christian summer camp would involve ("Yousaf"). Keeping in mind that she agrees with Marx's classical dictum that "Religion is the opium of the people" renders it less shocking that she would even like to take the risk that Paige might turn to alcohol and drugs, if she's forbidden to take part in church activities, as Philip warns.

When Paige confronts her parents with her apprehension about their strange behavior, the relationship between them fundamentally changes and her parents reveal their secret ("Stingers"). Insecure about the whole situation, Philip and Elizabeth now have to figure out how much knowledge about their secret activities her daughter can handle. For the longest time, they have seemed rather thoughtless about their children's future. Only occasionally, when forced by the circumstances, did they reflect on the risks their actions as KGB agents confer on their children and how they might get through life without them. Again, it's the circumstances that force them to deepen their relationship with her daughter and to decide whether they want her to follow in their footsteps, limiting Paige's ability to live an autonomous life. Philip and Elizabeth seem to have different opinions about the nature of a good life for her daughter: Whereas Philip shows very little ambition to limit Paige's liberty and force a secretive and dishonest life on her, Elizabeth rather seems to appreciate the idea that Paige in one form or another participates in the ongoing class struggle.

A Good Life After All

Do Philip and Elizabeth live a good life, although they have to maintain the fiction of a normal American family and do horrible things to innocent people? Looking at their actions as secret agents fighting for the interests of the Soviet Union, their dirty hands might be washed clean by both their good intentions and the conditions of the Cold War. The greater good for the proletariat of all countries might even silence their conscience.

But it wasn't Adorno's intention to evaluate individual moral decisions. He was often concerned with the ancient idea of a good life—a life with truthful, deep, and honest relationships with other people. Lacking the opportunity to live in accordance with their cultural identity, being forced to be secretive and dishonest in relationship with others and in constant fear of being discovered, their opportunity to live such a good life is rather limited. Nonetheless, Nadezhda and Mischa struggle for it—for themselves, in their partnership and in their relationship with their children. At times, they manage to live a good life after all.

16
Dangerous Conscience?

KEVIN MEEKER

Can conscience be dangerous? According to Gabriel, it can. Gabriel's a liaison between the Soviet government and spies Philip and Elizabeth Jennings, who are living in America during the Cold War. In the episode "Salang Pass," Philip's wrestling with the morality of a job that might require him to develop a relationship with a young fifteen-year-old girl, Kimberly. Although Gabriel acknowledges the acceptability of wrestling with your conscience in such situations, he also insists that conscience can be dangerous.

But isn't *ignoring* conscience supposed to be dangerous? We often shudder to think about what havoc people with no conscience could wreak. *Dangerous* might be too tame a word for that possibility. So why does Gabriel suggest that *listening* to conscience can be dangerous? Is he just blowing smoke and trying to manipulate Philip into following his orders? Or is there more to it than that? What is Gabriel, or *The Americans*, trying to tell us?

Gabriel never explains what he thinks a conscience is. And no one else in *The Americans* comes close to pinning down this difficult idea. That's not surprising. Philosophers have long debated various views about conscience and there's no agreement about how to understand the debates in this area. But conscience is still an incredibly important topic for philosophy and everyday life. And many of the most

171

interesting issues about conscience seem to surface in crucial times for the central characters. So without some idea of what it is that they are dealing with—or what they think they are dealing with—we might be missing some of the most thought-provoking subtleties of how *The Americans* handles this vital topic.

Speaking in very broad terms, we can understand at least some of *The Americans* as portraying a powerful clash between two opposing views about conscience. The show drops some fascinating hints about these views on conscience and their conflicting implications by showing how the main characters discuss and wrestle with their consciences. Piecing together these scattered clues, we can glimpse a picture of the philosophical issues that motivate some of the most riveting narratives of the show. With this broader perspective in view, we also might be able to understand better the question of the danger of conscience, provocatively raised by Gabriel in his conversation with Philip.

Conscience, Conscience Everywhere

All of the Jenningses wrestle with issues of conscience. But they're not the only ones. Stan Beeman, the FBI counter-intelligence agent who lives across the street, clearly has a guilty conscience. His former supervisor, Frank Gaad, confronts him about his conscience in "The Magic of David Copperfield V: The Statue of Liberty Disappears." Stan's conscience is bothering him because of his relationship with Nina Krilova, a Soviet informant who had been working in the Rezidentura. Just as Gabriel warned Philip about the dangers of conscience, so too Gaad cautions Stan that his conscience can get in the way of his job and that he needs to remember who the Soviets really are.

After thinking about Gaad's message, in "Dinner for Seven" Stan simply cuts off contact with Oleg Burov, another Soviet from the Rezidentura, telling him: "I don't want you on my conscience too." Here Stan seems to be agreeing with certain philosophers, such as the medieval thinker Aquinas, who see conscience as focused inward. Your conscience is guilty when it judges that you have not lived up to your own moral standards. In such a case, according to Aquinas, conscience can torment us for our moral lapses. This inward assessment view would explain why some people use phrases like "pangs of guilt" and "pangs of conscience" interchangeably. But there's more to this view, as we'll see.

Like Stan, the Jenningses' children, Paige and Henry, also grapple with the torment of failing to live up to their own moral code. In "New Car," Henry expresses remorse after being caught sneaking into their neighbor's house to play a video game. Nevertheless, he insists that he is a good person and wails that he knows "the difference between right and wrong." Some philosophers could interpret Henry's point as the view that conscience tells us what the right thing to do really is. To many Christian philosophers, such as Augustine and Aquinas, conscience is also a source of our moral knowledge. It tells us some objective truth about moral standards; it's akin to a moral law encoded into us. Conscience is not simply an indicator of how we measure up to our own subjective standards of behavior.

Paige's struggles with her tormented conscience are more pronounced and affect the narrative much more dramatically. After she finds out the stunning truth that her parents are really Soviet spies, she's forced to promise not to tell anyone. But she is supposed to do more than simply refrain from telling the truth. At crucial times, she must deceive others. In "March 8, 1983," Paige and Elizabeth visit Germany so that Elizabeth can see her mother (the grandmother Paige never knew existed) one last time before she dies. After they return, Paige is expected to lie about the purpose of their trip.

Realizing that the lies would never stop, Paige tells Elizabeth: "To lie for the rest of my life . . . that's not who I am." Her conscience is rebuking her for failing to live up to her moral standards of truthfulness and integrity. Although Elizabeth tries to calm her down by telling her that everyone lies, Paige is unenthusiastic, to say the least. Plagued by the thought of a life full of lies, her tormented conscience forces her over the edge in the riveting climax to the episode and she calls her pastor to reveal to him her parents' secret Soviet identity.

Stan, Henry, and especially Paige seem to portray or represent something like an inward-looking, objective moral code measuring view of conscience. But what about Philip and Elizabeth? We've already mentioned Philip's qualms over the Kimberly assignment. Perhaps the most heartfelt discussion of his pangs of conscience also occur on March 8th, 1983. Philip kills Gene, the FBI computer guru, and makes it look like a suicide so that the FBI will suspect that Gene bugged Gaad's office—not Martha, the secretary Philip has married as a ruse. He confesses to Elizabeth: "This guy, today, his apartment, had all this kids' stuff. Games, you know, stuff Henry plays with. It was hard." A more tortured conscience is difficult to imagine. And we glimpse this struggle, ironically, in a scene interspersed with Paige's conscience-driven phone call to her pastor.

Elizabeth, though, seems to be more concerned about Martha's conscience than her own. When Elizabeth asks whether he told Martha what he was going to do, Philip responds: "No. . . .When she finds out he's dead, she'll come to me and tell me how much she needs to know about it." Elizabeth is worried: "A woman like that with this on her conscience . . . I don't think you're seeing things clearly." But perhaps it's Philip's conscience that's preventing him from seeing things as Elizabeth does. He again struggles to express his pangs of guilt to Elizabeth: "I almost feel like when I do this stuff, if I don't . . . I just feel like from now on I need to be able to know what I'm doing better . . ." But Elizabeth cuts off his inarticulate musings to focus on a TV speech by Ronald Reagan, during which Reagan calls the Soviet Union the "Evil Empire." So Elizabeth is concerned about Martha's conscience but apparently not Philip's. Could Elizabeth be thinking of, and thus represent a different view of, conscience?

Feelings, Nothing More than Feelings?

Elizabeth seems concerned about Martha's conscience because it could spur Martha to do something that affects their spying mission. So Elizabeth appears to agree with Gabriel that conscience can be dangerous—for their goals. On the other hand, she's not above exploiting people's consciences when it fits her purposes. In "Munchkins," we learn that Paige's pastor and wife, Tim and Alice, "feel really bad" about accusations Alice made against the Jenningses when Tim mysteriously disappeared in Africa. In "Dinner for Seven," Elizabeth tells Paige to pretend to forgive them, presumably to manipulate their guilty feelings and make them feel more like allies.

The "Munchkins" episode also presents us with a pivotal conversation between Elizabeth and Gabriel. Elizabeth is clearly feeling guilty about the harm she has caused to people that she's befriended. Gabriel tells her: "Your feelings matter." Elizabeth immediately retorts: "They shouldn't." Elizabeth seems to be expressing an idea about the misleadingness of conscience that is sometimes associated with philosophers such as Friedrich Nietzsche and psychologists such as Sigmund Freud (although, as with so many areas of philosophy, these are controversial interpretations).

The idea is that a guilty conscience is nothing but the result of an unhealthy internalization of someone else's rules—parents, say, or society. These internalized rules are mistaken for some objective moral code. We mistake the subjective for the objective. We don't recognize the arbitrariness of such rules. Feelings of guilt for failing to live up to these internal rules, that masquerade as objective moral truths, thus impede your life and often prevent you from doing what you should. That's why guilty feelings shouldn't matter—ever. We shouldn't give in to or be deceived by our guilt. Conscience is nothing more than feelings that fail to reflect any objective moral order in the world. From this perspective, perhaps Elizabeth is concerned about the conscience of Martha, Tim and Alice because of how it can help her, but she's not as concerned with Philip's conscience because she assumes his training will, and should, override his misleading pangs of conscience—as hers does.

We can contrast the views of Elizabeth and Gabriel in the following way: Elizabeth seems to be expressing the philosophical view that conscience is *always* dangerous. It provides us with false standards and feelings, robbing our joy in life by tormenting us when we fail to live up to our arbitrary code. For Gabriel conscience *can* be dangerous and misleading, but not always. When Elizabeth claims that feeling shouldn't matter, he serenely replies: "They can sometimes." This response indicates that Gabriel is closer to the camp of Stan, Henry, and Paige when it comes to conscience. For Gabriel, we should feel guilty when we fail to live up to our code. But too much guilt, or misplaced guilt, can be a problem and even dangerous perhaps. I suggest, then, that the main clash in *The Americans* is between Gabriel's "guilty feelings can be important" view and Elizabeth's "guilty feelings are always irrelevant" view.

There Be Monsters

Despite her view that feelings shouldn't matter, Elizabeth is often intensely tortured by them even if she's better at hiding them than Philip is. One of the earliest signs of these pangs of conscience is the episode "Covert War." After the killing of her friend Vijktor Zhukov, Elizabeth seeks revenge on the CIA's Richard Patterson, whom she partially blames for Zhukov's death. After kidnapping and tying up Patterson with the intention of killing him, Patterson verbally lashes out at Elizabeth: "You have no heart, no soul, no conscience . . . Do you care about anything? Do you love anyone?" Shaken, Elizabeth decides not to kill him and flees the room.

Why? She's killed many times before. If she thinks that conscience is always dangerous then who cares? You know the saying: "Sticks and stones . . ." But Patterson's words strike deeply and reveal Elizabeth's inner state more than she is willing to let on, perhaps even to herself. Essentially

Patterson's accusing her of being a monster—an inhumane, immoral monster. Elizabeth seems to put this incident behind her fairly quickly. But such accusations crop up quite frequently in *The Americans*. For example, in "The Deal," when Philip is kidnapping him, Anton Baklanov calls Philip a monster who has had his humanity and feeling trained out of him.

The Soviets also are not above hurling such an epithet. When informing Elizabeth of Zhukov's murder by the CIA in "Covert War," Claudia hisses: "Monsters is what they are. Assassins with federal ID badges." In "Arpanet," Elizabeth says of CIA informant Larrick: "Larrick is a monster, but he's our monster." Larrick's *our* monster? If we try to eradicate our misleading and dangerous conscience, then how does that not make us monsters? Elizabeth seems to accept Larrick's monstrosities when they advance her cause's agenda. So are there good monsters and bad monsters? What's the difference?

Do Spies Dream of Monsters without a Conscience?

Perhaps the most riveting, emotionally draining, yet revealing scene in *The Americans* occurs in "Do Mail Robots Dream of Electric Sheep?" After breaking into a repair shop to plant a bug in a mail robot that circles the halls of the FBI (without wearing disguises for some reason!), Philip and Elizabeth hear a noise. Upon investigation, an undisguised Elizabeth finds Betty, a widowed lady who helps run the company. She pays the bills at this late hour, we learn, because this is the time of day that she feels closest to her deceased husband. And she tells Elizabeth the story of their lives, his experiences in World War II, the effects these experiences had on his religious beliefs, their divorce and remarriage, and how they came to run the repair shop.

But this is not a monologue. Betty also asks Elizabeth some questions about her life and family. Knowing that she is going to kill Betty, Elizabeth answers honestly. When Betty realizes that Elizabeth is a Russian well-trained to speak English, the terrible light dawns on her. "You aren't going to let me leave. Are you?" Betty asks. "It's not possible, no," Elizabeth answers. Betty then muses: "This is not how I expected it to end, the story. I'm not afraid of leaving the world. I don't know why, but I'm not."

Elizabeth decides to kill Betty by making her overdose on her medication. Although Betty is not anxious to die, she compliantly begins to take the pills. But she is not done asking questions of Elizabeth. She is shocked to discover that Elizabeth has children and that her husband also kills people as part of their spy gig. "You think doing this to me will make the world a better place?" Betty pointedly asks just before she expires. Elizabeth replies affirmatively and in her last breath, Betty hauntingly shoots an arrow into the icy core of Elizabeth: "That's what evil people tell themselves when they do evil things." After watching Betty die, Elizabeth dejectedly returns to Philip; but she's quietly shedding emotional tears for one of the few times in the series.

Why now? As we've said, she's killed before. Why does this killing hurt her so deeply? If she thinks that conscience and guilty feelings are impediments, why does she let them affect her in this case?

The Face of Conscience?

The philosopher Emmanuel Levinas made a distinction between ethics and morality. Ethics comes first, morality second. More specifically, ethics arise from our face-to-face encounters. When we encounter the face of other human beings, we are confronted with the responsibility that we have towards them. More basically, then, we derive some of our most fundamental knowledge of what's right and wrong from the face-to-face personal encounters with another human. Morality moves beyond ethics: it's a system of rules that arises after the face-to-face encounter, to order interactions among many different people.

Gabriel seems to share something like this view. As we've seen, he's talked positively about the feelings that Philip and

Elizabeth have developed for some of the people they must betray. As he puts it in "Clark's Place": "You two still care about people. It's what makes you such good officers." For Gabriel, as with Levinas, our ethically appropriate feelings for others often arise through our face-to-face encounters with others.

In the episode "A Roy Rogers in Franconia," the Soviet spy William is wavering about his commitment to steal bioweapons, and Gabriel tries to steel his resolve to complete his mission. His pep talk is instructive: "It is hard to believe in things that kill people. You haven't seen the people that you are defending in too long. You have to see them, William." He's not appealing to some abstract, impersonal concept of the "greater good" to motivate William. Instead, Gabriel wants William to see the people he's "defending." Gabriel could always show William *pictures* of those "back home." But clearly that's not enough. Gabriel is implying that William needs to see them in person, *face-to-face*.

Gabriel is not the only one who implies that a personal, face-to-face encounter is ethically important. When Philip is kidnapping Anton Baklanov, Baklanov pleads with Philip to look at him—with the camera eerily peering at Philip's darting eyes in the rear view mirror of the car that he's driving. Baklanov's point, I take it, is that in looking on his face, Philip will see the inhumanity of what he is doing and his conscience will prevent him from sending Baklanov back to the Soviet Union. Even Elizabeth recognizes the importance of the face. In "The Magic of David Copperfield V: The Statue of Liberty Disappears," Elizabeth dredges up some deeply rooted hostility toward Philip and reminds him that he "lied to her face" about his relationship with the mother of his son, Misha. Not just lied—but lied *to her face*.

And perhaps this explains the encounter with Betty. Elizabeth often kills people during some kind of physical altercation. Betty, though, calmly consumes the pills that will kill her, while serenely looking at Elizabeth's face. I suspect that *The Americans* is suggesting that this haunts Elizabeth's conscience so severely because of the face-to-face encounter in which Elizabeth is painfully aware of the inhumanity of what she is going to do to this fellow human. This suggestion can be seen not only in the discussions that we have cited but also in viewing the haunting scene between Elizabeth and Betty, including Elizabeth's poignant facial expressions.

Walking the Line

The show *The Americans*, then, seems to be favoring the view of Levinas and Gabriel as opposed to that of Elizabeth and (perhaps?) Nietzsche. Conscience is important, especially conscience informed by or shaped by face-to-face encounters with other human beings. But we're still left with our original puzzle. Why exactly does Gabriel say that conscience is dangerous? Isn't the conscience, formed by face-to-face encounters, supposed to tell us what the right thing to do really is and warn us when we are not doing it? Since the show seems to agree with Gabriel, what is *The Americans* trying to tell us about the dangers of conscience?

Throughout the series, the Jenningses constantly justify their deceptions, killings, and other horrible actions as serving the greater good of humanity and they sometimes characterize their enemies as monsters. But how far can we go in the name of a greater good? We generally agree that killing in self-defense is good and both sides seem to think that it is okay to kill for their country. But where's the line? Killing in defense is justified only when it's necessary.

The problem for Elizabeth in particular is that she holds others to standards that she herself seems to violate. She appears to agree with Claudia in "Covert War" when Claudia grouses: "I thought that the Americans understood that even covert wars have rules. I was wrong." More clearly, in "New Car" Elizabeth rages about Ronald Reagan as he appears on TV: "Look at him. He'll do anything—he doesn't care. Kids, nuns, journalists. He doesn't care." But we could add "elderly ladies" to the list and immediately recognize that Elizabeth herself may "do anything." And when we factor in her (perhaps) Nietzschean "(guilty) feelings shouldn't matter" mantra, it seems as though she doesn't—or *shouldn't*—really care either. Perhaps her conscience becomes so overwhelming because she fails to live up to the standards that she constructs for her enemies. And maybe it takes her longer to arrive at this point than, say, Philip and Stan because of her negative views about feelings arising from conscience.

One important question that *The Americans* raises is this: if during war we can justifiably kill, lie, and commit other acts generally considered wrong or evil, is there *any* limit on our actions? Perhaps conscience can be dangerous if it prevents us from performing necessary duties in time of war, as Gabriel— and Gaad—indicate. But *The Americans* suggests that a total disregard for conscience is the greater danger. Killing in the name of the "greater good" becomes so second nature that it becomes easy to kill and *think* that it is necessary.

We can rationalize our own behavior when we find the same behavior monstrous when done by our enemies. The poignant portrayals of spies dealing with face-to-face encounters of those they "must" kill vividly confronts us emotionally and philosophically with some thought-provoking scenarios that alert us to the possibility that conscience might need a seat at the table in these dire situations. Ignoring issues raised by conscience in war may be the greatest danger of all.

17
Ethical Spying

JAI GALLIOTT

For certain political parties, a soap opera about Soviet-born spies, trained to pass for a typical American suburban family, couldn't have come at a better time. Indeed, some would have us think that while the Cold War was over, there has been something of a Russian revival in recent times.

We've been led to believe that there are Russians in the closet, Russians in the pantry, Russians in the garage, and behind the neighbor's every suspicious step. Russians, Russians everywhere—but not a single one to see. Yet for all the talk about national security, Russians compromising the political process, and false testimony aimed at hiding Russia's influence on presidential appointments and administrations, most Americans know and take this for what it is. Politics. And while some of the rhetoric may be true, the politics of today is not decent and it's hardly moral.

The show's ex-CIA creator, Joe Weisberg, undoubtedly knows that the recent Washington storyline about the Trump administration and the Russians helps his show and fuels the hysteria. Although the FX series has been praised for its nuance, it creates a cloak-and-dagger world where its tools almost never fail, master plans almost always work and the best spies always win. Of course, real spies and others familiar with the intelligence domain will know that this world is largely make-believe in much the same way that average Americans know they need to be wary of political rhetoric. Still, when those in the intelligence community are done lurking in shadows—or typing away in their cubicles, as is more likely the case for the modern day spy or analyst— many often come home and turn on the show about the Soviet sleeper spies posing as a married couple, just across the street from their FBI friend and with the knowledge of their daughter's pastor.

Why? While the show depicts an idealized intelligence world that's very different from the genuine day-to-day intelligence life, reviews of the show by known intelligence officials praise it for the one important way in which it rings true: the sense that spying is in some cases morally justified and spooks have internalized, and abide by, a set of generally agreed upon rules.

Yes, they murder people, wear disguises and steal other nations' secrets, but not for fun. They are professionals. Yes, they occasionally use their 1980s sex appeal to lure capitalist fools into their Soviet spy web, compromise them, turn them and ruin their lives in the process. But these "Americans" have morals, even if they're a bit lose at times. They're decent parents who care enough about their children to take them to Disney World. They also stay awake at night, occasionally worrying about their past day's actions and whispering quietly between themselves about their kids' wellbeing, just like real American parents who aren't agents of a foreign socialist republic.

They think before they kill people, and wait until it's absolutely necessary, especially when their target is another spy. They acknowledge their faulty assumptions, identifying that America was creating genetically modified crops resistant to bugs to help impoverished countries, rather than developing super pests to destroy what few crops survived in the East, which could have led to World War III ("Episode here"). They didn't spill the stolen bio-weapons in Alexandria and wipe out of half of the East Coast, even though they easily could have done so to the benefit of the USSR ("Episode here"). They are killer Russian spies, with some morals.

Morals, Really?

You might be forgiven for thinking that, by definition, the very characteristics that make for a successful spy violate all common moral principles. How could we justify lying and deceiving people, especially when our common moral beliefs are Christian and Christians teach that such actions are sin? I'll let others answer this question as it pertains to religion, but it needs to be recognized that spying among nations is an exceptionally old and extensive human endeavor. It's often said that spying is the second oldest professional when, in fact, the first and second oldest professions are closely intertwined, as Philip and Elizabeth demonstrate every other week. In times of war and peace, a significant slice of states' resources is typically allocated to intelligence organizations, even to the detriment of other social goods like health and social security. This is because espionage is aimed at avoiding harm, potential or actual.

Surprisingly, this costly yet potentially advantageous activity is often seen to lack a clear academic justification or a set of rules to govern it. But that's not to say that these morals are unwarranted, non-existent, or impossible to develop. Until recently, legal and philosophical scholarship was almost exclusively focused on understanding the legitimacy of war among nations, and the proper legal framework for regulating war. Scholars have also rigorously debated the legitimacy of the domestic use of government force. Yet when it comes to spying, a lot of moral theorists are as soundless as the spies themselves, perhaps because of the above view that spying is non-moral.

If or when espionage is discussed, it is generally perceived as an extra-moral activity, one that goes beyond the boundaries of ethics. Espionage is frequently associated with a questionable sphere in which the gravitational pull of states' ultimate interests bends the standard contours of moral space in a typically realist-type manner. This ignores the role that moral theories concerning warfare can play as an appropriate ethical regulator for espionage. To reconcile the moral dilemmas without gleefully dismissing potential for abuse or the moral quandaries is no easy task, of course.

The starting point must be to recognize that the principal reason for espionage, like the use of force, is the presence of evil in the world. Once this is established, we can draw parallels between the principles and values of the Just War tradition started by robe-wearing great thinkers centuries ago, and apply those values and principles to espionage. This is because, just as the case for making decisions concerning the use of lethal force in wartime hinge on considerations of proportionality and discrimination, both of which are central principles of Just War theory, so too are those considerations centrally applicable in the determination to undertake covert action of the kind in which Directorate S is involved.

Such justifications make the constituent aspects of espionage, such as deception and killing, morally acceptable when practiced in the pursuit of higher good by a nation, namely fighting evil. If we are to reflect wisely on the practice of espionage, we cannot afford to presume that the ethical tradition governing war—the just war tradition—has nothing to say about it. War is harmful in the same way and is fought for the same good reason. Crossing this bridge is vital for those of moral conviction determined to avoid morally unacceptable choices in defence of justice, peace, and order. As a part of the arsenal of a nation in which democracy thrives, espionage like that so well portrayed by Philip and Elizabeth can, it turns out, be judged (if not justified) in ethical terms.

Just War Theory for Clandestine Operations

A few select authors, including former spooks such as August Cole and many academics who probably aspire to be spies, have used the existing Just War literature to establish a moral basis for conducting clandestine intelligence operations. Although Just War theory is usually concerned with what is and is not permissible in war, it can still contribute to an understanding of the morality of potentially harmful intelligence activities during peacetime.

War is probably as close as you can get to hell on Earth, though life in a Soviet Gulag may well have been worse. Killing is not only allowed, but is often considered a patriotic duty. This is one reason why many people believe that war is a place where no moral constraints or laws apply. Cicero (106–43 B.C.E.) summed up this view nicely in saying that "in times of war, the laws fall mute." Yet, all is not fair in love and war. Just War theory says that there are times when killing and other atrocious acts are morally justified. In abstract terms, it seeks to discern the difference between a just and unjust cause, usually related to self-defense or collective defense, and just and unjust means of supporting that cause. There is a common assumption that the opposing party is always in the wrong and that the enemy's attack or threat of force is unjustified. Of course, in both history and objectively viewed modern reality, there are many more cases of conflict in which both sides have accused the other of unjust aggression or where both parties seem to have some genuine moral claim to defend and thus support what would otherwise be purely offensive action.

In finding a middle ground between the Machiavellian position that there ought to be no moral restriction and the absolute view that no immoral act is ever justified, at any time or anywhere, Just War theory allows for measured and unwavering acts in the support of a more peaceful world, but does so in the face of immorality. The rationale it employs permits "absolute" values to be contradicted under extreme circumstances, while maintaining that the very values violated remain absolute in the universal sense.

We might, therefore, accept commandments such as "Thou shalt not kill," "Thou shalt not steal," and "Thou shalt not bear false witness against thy neighbor" as "absolute" obligations, while maintaining that all three circumstances might be tolerated in certain defined circumstances. These imperatives remain absolute, because it is agreed that such acts are evil even when they are justifiably performed. In such cases, a moral law is broken out of necessity. We do evil deeds only in so far as they are required to avert greater evil. Even though this would have many Kantians rolling in their graves, it is not as though evil deeds cease to be evil if urgent public interest makes them necessary. This philosophy underpins Just War theory, the function of which is not necessarily to justify warfare, but rather to offer a guide and judge conflicts.

The criteria for judging acts of war to be forbidden or allowable have developed over centuries from ancient moral and theological ideas. One of two major Indian epics, the *Mahabharata* offers one of the first written discussions of whether the suffering caused by war can ever be justified. Parts of the Bible also tend to encourage ethical behavior in war and hint at the concept of *just cause* in suggesting that war should only be fought for certain divinely approved reasons. Saint Augustine (354–430 C.E.) also wrote about the morality of war from a Christian perspective, warning us of the love of violence that war often engenders. However, it was Saint Thomas Aquinas (1225–1274) who gave the general outline of the Just War theory that is taught to the military officers and philosophers of today.

Aquinas not only discusses the justification for war, but also expands on what sorts of activities Christians ought to perform in war. Of course, the Soviets had no respect for religion. It is important, then, that other robe-wearing scholars from the good ol' days, such as Francisco de Vitoria (1486–1546), Hugo Grotius (1583–1645), and Emerich de Vattel (1714–1767), secularized the moral principles proposed by earlier Christian scholars. Each of these scholars wanted to limit unnecessary suffering and destruction, while not impeding the pursuit of just outcomes.

Modern scholars have expanded on these principles to the point that we now have a generally coherent set of conditions, all of which are required to met:

1. **JUST CAUSE.** Aggression is inherently evil and only action defensive action is legitimate.

2. **Right Intent.** Nations must seek a better state of peace. This rules out revenge, conquest, economic gain, or ideological supremacy.

3. **Last Resort.** War is acceptable only when all other options have been exhausted.

4. **Legitimate Authority.** As war is the prerogative of governments, legitimate authorities must formally declare a state of war.

5. **Probability of Success.** Given that aggression is inherently evil, objectives must be likely to derive the overarching goal of war: peace.

6. **Proportionality.** Nations should limit their actions and use of force to what is necessary to stop aggression and secure a just peace.

7. **Discrimination.** Only those who are official agents of government may fight justly; individuals not actively engaged in combat should be immune from attack.

These conditions apply at different levels to different people and are purposely onerous. The Just War theorist accepts the need for conflict reluctantly and with regret, concluding that participation in war is sometimes the lesser of two evils. To Just War theorists, war is not a matter of choice but rather one of necessity, arising from the need to control violence in our imperfect world.

Both the intelligence world portrayed in *The Americans* and that which exists between nations today are obviously imperfect in many ways. One can successfully incorporate espionage and covert interference in the affairs of foreign nations under the penumbra of Just War theory if one understands that espionage is utilized as a means of government survival in a chaotic world. For any nation, the citizens' lives and wellbeing are closely tied to the military and economic prosperity of their nation and the broader international community.

Just War theory contains an implied basis for the existence of organisations like Directorate S. The principles of Just War theory ground the right of governments to interfere in the affairs of foreign nations, so long as the principles of Just Cause, Right Intent, Probability of Success, and Proportionality prevail. The principles will not always prevail, of course, as statecraft is in the hands of fallible human beings and the bar is justifiably high in establishing the rules of engagement for the personnel that undertake espionage in defense of the nation.

Some will flout the rules. Indeed, the job of the intelligence professional is fraught with temptations for extreme abuses due to often operating in the shadows. Any person involved in espionage must be a person above reproach and of the highest integrity or abuse is almost certain to follow.

Philip and Elizabeth seem to fit this description. Take what occurred in "Amber Waves," *The Americans'* Season Five premiere. Its entire final segment is devoted to the detailed work of Philip, Elizabeth, their young South African protégé Hans, and a team of spies digging up the unmarked grave of William, the bioweapons expert who deliberately infected himself with a lethal contagion rather than give up their secrets to his American captives.

After getting the lay of the land from an anonymous driver outside the facility's perimeter, they cut through Fort Dietrich's fence, find a patch of grass beneath a hill, unpack a tarp and tools and shovels, and methodically start digging. In some ways, this represents the methodical mindset required to meet the demands of Just War theory. When Hans loses his balance on the lip of the grave, he falls in, slicing his hand open with the knife and landing right on top of William's body, from which they were trying to retrieve a sample for testing. Elizabeth reassures him that it's okay, he asserts that the wound doesn't hurt, and Philip gives him leave to climb back out and leave the rest of the job to them. Once he turns away, they shoot him in the head.

It seems cold and might seem immoral. However, they were on a mission that revolved around understanding the chemical weapons threat posed to the USSR, seemingly a just cause. They had the right intent and they would not have resorted to carefully cultivating William as an asset if they had other means of circumventing the threat. Hans's killing was also just in that he was a foreign operative, someone who knew that his life would be over if he ever posed a risk to his nation, and discriminating and proportional in that the killing was better done in the hole so that his body could be put in the coffin to prevent the spread of the contagion that could have killed much of the local civilian population. The probability of success in taking the immediate lethal action was also high and perhaps even quite noble, considering that the killing represented the death of an ally to save the citizens of a nation they despise on ideological grounds. Elizabeth and Philip were, in more ways than one, dealing with the problem of dirty hands.

In other cases, though, we see that Elizabeth and Philip's espionage activities bring them close to conflict with the requirements of Just War applied to intelligence theory. On several occasions, the duo is faced with the decision to kill "innocent" characters, people who are not actively involved in spying, but who are involved in the military-industrial complex in some way and might endanger their safety if permitted to live.

During the Season Two episode, "Arpanet," Philip is forced to shoot a programmer when the worker inadvertently catches him in the act of bugging Arpanet, the military precursor of the Internet. Some will maintain defense workers like this, and even administrators like Martha, ought to be viewed as innocents and their deaths considered indiscriminate. But what principled reason could we offer for excluding those and others who make a causal contribution to the intelligence collection or military-industrial effort in an indirect but important manner? The contributions of these individuals are essential to the harms inflicted on the frontline in combat or in the intelligence world.

More generally, we might say that all espionage activity is unjust and unethical because the element of formal declaration of conflict is missing. However, there are two ways to respond to this complaint. The first is to point out that the absolutes that are breached by intelligence activity are presumably less stringent than those that might exist for a declaration of war, meaning that Just War requirements might be somewhat relaxed as they pertain to intelligence. The second, and linked, response is that intelligence professionals can be both declared and non-declared officers. That is, foreign governments effectively know that spies are on their territory seeking to exploit holes in their counter-espionage defenses. There is also the fact that virtually every nation has its own intelligence collection resources, and that it is everyone's interest to have their spies abide by a set of common "rules," especially when many spies are morally compromised individuals like Agent Beeman.

Russians in Cyber Space

In the Season Three finale, references to the Cold War converge with the show's dramatic narrative about good and evil during an eye-catching scene which intercuts between Philip and Elizabeth watching Ronald Reagan's infamous "Evil Empire" speech, Henry and Stan playing a board game and Paige confiding in her pastor that her parents are foreign operatives. Whereas Reagan warns against the "aggressive impulses of an evil empire" and describes the conflict between the United States and the USSR as a "struggle between right and wrong and good and evil," *The Americans* provides some insight into how intelligence professionals concern themselves with questions of justice. Simplistic narratives about good and evil cannot be sustained in our age, so we must recognize when a seemingly simple narrative might be presenting us with a nuanced picture filled with human actors and complex concerns and motivations.

This will become increasingly true as we move forward. The Just War theory which can be applied to the Cold War–era intelligence world can also apply to intelligence collection efforts underway today. Russian spies are doing what they have always done, but they are now doing it in cyberspace. The Arpanet attack might not have been all fiction!

Increasingly, cyber espionage is being combined with human espionage to research targets and work out whom to approach and how. It will be important to consider the impact that cyber espionage will have on adherence to the Just War concepts and their regulation of intelligence activity. While cyber might well be more discriminating and proportionate in that it could, in theory, involve reduced infrastructural damage and reduced casualties, and perhaps even prolonged peace, it is not without its problems.

It's difficult to determine the source of cyber infiltrations and this leads to an "attribution problem." This fact would give many cyber spies credible deniability, but poses issues for the principle of legitimate authority and gives rise to a host of concerns regarding how to respond ethically to espionage efforts when it is not possible to determine who is behind them.

V

Rules of Engagement

18
Bypassing Humans, Exploiting Machines

Louis Melançon

There are different types of roles for an actor: leading roles which carry the story, supporting roles which propel the story, or bit roles that don't really interact much with the others, they're just sort of there. Of course, most of these definitions rely on how much dialogue with others an actor has.

I think that's hooey, because in *The Americans* there is one actor whose lines are only uttered by others but is a pivotal point for propelling arcs and development of almost every major character: Stan, Philip, Elizabeth, Martha, and even Oleg. When the frame of the television screen includes this actor, the viewer knows it, even when it's just rolling across in the background. That's right, I'm talking about Mail-bot, the best supporting actor on television!

"Surely you jest, that's not an actor, that's a *prop!*" But good old Mail-bot is more than a prop. Tell me you don't smile just a bit when it rumbles down the hallway when Martha is feeling like the walls are closing in. Or when it can so fully empathize with Gaad when he just kicks, and kicks, and kicks Mail-bot out of frustration with all the things going wrong in his life ("Divestment"). Mail-bot has become more than a prop, more than just Chekhov's gun waiting to discharge (Chekhov, you'll remember, first stated the principle that if a gun is introduced into a play, the gun absolutely must be fired some time later in the story).

While Mail-bot is an object on which people base actions it has also become something with which they interact. This opens a window for us to see a potential trap in the world of intelligence where people are dehumanized. This can happen just by the way people are treated, how Martha's constant droning becomes like the hum of Mail-bot's drive motor to Philip, merely background noise in the world. But this can also happen, through the use of technology, in an unintentional fashion.

Mail-bot is more than just a prop. It's not so much that Mail-bot has been promoted to human, but that all the other characters are demoted down to something less than human. In the real world, to gain insights and reveal secret information, the use of technology has been advocated as being somehow easier to ethically justify. But is it really, or does it dehumanize just like Mail-bot does with its fellow actors?

The Truth Is in the Transcript

The first time Mail-bot really has any lines, they're spoken by others. When Oleg and Tatiana are presented with reams and reams of transcripts from the bug planted inside Mail-bot, they are confused. "Beep, beep, beep?" The conversations seem disjointed as the transcripts have at least three speakers: two FBI agents and this beeping character ("A Day in the Life of Anton Baklanov"). Are the beeps in response to statements or questions? Is there interaction? Slowly and amusingly, they start to realize: these precious lines of communication from our hero Mail-bot are nothing more than the background noise that the translators/transcribers failed to scrub out. They have no more meaning to the conversation being recorded than would the tweets of a songbird right outside the window or the honks and engine noises of traffic from the street below. Yet for just a brief moment, before they burst into laughter, Oleg and Tatiana had put Mail-bot on an equal footing with the humans conversing near the microphone. The question becomes, did that raise Mail-bot up, or bring the humans down?

At the core of this question is the context of what was being accomplished. In this case, it was all about discovering FBI secrets such as: Who was being placed under surveillance? Who was under suspicion of spying for the Soviets? When, where, and by whom were surveillance teams dispatched? Mail-bot had the placement and access to provide answers to these and so many more questions. From the KGB perspective, it was a stroke of genius to plant a listening device there. This unleashed a treasure trove for protecting KGB operations and determining how much risk was being taken on by the various Russian spies.

This isn't the first time that the Jenningses have used technical means to listen in on what was happening inside the US national security enterprise. Remember the clock they placed in the Undersecretary of Defense's library ("The Clock")? Or what about the tape recorder of the CIA Afghanistan Division Chief's bag ("Dimebag")? And perhaps the most impactful of all, at least from a plot driving perspective, Frank Gaad's pen ("The Oath")? Why they do this is self-explanatory: using technology allows for finding out secrets without the secret holder knowing that the information they are trying keep hidden has been revealed.

It doesn't just happen in the world of television: recall Secretary of State Colin Powell playing tapes of recorded telephone conversations between Iraqi military officers to the United Nations Security Council in the run-up to the second Gulf War, Operation Iraqi Freedom. Or the US Ambassador to the United Nations, Adlai Stevenson, showing high-altitude pictures of Cuba undergoing preparation for the emplacement of Soviet nuclear missiles. While this latter example deals with visual imagery, it's the same basic conceit as all the previously mentioned examples, both fictional and real: a technical mechanism is used to discover and reveal secrets that another party wants to keep hidden.

Bang for the Buck?

There's no question that these are efficient ways to discover secrets. If you can afford the technology and get it where it needs to be then you're able to have access to information that you really need to make better decisions, the whole point of intelligence (please see Chapter 22 for how I'm defining "intelligence"). Convincing someone to give you secrets can be difficult and time-consuming. How long does it take to find the human who could get you the secrets you need, determine how you need to manipulate that human to give you those secrets, and then convince the human to give you the secrets? Obviously there's no fixed answer, it will all depend on the circumstances. But as James McCargar pointed out in *A Short Course in the Secret War*, it's hard work. It often doesn't come quickly or easily, or if it does then you're walking into a trap.

But let's say you find that person or persons who can get you the information you need and you convince them to betray their peers. Could there be an issue with reliability and trustworthiness? Loch Johnson has proposed that this is a critical weakness of human intelligence: the people acting as assets on your behalf are unreliable or prone to tell you what you want to hear. If you're using technology instead of humans, you won't have to worry about all that, at least in theory. People can pass deceptive information; Elizabeth is almost captured in this way ("The Colonel"), but you can't deceive technology. Center believes this. That's why they push these programs so hard with Philip and Elizabeth. Those listening devices, whether the clock, the pen, or the valise, could be gold mines of information with a low risk that the entire take was a scripted deception by the Americans on the Soviets' or someone's personal agenda.

Some intelligence experts have argued that using technology is also morally superior to using humans. In the 1970s, Stansfield Turner, Director of Central Intelligence, in addition to making resource decisions to invest more heavily in satellites as part of a push for more technological collection of intelligence, also made the argument that these were ethically superior operations. This came on the heels of some serious scandals of inappropriate intelligence activities within the United States, culminating in several high profile investigations, such as the Rockefeller Commission and the Church Committee. There was a common trend across these various investigations: the concept of least intrusive means of surveillance.

This concept of least intrusive means was not without controversy. A variety of positions were staked out ranging from an extreme end of having the US cease conducting any of this dastardly intelligence business all the way to the other extreme of denying that there were any problems at all despite what the investigations revealed. Sitting somewhere in the middle is this notion of least intrusive means. The argument is that methods which intruded the least were less likely to access or reveal secrets that did not apply to the matter at hand, therefore not infringing, or less likely to infringe, on the right to privacy.

Underlying all of this was the fact that the discussions were centered around US persons being involved in some way. There are technical definitions about what constitutes a US person, but we aren't going to worry about that right now. We just need to know that this argument states that a method which intrudes least and likely will not reveal unrelated secrets and so becomes ethically superior and preferable to another method.

Shortly afterwards this general argument was extended by Turner and others such as Gary Marx to go beyond US persons. This extension still claims ethical superiority but adds a practical viability advantage. The argument is that in addition to the previous benefits, a less intrusive method is less likely to be detected and cut off by those protecting the secrets. This means a greater reliance on technology and an additional side benefit of not having to deal with those pesky humans in a potentially ethically shady fashion. So even beyond US persons, technological means of collection become the ethically superior and preferred method, especially when contrasted with old-fashioned human intelligence.

Louis Melançon

The Second Oldest Profession

Using human assets not only might be unreliable but can be ethically dubious. At its most extreme, it's about leveraging a person's flaws against them to have them do things on your behalf. The Jenningses could try to justify this, claiming that anyone who can be recruited is already corrupted, having them reveal secrets is not a great leap from the bad things they have already done.

Take Andrew Larrick. From the Soviet perspective he was doubly compromised: homosexual and hiding it. Center was able to blackmail him based on what they believed to be his ethical weakness, homosexuality. His actual ethical weakness was that he was a cold-blooded killer who did not feel he was bound by the norms and laws of society when it came to taking life ("Behind the Red Door"). There's a difference between killing on a battlefield, which he did in Vietnam, and ambushing KGB support personnel in their homes, which he also did. Larrick has poor moral character, but just not in the way Center thought. In the real world assets are often recruited from those with questionable moral fiber: criminals, politicians, and (shudder) lawyers. But, dealing with these deplorables isn't the true ethical issue with human intelligence.

The real issue deals with the relationship between the person trying to get the intelligence, say Stan, and the person being recruited, say Nina. This is a relationship based on manipulation. One person finds a weakness, like smuggling electronics into the USSR, and uses that as leverage to control the other person to gain what they want, access to secrets ("The Clock"). The other person in that equation, the one being controlled, becomes nothing more than a means to an end. Kant would roll over in his grave. Even John Stuart Mill would be a bit leery—even if the action could be demonstrated to show a greater utility for the society at large. Because what we're seeing is the dehumanization of the individual. The language used by practitioners reflects this: a recruited person is an "asset," not a spy, not a colleague, but an "asset," a resource, a thing.

But if the person you're dealing with is already morally questionable, does it really matter if they're being exploited? Well, yes. Even bad people still have value. This is why recruiting assets can damage the recruiter. Heck, that might be the leitmotif of *The Americans*. We see that happen to Stan. He leverages Nina's weakness to control her and get her to provide information about the Soviet embassy. But it's not just this initial interaction with Nina that has damaged Stan. Stan spent years undercover with the neo-Nazis and being partnered with Amador the ladies' man didn't help. When your job is deception and manipulation, it's hard to keep your moral compass calibrated. This led to his turning a professional relationship with Nina into something more intimate, and by intimate I mean naked, sexxxxxxy times ("Duty and Honor"). Which, of course, turned into being controlled by Nina and Oleg ("The Cardinal"). Yes, Stan presents an extreme example, becoming a double agent for the Soviets, but the threat of moral damage to those other Stans out there, like Elizabeth and Philip, are all too real.

It's hard to determine where to even start with how it's affected Elizabeth. The damage to her moral compass allows her to enable and exploit Lisa's alcoholism ("Martial Eagle"), force Betty to overdose ("Do Mail Robots Dream of Electric Sheep?"), and create the conditions that destroyed Don's life ("Dinner for Seven"). This business of exploiting other humans clearly has risk to those being employed to do it. Lisa, Betty, and Don aren't the only ones to suffer; this is clearly taking a toll on Elizabeth's soul as well.

This supports the least intrusive argument. By placing the method of secret revelation, the technology, between the secret holder and the secret seeker, a prophylactic for the soul of the secret seeker is created. You might think, and the argument goes, that since they aren't trying to manipulate another person there isn't the opportunity to dehumanize the asset or damage the secret seeker's soul. If only this rationalization was truly sound! But I think that using Mail-bot, or really any technology, as an asset can be just as damaging to the secret seeker, just a different type of damage.

The Machines Are No Better

Let's go back to Oleg and Tatiana reading through the transcripts from Mail-bot. The initial read by the Soviets treated
the machine as an equal in the conversation, until they realized what was happening. At that point, beyond being
amused, they became more interested in what was being said
as they realized they had unfettered insight into the FBI
counterintelligence division. The prophylactic of Mail-bot
means that Oleg didn't have to manipulate an asset to get
these secrets. But there is a different type of damage, and it
rests on the agency of the individual possessing the secret.

With the interaction and exploitation between two humans, it's pretty apparent where we can get damage: leveraging another's weaknesses. But even then, there is an
internal agency, the one being leveraged could simply walk
away. When Oleg attempts to leverage Stan over Nina's
safety, each has agency over the potential damage. Oleg
makes the decision to utilize Stan as an asset accepting the
damage to himself. Stan is somewhat dehumanized, being
blackmailed over his relationship with Nina, but he still has
the element of choice. He can, and eventually did, demonstrate his own agency over revealing secrets; he walked away
and let Nina suffer the consequences rather than suffer the
moral damage of revealing US stealth technology ("Echo").
Both Stan and Oleg demonstrated agency over their own
destiny, they made choices about risking moral damage to
their own or another's soul.

Since in technical collection of information the machine
becomes the one collecting the secret, it is the one conducting
the revelation of the secret and the receiving humans merely
accept the information through their senses, it would seem
the possibility of moral damage would disappear. But the humans being observed still become merely a means to another's end. Only this time they have no agency to potentially
retain concealment of the desired secrets. That's something
of a problem, the loss of agency is itself a form of damage. By
not getting to choose what or if any secrets will be revealed,
the actors possessing the secrets can't make the decision

about betraying those who entrusted them with secrets. Yet the secrets are still revealed. Unless the individuals in question are being exceptionally careless, like whatever goofball keeps leaving classified material on top of Mail-bot, we can't really assign blame to these individuals. All in all, this is rather trivial, but it leads us down a trail to examining those on the receiving end of the technology.

As we've seen, the people relying on the machine are lucky enough to avoid the moral damage of directly manipulating other humans; but there remains a tendency to dehumanize those they are observing. By removing the agency of the secret keepers and placing the machine as the means of revelation, it becomes quite easy to forget that we're still dealing with real people; they are a someone not a "something" that is just a means to an end. This dehumanization by loss of agency might be trivial to the secret keeper, but it can insidiously impact the observers.

This is exactly the trap that Oleg and Tatiana fell into as they read the transcripts and begin to laugh as they realize that the beeps were not part of the conversation, just background noise. For that brief moment in time, Mail-bot was the equal of the various FBI agents around it. Not because Mail-bot was elevated to the status of human, but because the FBI agents had been demoted to something less than human, something that simply made noises that could be understood by the humans Oleg and Tatiana. True, those FBI agents didn't suffer any moral damage as they weren't asked to betray the US the way Stan almost stole stealth research, but Oleg and Tatiana still incurred a moral taint. Though not as blatant and obvious as the direct manipulation of another human, there is still the potential for the damage, though subtle, to occur as the technology degraded and eliminated the humanity of those they were listening to.

Just Stop?

In the years since the scandals of the 1970s, the risk in human intelligence collection is a constant, dominant theme in ethical examinations of intelligence. The dehumanization risk in technical collection isn't really addressed in the literature. Could it be the arguments of the 1970s were right? Governments and persons could avoid the more obvious risk if they stayed away from the human aspect and focused on the technical? That answer seems too pat and unsatisfactory. But going to the extreme and simply not dealing with intelligence doesn't work either; there's a valid need for governments to gain information to be able to make the best decisions. This is what drives all of our favorite characters from this show, from Philip Jennings to Frank Gaad.

Perhaps what's needed is to recognize that regardless of the method, intelligence collection always carries a risk of moral damage of some form. Technical is not superior to human collection because it doesn't have the potential for damage, the stance taken by most advocates, it just has a different type of damage risk. What is important is going into the act of gathering intelligence fully cognizant of what the ethical risks may be and then making the conscious decision about what risks are acceptable.

Despite all these ethical risks in intelligence, I know of one assignment that is risk-free: getting an Emmy for Mailbot. It's simply the best supporting actor out there.

19
Do unto Others Before They Do It unto You

DAVE WOLYNSKI

In *The Americans*, the struggle for influence and power between the KGB and the FBI plays out in Washington, DC during the height of the Cold War in the 1980s. Power struggles are not new. Niccolò Machiavelli in the early 1500s in Italy, and Thomas Hobbes in the 1600s in England, could directly relate since they participated in similar power competitions in their days as advisors to kings, princes, and ruling families. If Machiavelli and Hobbes were alive, what advice would they offer? How would they frame the Cold War contest between the KGB and the FBI?

Realist Perspectives

Machiavelli is known as a "realist" philosopher because he preferred to examine the real nature of government and individual behaviors as opposed to speculating on what an ideal government or utopian society would look like. Machiavelli thought understanding the good, the bad, and the ugly nature of governments and humans was more practical and reasonable than singing kumbaya or standing around and offering "Wouldn't it be nice if . . . ?" approaches. Machiavelli advertised himself as someone who understood how to really get things done and outmaneuver your opponents—important insight for the competing ruling families, individuals and city-states in 1500s Italy. Flowery idealism is nice: in your enemy.

In Machiavelli's view, the competition for power doesn't favor virtuous people exactly because they are good people who act virtuously. Only the result of a person's actions matter. To obtain power or keep it, you don't need to be honest, or show integrity, or act fairly. Machiavelli thought just the *appearance* of having these qualities is what you need to show. Even if you actually do possess these qualities, Machiavelli argued that leaders need to be able to abandon them when the circumstances require. Sometimes you have to get your hands dirty in order to achieve good things.

Hobbes also explored the "real" nature of humans and human society in seventeenth-century England. He proposed an ideal government, but it was not flowery. He lived during an extremely violent time. Losers in the competition for power were routinely tortured or killed. Like Machiavelli, he saw himself as an advisor to the political elites, in this case, the would-be kings and queens who sought the English throne. Hobbes's experiences led him to believe that the only government capable of sustaining power and keeping the peace between selfish and violent individuals would be a Sovereign with absolute power.

Wrong Place, Wrong Time—Wrong to Kill?

As KGB officers, Elizabeth and Philip Jennings sometimes get their hands dirty and use violence in their operations against the FBI and the US government. Yet they also repeatedly question the need to be violent. In one situation, Elizabeth and Philip go to a company repair shop late at night in order to bug the FBI's Mail-bot machine. While bugging the machine, Elizabeth unexpectedly runs into the elderly mother of the shop's owner. Elizabeth agonizes over killing the innocent woman, but Philip convinces her that the woman is in the wrong place at the wrong time, and unfortunately needs to be killed.

Philip also kills innocent people due to bad timing. When stealing the key components to ARPANET (yes, the real precursor to the Internet!), Philip kills an innocent student who walked into the computer lab just as Philip was finishing the job. After his ARPANET mission is over, Philip has a drink at a bar and seems to question if he really needed to kill the student in order to successfully complete the operation.

In both of these situations, Machiavelli would advise Elizabeth and Philip that they did the right thing. To defeat the FBI, it's sometimes necessary to kill innocents or do other things that you might find personally distasteful. As servants of the state, your own individual needs or personal feelings are not relevant. The KGB has determined that successfully bugging Mail-bot is necessary in its fight against the FBI, and thus you need to do whatever is necessary to successfully bug Mail-bot. Stealing ARPANET will give Soviet scientists essential information on US military technology which will again preserve the Soviet Union's power and ensure its survival. That unlucky student was in the way.

Machiavelli would not condone violence for no reason. He would support these violent acts in the sense that they help accomplish the "good" thing in the end, which is the FBI's defeat. Machiavelli would be frank with Elizabeth and Philip: if you act "virtuously" in every way against the FBI, you'll be defeated when FBI agents resort to dirty acts themselves. The choice is yours: a "hands-clean" approach and be defeated or do what you have to do in order to win.

Kudos to Claudia

Early on, the KGB is aware of a mole in its Washington DC rezidentura, but doesn't know exactly who it is. Claudia, the handler of Elizabeth and Philip, is tasked by Center to help find the mole. It could be anyone. Claudia kidnaps Elizabeth and Philip and subjects them to mental and physical torture. It might be one of them. Claudia eventually frees them after finally being convinced that neither of them are the mole. Rather than praising Claudia for taking the needed dramatic actions to find the mole, Elizabeth and Philip are furious with her.

Elizabeth savagely beats Claudia to within an inch of her life. Machiavelli, however, would applaud Claudia's actions. She did what was necessary. Finding the mole (and therefore protecting the interests of the KGB and the USSR) trumped any personal loyalty interests Claudia had toward Elizabeth and Philip. In his writings, Machiavelli praised ancient Romans who served the state instead of furthering their own private ambitions. Machiavelli would also chastise Elizabeth and Philip and tell them to calm down and grow up. Claudia did what was necessary—just like Philip and Elizabeth have done so many times before—in service to the Soviet Union. Torturing your fellow agents and friends is justified if that's what it takes to protect the state. Moreover, serving the state in difficult circumstances is a patriotic duty, and patriotic duty in itself would be praised by Machiavelli.

Yet Elizabeth and Philip could legitimately ask if they are just tools wielded by Center which has the true Machiavellian power and control. It is Center which has the force to compel the Jenningses to do what it wants, not the other way around. The arrest and killing of Nina by Center showed other KGB officers what happens when you fail to do what Center wants you to do.

Stan: A Disappointment to Machiavelli

On the FBI side, Agent Stan Beeman is a key player in the fight for power and influence against the KGB. For a while, Machiavelli might have liked him. He was an excellent counter-intelligence officer, Gaad's "go-to" agent and looked to be on the fast track. Stan came out on top even in very dangerous situations, such as his last assignment undercover in a violent supremacist group. Whatever Beeman needed to succeed he had. Machiavelli called all of this "virtù." Sort of like a "vital spirit," virtù is embodied by men like Stan who are able to use their talents when the opportunities arise to mold events to their advantage. Having virtù means you're not content with just sitting on the couch and watching TV (Machiavelli detested laziness in particular). You want to be out in the center of the action like Stan. Machiavelli argued you gained and maintained power by your virtù.

Yet, as Stan develops feelings for Nina, the Russian agent he's responsible for running, his virtù seems to leave him. His marriage falls apart and he kills a KGB agent in an unsanctioned act. Machiavelli would shake his head in disgust at how low Stan has fallen. In Machiavelli's view, Stan is yet another example of someone who puts his own selfish interests above the interests of his country (Machiavelli thought this happens all the time). Yet even at his low point, Stan shows flickers of virtù as he concocts a scheme with Oleg to out a KGB officer to win Nina's freedom and yet keep his own career intact. Similar to a cat that always lands on its legs, having virtù means you can outmaneuver whatever fate (or your opponents) throws at you.

Machiavelli and Hobbes on Pastor Tim: Not. A. Fan

In the competition for power and influence, there are always pesky irritants who seek to challenge you. For both Machiavelli and Hobbes, religious authorities were such irritants. In *The Americans*, Elizabeth and Philip have the same problem with Pastor Tim, a preacher who, thanks to Paige, knows that Elizabeth and Philip are secretly Russian spies. When Paige starts to attend Pastor Tim's church, Elizabeth and Philip are wary of the church's possible power and control over Paige. Machiavelli and Hobbes would share their concerns.

Machiavelli saw religions as social organizations that could help keep the people under control. As long as religious organizations didn't compete with the state for power or influence, they could be tolerated. So, as the civil disobedient missions of Pastor Tim's church became increasingly clear, Machiavelli would view Pastor Tim more and more as a threat. He would see Pastor Tim's civil disobedient actions (such as demonstrating against nuclear weapons) as challenging the state's power and thus needing to be squashed. To add fuel to the fire, Tim views baptism itself as a subversive act aimed directly at the state.

Hobbes would also not be a fan of Pastor Tim and his civil disobedience. Hobbes lived through the English Civil War, a period of violence and bloodshed between religious factions, as well as between supporters of the King and supporters of the Parliament. Hobbes blamed religious sects for inflaming the English populace with pointless religious disagreements. Hobbes would recommend Elizabeth and Philip to take whatever actions are necessary against Pastor Tim, not just because Pastor Tim knows they are Russians, but because if Pastor Tim goes unchecked, he will spur more religious fervor among the population that will ultimately lead to civil disorder and chaos. And this civil disorder and chaos could lead to war between the US and the Soviet Union. In a broader sense, Hobbes would argue that Pastor Tim is an example of why a Sovereign needed unchecked power. This Sovereign could then crush such religious clergy and keep the peace.

A War of All Against All

So, what happens when there isn't a Sovereign or anyone able to impose order over everyone else? How will Elizabeth, Philip, Stan, Gaad, and the other power contenders treat each other if they can do what they want without worrying about their superiors, the law, or international repercussions?

Hobbes thought there were three main causes of conflict in human nature. The first is competition. For example, Stan and Oleg are both romantically interested in Nina. Hobbes argued that competition like this (when they both can't have what they want) leads to the two naturally becoming enemies. As such, both plot the downfall of the other.

A second cause of conflict is diffidence, or mistrust. Elizabeth and Philip debate whether to flee or take other protective measures against Gabriel once they learn of Center's desire to recruit Paige. Elizabeth and Philip don't trust Gabriel's intentions in looking after Paige's best interests.

A third cause of conflict is the old-fashioned one: glory. Stan takes pleasure in being the lead agent in pursuing the Soviet Directorate S officers at the expense of his fellow FBI agents. Arkady basks in Nina's success in running Stan as a double agent (enhancing his own reputation) yet is suspicious of Tatiana as her limelight starts to intrude on Arkady's.

If there's no higher authority that has the power to keep these individual conflicts under control, Hobbes argued you were in a "state of nature." Hobbes famously argued that this state of nature would be a "war of all against all," while life was "solitary, poor, nasty, brutish and short." Why is life in the state of nature so miserable? Hobbes says it is simply because there's no higher authority to maintain order.

Hobbes didn't coin the term "Cold War" but he could have. War is anytime when you live without peace, without security. The Jenningses are at war. Yes, there would be times when people would use force and violence. Yet, what made the state of nature so destabilizing was that force and violence could be applied to anyone, at any time, without warning. Without a sovereign powerful enough to impose order, no human is ever really safe. Lack of order made life "nasty" and "brutish." Other people made life "short."

KGB versus FBI in a State of Nature

Similar to the state of nature that can exist between individuals, Hobbes argued that states exist in a state of nature relative to each other. The KGB and the FBI are equally matched and conflicting powers. Predictably they spiral downward into constant conflict and tit-for-tat killings. The KGB targets US scientists for assassination in a move that ends up killing several FBI agents. In response, the FBI and CIA kill a senior KGB officer in Moscow. Stan kidnaps and kills a KGB officer after his FBI partner was killed by Elizabeth and Philip. Both organizations see the other as at fault for the escalating violence. Moreover, both organizations take what they perceive as defensive or retaliatory measures which only end up feeding the vicious cycle.

Machiavelli would also agree with Hobbes's characterization of ungoverned competition between states, yet in his view, states exist because of their strength and power relative to others. Rulers and citizens with virtù take advantage of weaker states. Machiavelli would argue that the state doesn't exist to provide a "safe space" from the state of nature (like Hobbes would argue). Rather it is a platform to expand the ruler's own power and influence.

Establishing "Rules" in the Power Game

Arkady, the KGB resident and FBI Special Agent Gaad meet outside of Gaad's house in Washington, DC. Arkady tells Gaad that the KGB has agreed to Gaad's fictitious explanation of how a KGB officer has died. The KGB accepts a false explanation that their agent was killed in a random act of street crime. With this agreement, the KGB and the FBI can move past killing each other's officers and go back to the old rules and focus on intelligence gathering. Because there is no absolute Sovereign that can keep the peace between the KGB and the FBI, both organizations voluntarily agree to rules that both sides acknowledge have no force behind them.

Gaad is relieved to hear about Arkady's acceptance, as he also understands that it's in his and the FBI's interests to try to establish some "rules" while in the state of nature. Yet Gaad also threatens a return to violence with his comment to Arkady, "You target our people, we target yours" ("Yousaf").

Hobbes: That's Why We All Need a Sovereign

Hobbes would use Gaad's parting shot against Arkady to show why we as individuals need a Sovereign with absolute power. If such a Sovereign existed, it would be able to tell Gaad at the end of that scene, "No, that's not how it works around here. If you kill Arkady's agents, I will kill you. And if Arkady kills your agents, I will kill Arkady." And with that, the Sovereign keeps both Gaad and Arkady in line. Both Gaad and Arkady will fear what the Sovereign will do to them if they step out of line, so they will keep their disagreements civil.

In Hobbes's ideal government, there's just the Sovereign (with unchallenged power) and subjects (everyone else). Subjects agree between themselves to surrender their own power to do what they want (i.e., individually govern themselves) to the Sovereign, and in return, the Sovereign provides a common order and peace. This has been called Hobbes's "social contract."

Take Arkady and Gaad as an example. In Hobbes's social contract, each of them agrees to submit to the rule of a higher authority, *but only if* the other agrees to do the same. The contract won't work if just one party agrees to it. Each party needs the assurance that the other party can no longer use force and violence at will. They have to be given up by both, otherwise they remain in a state of nature. By submitting to the rule of the higher authority (the Sovereign) they give unquestioned obedience. There's no moral basis for a revolt, even if the Sovereign is cruel or murderous. Hobbes would argue that this is better than the alternative, which is the state of nature, with its war of all against all.

Who Is This Sovereign?

Hobbes's Sovereign needed to have unchecked power in order to force his will upon everyone else and ensure peace. Hobbes saw an analogy to this degree of ultimate power by the biblical creature called the Leviathan, a fearsome animal which, according to the Book of Job, only God had the power to subdue. Hence, Hobbes named his great work on political power *Leviathan*. However, Hobbes didn't mean for his Sovereign to submit to the will of God on earth, as expressed by religious authorities. Rather, he saw his Sovereign as the ultimate civil authority which could dictate the right roles and responsibilities of everyone (including unruly clergy like Pastor Tim).

On the idea of a Sovereign, Machiavelli, however, was a bit contradictory. He saw plenty of examples of ruling princes (and Roman tyrants) who would do wrong "when there is nothing to prevent them from doing wrong." He in fact was tortured and exiled by one prince (which of course fed his anti-prince feelings). Yet he argued that governments had to have a monopoly on power (especially military power), otherwise they would either rot away or be swallowed up by their rivals. Additionally, Machiavelli saw utility in having a single autocrat when the state was in crisis, the crisis stemming from either internal or external factors.

It's the Same Struggle for Power

Both Hobbes and Machiavelli would recognize the struggles between the FBI, KGB and its assorted players as the same sort of power contests that existed in sixteenth-century Italy and seventeenth-cenury England. They would pass along the same lessons that they provided the competing princes and wannabe kings of their day.

Do the dirty things that you need to do to defeat your opponents, otherwise they will do them to you. Build your own virtù so you can take advantage of opportunities and your opponents' weaknesses when they present themselves. Understand the state-of-nature environment that you live in so you can protect yourself and come out on top.

After all, winners are winners, and losers, are well, losers.

20
The Immorality of Bio-Weapons

ADAM BARKMAN AND
SABINA TOKOBERGENOVA

Season Four of *The Americans* introduces two kinds of biological weapons—Glanders and Lassa.

Glanders is a fatal horse disease that has been genetically
altered to infect humans ("Glanders"). Glanders brings only
trouble to Philip, Elizabeth, William, and Gabriel. Philip, a
KGB officer, is unable to send it to Russia because the pilot
who was supposed to deliver it was too afraid to do so ("Pastor Tim"). As a result, Philip has to give the sample of Glanders back to Gabriel. Later, Gabriel, a KGB supervisor, gets
infected with Glanders in his apartment.

When Philip and Elizabeth discover Gabriel infected on
the floor, they become infected as well. Even though William
provides everyone with vaccines, they had to remain quar-
antined in the apartment for the next thirty-six hours ("Experimental Prototype City of Tomorrow"). Gabriel suffered a
lot, while Elizabeth had a horrible reaction to the vaccine.
The suffering of both was so severe that both of them con-
templated the idea that they might not survive.

The Lassa virus is even worse than Glanders. This deadly
bio-weapon makes Glanders look like chicken pox. It causes
a hemorrhagic fever that liquefies a person's organs, causing
blood to seep through the skin. William tells us that Lassa
is a very undignified way to die because if infected, people
would dissolve inside and would squirt themselves out of

their asses in liquid form. "First it's woosh, then it's a trickle," explains William ("A Roy Rogers in Franconia").

You wouldn't wish death by Glanders or Lassa on your worst enemy. It seems that to be killed in this indiscriminate, undignified, and unnecessarily painful way could never be right. This should violate Kant's Categorical Imperative, which, in one form, says that a person should always act according to a rule that that that person would will to be a rule for *all* people. Another way to say this is that there are no exceptions to the indiscriminate and undignified method of killing that is the use of Glanders or Lassa. If one were to imagine an exception, say, in the case of killing a terrorist, it would be difficult to maintain the wrongness of Glanders and Lassa in potentially hundreds of other cases. The reason for this is simple: since the "categorical" part of Kant's Categorical Imperative is stated as a universal negative proposition, something like, "No undignified killing is just killing," any exception to this would set up a contradiction, namely, the particular affirmative proposition, "Some undignified killing is just killing." But since these can't both be true at the same time, we must choose: Is some undignified killing just? Kant didn't think so, and neither do we.

William the Mean

Being a member of Directorate S is not fun for the Soviet agent William Crandall, as he has to lead a lonely and dangerous life with no one to talk to. He works undercover in the US Army's biological defense program at Fort Derrick. His wife, Eliza, was sent back to Russia. Gabriel views William as just a tool to provide Center with samples of bioweapons. "I've gotten so many vaccines because of what I have to do. It's given me all these allergies. I've got no sense of smell. My skin has no natural lubricants. And I don't have anybody to talk to about it," confesses William ("Experimental Prototype City of Tomorrow"). Even though William had to live for twenty-five years in isolation, paranoia, and under the effect of endless vaccinations, which damaged his physical health, Gabriel and the Jenningses don't feel sympathy for him.

It's understandable that William doesn't want to lead this kind of life anymore, but sadly he's not free to quit his job as a spy or a scientist. Gabriel forces him to keep working at the US Army's biological defense program and uses him as a pawn in the Soviet game. It's clear that William has no freedom and can only serve as a Soviet tool when he admits that he doesn't remember what freedom feels like ("The Day After"). We can see that he is a compassionate man when he is concerned about Martha being sent to Russia. He asks Philip if she will be able to adapt, to which Philip replies that she'll be free. William has a pained expression on his face as he says, "Free? Can't remember what that feels like" ("The Day After"). This scene proves that Crandall is a slave to KGB and he is unhappy about it.

When William tries to oppose Gabriel and confesses to him that he doesn't want to steal the sample of Lassa virus, Gabriel persuades him to stay loyal to his country ("A Roy Rogers in Franconia"). Gabriel doesn't let William quit. He says, "You'll do this one thing"—he is not asking but commanding. Another version of Kant's Categorical Imperative states that we should treat people as ends in themselves and never merely a means to an end. Applied to our case, we can see that the KGB's use of William as a mere pawn or a means to an end is immoral.

But why is it immoral to treat a person merely as a means to an end? This has to do with reason and propriety. If all people are equal as people—if all people are equals as beings able to reason and discern the moral law qua the Categorical Imperative—then to treat someone who is so capable as if they were not is to imagine they are not human. But this is a failure of both reason and justice. Consequently, we can't ever imagine an equal not to be an equal; to start down this road is to be indiscriminate in how we treat people, and this is both irrational (since reason teaches us we are rational beings) and unjust (since we should treat equals as equals). So once again, treating people as ends in themselves is essential to morality and is an argument against bio-weapons.

Categorical Nonsense?

Of course, Gabriel and the Russian government are not Kantians. They follow a different morality, the morality of Fredrick Nietzsche (1844–1900). According to Nietzsche, people must reject pity and strive for power as a way to happiness. Thus, on Nietzsche's account, Gabriel is doing the right thing; he doesn't pity William and forces him to steal the sample of Lassa against his will.

Pity, according to Nietzsche, is nothing less than the multiplication of suffering, draining us of our strength and will to power. Nietzsche argues that power is essential for people because we can't achieve happiness without power. All that heightens the feeling of power is good; all that is born of weakness is bad. In *The Americans,* the bio-weapon is the source of power that the Russian government needs and Crandall is the tool that could provide them with this power. The fact that William is unwilling to steal the Lassa virus would be seen as a weakness in Nietzschean philosophy. If Gabriel leads a Nietzschean way of life, he could use anyone in order to achieve his will which is a direct violation of Kant's Categorical Imperative. Gabriel is making empty promises to William that he would return home a hero, find a wife and have a family. He knows how lonely William is and that all he wants is a family, so he controls him by promising that by obtaining Lassa virus his dream of the family would come true. By controlling William with the promise of future rewards to achieve his goal, Gabriel is using him as means to an end. William died in the end without getting the promised rewards ("Persona Non Grata"). In order to save the information about the KGB, William infected himself with Lassa. By sacrificing himself to prevent using others as a means to an end, William proves himself to be a good Kantian. He died all alone, in terrible suffering and with no one by his side. William's last words were heartbreaking as he confessed to the FBI agents that his job became a curse. "I wish I was like them [Philip and Elizabeth]. Had a wife. A couple of kids," William whispers as he dies ("Persona Non Grata"). A good man's life is ended for the sake of the bio-weapons because he was used purely as means to an end.

Furthermore, Gabriel might even think that William doesn't lead a bad life as his life is full of danger. A dangerous life is a good life according to Nietzsche, for only through creativity and risk can you be your true self. For Gabriel, William should accept his responsibilities as a KGB undercover agent, stop complaining about his loneliness and health problems, and risk his life to steal biological weapons. This is a very convenient philosophy for Gabriel when he forces William to steal the Lassa virus ("A Roy Rogers in Franconia"), but again, would Kant agree? Can we can do whatever we like to achieve power? And is creativity and risk necessary for the moral life? Not according to Kant. The limits of our actions are the limits of what would be right for all people, not just for some—however creative and powerful they may be. And risks in themselves aren't value, but, on the contrary, can promote needless immorality since even endangering oneself is immoral according to Kant.

Why Killing the Innocent Is Wrong

Let's not forget about the consequences the Lassa virus would bring if it were released on the general population. "Lassa is one of the deadliest pathogens on the planet. Just say it actually gets out there. And I play a part in that?" William contemplates ("A Roy Rogers in Franconia"). William is not just worried about himself, but also cares about other people and doesn't want to be responsible for so many deaths.

Neither William nor Oleg trust their government with this deadly weapon. This is the reason why Oleg tells Stan Beeman, an FBI agent, that someone from the KGB works at the US Army's biological defense program ("A Roy Rogers in Franconia"). Tatiana Ruslanova, is originally a member of the Directorate S, but by Season Four she is revealed to be secretly working with Department 12. Department 12 is the USSR's undercover "seventh floor" germ warfare department—a project so secretive and politically controversial that even the Rezident Arkady does not know who, or what, it involves. Tatiana informed Oleg that members of the KGB in Nairobi might kill half of the people on the Eastern seaboard in the next week or so because of the Lassa virus.

So, another reason why Kant would oppose bio-weapons like Glanders and Lassa is because they will inevitably kill innocent people—people who will be treated as means to an end. It is assumed that as a part of Department 12, Tatiana is in some capacity related to the supply-chain involving William's samples being studied in the USSR. But why is this bad? Well, to kill an innocent person—even painlessly—would be to treat people (the innocent people) as a means to an end (the Soviet's agenda or will to power). Killing people is only permissible in cases of just war (where soliders are killed, not innocent civilians) or capital punishment, where the person being killed is being treated as an end in themselves (the murderer's choice to murder is respected and the consequence of that choice—to be killed in return—is rendered unto him).

Kantian Prude or Kantian Prudence?

When Philip develops some doubts about the bio-weapons, Elizabeth retorts that the US is "making that poison for us, to destroy us. We have to be able to defend ourselves" ("The Day After"). The Soviets are trailing behind the Americans in bio-weaponry, and Elizabeth thinks that beating the Americans is more crucial than the inherent immorality of the weapons. Elizabeth would think that objecting to bio-weapons is prudish; a symptom of an outdated and ineffective morality. But Kant would call restraint on using bio-weapons *prudence* or practical wisdom—it is the applying of moral theory, such as the Categorical Imperative, to concrete situations. Thus, if in theory bio-weapons are likely to cause the innocent to suffer and to inflict an excessive amount of suffering (on the innocent or otherwise), then the prudent man or woman must decide if in *this* case the theory applies. In the case that the KGB proposes, to potentially use the bio-weapons in Africa, it seems that the wise or prudent person would see the theory as applicable and clear: bio-weapons should not be used.

Or again, consider the case of William and Oleg. They rightly fear that Soviet scientists would misuse the virus. When Philip asks William why he told him about the horrors of the Level 4 virus, Williams explains that he wants to make the right decision, and that is a big decision to make on your own ("The Day After"). In this scene, William wasn't sure if he should inform Centre about the Level 4 bio-weapon because he didn't want to steal it. He was using Kantian prudence—concrete moral reasoning—to decide what to do.

Prudence is skill in the choice of means to one's own greatest well-being. There is an imperative that refers to the choice of means to one's own happiness; this imperative is what Kant calls prudence. According to Kant, there are times when our desires often come into conflict with one another. William was very conflicted when he was trying to make the right choice. On the one hand, he needs to obey Centre and steal Lassa, but on the other hand, he wants innocent people to be safe from the release of the biological weapon. William realizes that his choice of whether to steal Lassa or not would impact his well-being. If he steals the virus, he thinks he might go back to Russia and achieve happiness, at the same time if he doesn't steal it, his conscience would be clear which would result in a different kind of happiness.

Lying and Means to an End

It is very hard to get your hands on deadly pathogens. Many sacrifices have to be made in the process. As a Kantian, William makes sacrifices, and as a Nietzschean, Gabriel sacrifices William. For obvious reasons, Level 4 bio-weapons are protected by a code, so in order to get the code, Elizabeth, like Gabriel, must sacrifice the innocent.

Being an undercover Soviet spy is a lonely profession, so even though Elizabeth has a family, she still needs friends. Using the name Patty, she befriends Young Hee, the wife of an American scientist. That friendship is built on lies, but Young Hee Seong is the closest thing to a real friend Elizabeth has had.

Young Hee's husband, Don, is a scientist who conducts research inside the US Army's top-level biological warfare laboratory, which means that he has access codes for the Level 4 bio-weapons. It's Elizabeth's mission to get the codes for William. As a result, Elizabeth must lie to Young Hee—must treat her as a simple means to an end—to succeed in her mission ("Dinner for Seven").

Elizabeth attempts to seduce Don, who, being a good man, refuses her advances. Desperate, Elizabeth drugs Don, strips him out of his clothes and puts him in bed. She gets in bed without her clothes on as well. When Don wakes up, Elizabeth tricks him into believing he has had sex with her. To make matters worse, she later lies to him that she is pregnant with his baby. Don is terrified and afraid to lose his family, so he asks her to have an abortion. Faking devastation and pain, Elizabeth storms out of the house, promising that she will take care of it herself. A while after, Philip, claiming to be Patty's brother, confronts Don at his office. He tells Don that Elizabeth committed suicide because of him and that he has to pay for her funeral. Overwhelmed with shame and fear, Don quickly agrees to pay for her funeral expenses. When Philip and Don go to the bank to take the money, Gabriel and Theresa (Philip's co-conspirators) stay behind and get the code from Don's computer.

The Seong family is ruined because the husband has to live with the thought that because of him their family friend died. As a result, Don becomes depressed and behaves differently, which in turn causes Young Hee to be worried and sad. To make matters worse, Young Hee doesn't have "Patty" to talk to anymore. When Elizabeth calls her answering service, she hears a tearful message from Young Hee. "I need to talk to you," Young Hee sobs. "Where did you go?" ("Dinner for Seven"). Kantian prudence would reason that Elizabeth's lies are clear instances of treating both Young Hee and Don as means to an end and so are immoral.

Disobeying an Immoral Order?

To Elizabeth's credit, she did try to avoid betraying Young Hee when she asked Gabriel to talk to Centre and find out if there was another way ("Munchkins"). Unfortunately, their government stated that there was no other way and commanded her to proceed with the mission to retrieve the code. Elizabeth could have avoided the destruction of the Seong family if she had disobeyed her superiors, which from her point of view would be disobeying her country.

Now true enough, the Categorical Imperative forbids lying, but would Kant be opposed to disobeying an immoral command? In a number of places, Kant makes it clear that the state (in Elizabeth's case, the Soviet Union) is a legitimate authority that binds people through a social contract. In this way, no citizen can rebel against their government, though citizens may be free to refuse to perform certain actions. More importantly, while in "The Doctrine of Right" Kant does state that citizens are obligated to their sovereigns, this extends to "whatever does not conflict with inner morality." Although it is not clear what Kant means by "inner morality," it probably has to do with freedom of conscience. Thus, if the will were too put-off by a certain act, it is free to refrain; or perhaps, if one would will that all persons in similar situations were to disobey the government, then this could be seen as an application of the Categorical Imperative. Whatever the case may be, Kant would make room for Elizabeth to disobey. But she didn't; and that was immoral.

Oh, and Don't Forget . . .

So far, Kant's Categorical Imperative and the prudent application of this has shown that bio-weapons are immoral not only in a direct way—causing excessive suffering and killing innocent people—but also in an indirect fashion: lying to obtain the weapons. But there is another indirect problem with bio-weapons: the inevitable environmental damage they would cause. In *The Americans*, America and Russia only seem to care about their cold war and who will ultimately emerge the winner. Both parties seem to forget the environmental harm bio-weapons can cause.

While many of the chemicals used in war break down relatively easily, bio-weapons are more of a question mark. Biological weapons are hard to detect and the spread of disease is enhanced by human and animal resistance to antibiotics. These weapons are a serious threat to agricultural ecosystems, wildlife, and their habitats. The possible effects of the biological weapons are subject to a high degree of uncertainty and unpredictability. Possible long-term effects of such warfare include chronic illness, delayed effects in people directly exposed (such as birth defects and cancer), and soil and air degradation. In the event that Glanders and Lassa were released, the environment might suffer catastrophic harm.

It's true that Kant isn't known for being super "green," but he'd certainly think it immoral to devastate the environment with bio-weapons. For one thing, harming the water, air and soil harms the small animals that are sustained by these, and these small animals, in turn, harm—when eaten—the larger animals that consume them. And since the largest animal of all in this sense is man, harming the environment harms man. Moreover, Kant thinks that while animals have no rights per se, it is wrong to harm animals in a careless fashion (as in the case of bio-weapons) since cruelty to animals promotes cruelty in the human soul. So, again—and again and again—Kantian prudence says "No" to bio-weapons.

21
I, Mail Robot

CHRISTOPHER M. COX

The title of a Season Three episode of *The Americans* asks "Do Mail Robots Dream of Electric Sheep?" The "mail robot" refers to the robotic device programmed to deliver mail within the FBI offices where Stan Beeman keeps a beat on potential spy activity. But while Stan is *keeping a beat*, the mail robot is *getting beat*. After fellow FBI agent Frank Gaad loses his cool and administers a beating to the mail robot that all but destroys the helpless device, it is sent to a shop for repairs.

When "Clark" learns from Martha the location of the repair shop, KGB agent Gabriel tasks Philip and Elizabeth with bugging the mail robot. At the repair shop, while Philip plants the bug, Elizabeth happens upon Betty, the shop's widowed bookkeeper who comes to the office at nights to work on the books. Betsy quickly realizes Elizabeth can't allow her to survive.

What ensues is a prolonged and very humane exchange. They swap stories about their personal lives, even as Elizabeth feeds Betsy the pills that will kill her. Betsy, stoic and unafraid of death, willingly takes the pills while recounting stories of her husband Gil, a machinist who opened the repair shop shortly after World War II. Betsy was a mathematician, albeit one disinclined towards computational technologies. "It wasn't calculators and robots then" she tells Elizabeth. "The world changes."

The Tech They Are A-Changin'

The world does indeed change, and with it the capabilities of our technologies undergo change, as do the complicated ways humans exist with technologies. Our lives are indeed increasingly bound up with computational calculation and robotics, capabilities and technologies that are empowered to perform an increasing number of tasks.

For some philosophers, technologies are instrumental; they are tools humans use. The mail robot simply delivers mail so that humans don't have to.

But, like humans, technological devices "perform" tasks. We might ask: "What other similarities are there between humans and technology?" Once we recognize that similarities exist, we begin to recognize that technology is not something apart from humans and the world we live in. Humans and technology mutually inhabit the world.

Through that mutual habitation we are intertwined with technology not only through physical contact and presence, but by sharing similar conditions and states of being. By asking: "Do Mail Robots Dream of Electric Sheep?", this episode hints at this dynamic, as well as the state of being that Elizabeth and the mail robot both dream about—their autonomy.

Putting the Me in Autonomy

Autonomy is the ability to make decisions about our lives free from coercion or constraint. It is tied to the concept of the "self," as in our ability to "self-determine" or "self-govern. The more I'm able to control or "self-govern" the circumstances of my life the greater my personal autonomy. And, the more autonomy I have, the more meaningful my life can become, according to the philosopher Immanuel Kant.

Kant considered autonomy to be "the basis of the dignity of human and of every rational nature." Autonomy is therefore not only the means to determine or govern the circumstances of our own life; it's the condition that can determine how much (or how little) dignity we feel.

As you probably already realize, many characters in *The Americans* face constraints that limit their personal autonomy—especially Elizabeth. Her life is meticulously orchestrated and controlled by the KGB. Whether it's her initiation into Russian espionage as a young adult or her arranged marriage to Philip or the identities she must perform in order to keep her cover, Elizabeth's life is often governed and determined by someone other than herself. Selflessly serving her Motherland may give her a degree of dignity, these constraints on exercising her autonomy also limit the amount of dignity she feels.

That's one of the reasons why the encounter between Elizabeth and Betsy is so important. Given the circumstances of this encounter, Elizabeth feels emboldened enough to dispense with a fabricated identity and come clean about her personal and professional life. She can determine, on her own, what to tell Betsy, or whether or not to tell her anything at all. What she chooses to tell is a series of truths and lies, all with the intent of easing the restrains on her personal autonomy while also easing Betsy through her final moments of life.

Responding to a series of personal questions posed by Betsy, Elizabeth confirms that she is from Russia (truth), works alongside her husband (truth), and has two children (truth). But she also chooses to disregard her atheistic beliefs when Betsy (slowing succumbing to the effects of the pills) asks "did Gil send you?" Elizabeth responds in the affirmative (lie), and when Betsy follows with the question "did he tell you I'm afraid of pain?" Elizabeth also affirms this question (lie).

Of course, she is under no external obligation to use this series of truths and lies to comfort Betsy. In other words, it's Elizabeth—and *only* Elizabeth—who gets to choose whether or not she tells only lies, only truths, or some combination of the two.

There are, however, different factors as to why she chose to first kill Betsy and then provide comfort to Betsy in the waning moments of her life. These factors tell us a great deal about how humans experience autonomy and, ultimately, how Mail-bot is also autonomous.

Understanding Autonomy Is Imperative

Elizabeth's decision to kill Betsy is a means to an end. If Betsy survives, she is likely to report the repair shop break-in to the police and thus potentially compromise the personal and professional lives of Elizabeth and Philip. This decision reflects what Kant referred to as a "hypothetical imperative."

A hypothetical imperative means that when we take action as a means to an end it's often because of something governing or controlling that action. For example, eating food achieves a very critical end—it means I will not die of starvation. My decision to eat food isn't much of a decision at all, since my human biology means that eating food is a necessary act for survival.

On the other hand, Elizabeth's decision to comfort Betsy is not necessarily a means to an end. Once Elizabeth knows Betsy is going to die, it doesn't matter for anyone other than Elizabeth whether or not Betsy feels greater ease about her inevitable death. Elizabeth makes this decision because she determines it to be the appropriate course of action, not because something other than herself necessitates that she behave this way. This decision to act based on what we determine is the appropriate way to act reflects what Kant called a "categorical imperative."

For Kant, autonomy is at the heart of the categorical imperative. Only when we're compelled to act because of what we self-determine to be the appropriate course of action (as Elizabeth does when she alternately tells truths and lies to Betsy) can we fully enact and experience a greater degree of autonomy.

You might have noticed, however, a similarity between the hypothetical imperative and our earlier discussion of technological instrumentality. They both share a common idea that something is a means to an end, whether it's using technology as a tool or performing a personal act that is necessary towards a particular objective.

We've seen that technology is much more than just an instrument. Technology is a part of us, just as our lives are intricately bound up with technology. So, if autonomy is best achieved not by instrumental actions (hypothetical imperative) but by making a determination as to the best course of action (categorical imperative), can technology also possess autonomy when it is capable of determining its actions?

The answer, is "yes." But there's more to it than that. Not only are technologies capable of autonomy; our own autonomy is often influenced by the autonomy of technologies. The more a machine experiences autonomy, the more we experience autonomy. At times, the autonomy of technology may restrict our autonomy in particular ways, while enabling our autonomy in other ways, as epitomized by an analogous relationship between Elizabeth and Mail-bot.

You've Got Mail-bot

One of the more skillful—and perhaps even unintentional—moves made by the creative writers of *The Americans* was to construct an analogous relationship between the circumstances of the mail robot and Elizabeth.

Elizabeth and Mail-bot have little (if any) direct interaction. So it might seem odd to suggest a profound relationship exists between them. But understanding their relationship is not about how they interact with one another. It's about the similar circumstances they face. These circumstances tell us a great deal about how our autonomy can be impacted by our relationship with technology.

Mail-bot is an autonomous technology, meaning that it can perform tasks and functions without being told to by a human being. It possesses autonomy because it has the means and will to do certain things related to movement and mail delivery, free from the direct control of human beings.

Mail-bot is not autonomous in all facets of its existence. As we already know, it can't repair itself. Its programmers apparently didn't think to account for Frank Gaad's scornful kicks. It also can't suddenly decide it's a coffee maker. Its autonomy is limited, but there are also limits to our human autonomy if our will to act is beyond our control. Even though we barely see Mail-bot, we learn something more profound—the way Elizabeth's personal autonomy corresponds to Mail-bot's.

On the surface, it may seem as if Elizabeth's autonomy becomes heightened at the expense of the mail robot. After all, it's in disrepair, and therefore incapable of performing its functions, autonomous or otherwise. If this machine breaks down, and then Elizabeth feels emboldened enough to dispense with personal details and provide comfort to Betsy, doesn't her renewed sense of autonomy come at the expense of the mail robot's autonomy? Not exactly.

Breaking Down the Breakdown

Mail-bot's breakdown shows us how Elizabeth has more autonomy at her disposal when the circumstances that restrict her autonomy also break down. Just as Mail-bot undertakes various technological performances, Elizabeth also undertakes various social performances. Frequently she must perform a fabricated identity in order to carry out her mission. She must also perform in accordance with Center's wishes in order to maintain her status as a professional spy and to stay alive. Even in her own home, she must perform duties as a mother and caretaker of two children, which includes performing the elaborate front that they are a typical American family.

All of these performances are a means to an end—she does them to stay alive, remain in Center's good graces, and shield her children from the dangers of geopolitical espionage. In the repair shop, alone with Betsy, Elizabeth is not restricted by the hypothetical imperative of these performances. In this moment, she no longer has to perform a falsified identity, carry out Center's edicts, or maintain parental oversight. Here, we see the analogous relationship between Elizabeth and Mail-bot—they both cease to perform.

It is through this ceasing—this breakdown—that we see the correlation between Elizabeth and Mail-bot. Both experience a breakdown. It no longer performs its technological functions. She no longer performs her professional, social, and domestic identities.

What this analogy helps us to understand is that our own ability to experience greater (or lesser) autonomy often occurs alongside the conditions and circumstances we share with technology. Our personal autonomy is not separate from technology. It's also not an either-or situation. Saying that the more autonomy possessed by a human or a machine makes the other invariably increase or decrease isn't necessarily true. Instead, the more our lives become bound with technologies, and the more we have in common with technologies, the more we are subject to newfound opportunities to exercise autonomy.

Understanding this analogy is no mere pedantic exercise. The mention of an autonomous mail robot may bring to mind other autonomous technologies we increasingly hear about in everyday life, such as autonomous cars. Even though *The Americans* is a fictionalized account of our historical past, the dynamics of Elizabeth's and Mail-bot's autonomy has direct implications for our contemporary real world, a world in which technologies increasingly possess autonomous capabilities.

A Little Buggy?

At the repair shop, while Elizabeth takes care of Betsy, Philip is busy attaching a tracking bug to the mail robot. The idea is that, once Mail-bot is functional again, Elizabeth and Philip will have a way to listen in on the activities of Stan and other FBI agents. Philip is ultimately successful. The bugged robot plays a critical role in monitoring FBI operations.

Turning Mail-bot into an asset plays another critical role. It shows us how we may experience newfound degrees of personal autonomy as technology becomes increasingly capable of autonomously carrying out its various functions. This is especially true when technologies we commonly interact with increase the number of things we can do with them.

Mail-bot's function is to deliver mail in the FBI offices. This is what it was designed to do. It has a job to do in the office just like all the human FBI personnel. But, when Philip plants the tracking bug, it undergoes a change. Now, it not only delivers mail, it facilitates the ability of Elizabeth and Philip to spy on the FBI. It retains its typical function (delivering mail), while also taking on new capabilities (audio surveillance).

Understanding the analogous relationships among human and robot autonomy gives us deeper insights into this episode and *The Americans* in general. It also helps us to think about the analogous relationship between our everyday life and technologies we interact with in the real world. In that way, it helps us understand how we can experience heightened degrees of autonomy as technology expands its capabilities. The potential for our interaction with autonomous cars perfectly illustrates this point.

Get out of My Dreams, Get into My Autonomous Car

For the better part of a century cars have served an instrumental function—they enable us to get where we need to go. But our cars can be more than just a means to an end. Some people enjoy the act of driving itself, of being on the open road with no particular destination in mind. Others enjoy modifying and tinkering with their cars. The way we interact with a car—when cruising, tinkering, or modifying— reflects the autonomous choices we make, whether its choosing to take it slow and easy in the right lane, customizing a paint design for a car, or adding chrome rims to the wheels.

Autonomous cars may seem to restrict our personal autonomy. After all, it may be argued, they are self-driving machines. If they do the driving for us, doesn't that diminish our autonomy? That's certainly a possibility. If you enjoy the act of driving because of what it offers beyond its instrumental use, it's very likely you'll feel less autonomy if the future of driving is the sole province of autonomous vehicles. But, the self-driving aspect of autonomous cars mean that, much like Mail-bot after it has been bugged, a long-standing technology takes on new capabilities. These capabilities are not only the technological performances of an autonomous car; it's what humans are capable of doing with cars when we no longer have to be their manual operators.

Mail-bot opens up new possibilities for how Elizabeth and Philip monitor the FBI. What does an autonomous car do for our personal autonomy here in the real world? There are many possibilities. Consider one of the more detrimental aspects of what some people do in their cars—texting and driving. Sending and receiving text messages while driving is a common form of "distracted driving," activities that distract from the primary task of navigating a vehicle.

Distracted driving has been linked to injuries and even fatalities. In a world of self-driving autonomous cars, texting while in a car poses less of an immediate risk to our bodily health. Once driving is something we are no longer distracted from, that opens up our ability to more freely text, and also opens up a lot of possibilities for what we choose to do in a car. If we no longer have to remain vigilant to the car's navigation, we are free not only to send and receive texts, but to do any number of things that can enhance our personal autonomy.

Being in a self-driving car means I can get things done if I'm stuck in traffic. I can re-watch episodes of *The Americans*, discuss these episodes with fellow fans on *The Americans* reddit board, and text with my friends about lingering plot threads. Or, if I'm en route to my job, I can choose to get a head start on my work or even join in conference calls, all with considerably less consequences since I no longer have to be vigilant of driving. Even if we think the self-driving aspect of an autonomous car lessens the autonomy we might experience as drivers, it also becomes clear we have the autonomy to do things previously off-limits in a car, whether it's beefing up on our knowledge of *The Americans* or getting a step ahead in our professional careers, not unlike the way Elizabeth and Philip stay one step ahead by planting the bug on the mail robot.

Dream On

Answering the question posed by "Do Mail Robots Dream Of Electric Sheep?" isn't yet possible. Our technologies can't yet literally tell us about the electric animals that populate their dreams. But, as this episode shows us, what a robot might dream about isn't really the point—the point is the suggestion that a mail robot has the ability to dream. To dream, if not as humans do, then in a way that illuminates that humans and machines are both dreaming entities and share many other similar states of being.

As we see through our understanding of Elizabeth's personal autonomy and the autonomous capabilities of the mail robot in this episode of *The Americans*, as technologies become more autonomous, we share a similar condition—we're also bound to experience newfound forms of autonomy.

22
Membership Has Its Privileges

Louis Melançon

Spy work keeps the Jenningses busy; Center keeps up a constant stream of requests and requirements for them to fulfill. This means that Philip and Elizabeth must always be recruiting new people who can get them needed information, continuing to work with those they have recruited, and occasionally crushing people under cars. That'll keep your daily calendar quite full.

What's worse, the demands of Center never slow down until a crisis point is reached, like Elizabeth getting shot ("The Colonel") or Martha almost getting arrested ("The Rat"). Had things gone just slightly differently, the Jenningses wouldn't be able to provide for Center at all because they'd be busy answering Stan's interrogation questions from a jail cell or just out and out dead. It really seems like a soul-crushing existence, doesn't it? It also raises an interesting question: why does Center run the Jenningses ragged and just to the point of failure?

The short answer, of which Karl Marx would be proud, deals with economics. Specifically a subset of economic thought, goods theory, which predicts how rational actors will behave based on the good in question. This means we need to understand the nature of intelligence as a good. For Philip and Elizabeth, as well as most literature on intelligence, it's assumed that we are talking about what's known as a public good. But when we look at Center, they seem to think this is a club good. Don't worry, we'll define these two shortly so we can see the differences. But as a clever reader, you've probably already figured out that if different understandings of the thing in question are in play, we're likely to see some disjointed interactions and tensions. Let's lessen the tensions here and work through some of these definitions so at least we have a common understanding, even if the Jenningses and Center don't.

What Is Intelligence?

The Jenningses are in the business of intelligence, they are spies. But what do we mean by this word intelligence? Most definitions center around a thing known as the intelligence cycle: information is collected, processed, analyzed, disseminated, feedback received and new requirements generated for the cycle to start again. This is the definition you'll find in Mark Lowenthal's intelligence studies primer as well as what the US Department of Defense uses. Information that passes through this cycle becomes intelligence. It's a very functional definition, but is it useful? It would be tremendously useful in storyboarding out an episode: Philip gets some information, the Rezidentura analyzes and passes it to Center for distribution to appropriate Soviet organizations. Then Center sends down new instructions. I'll take that executive producer credit, please. It really describes what is done by persons or organizations conducting intelligence work, but it doesn't tell us what intelligence really *is*.

If we go digging a bit into US history with intelligence, the 1955 Clark Task Force toyed with, but ultimately didn't use, a radically different definition. Paraphrasing a bit, intelligence is something you should know before taking an action. This definition is a bit fuzzier but more flexible, and so is more useful to us. It also hints that we should take a look into game theory. Don't worry, it won't be too painful, at least it's less painful than Philip having to sit through an *est* session with a full bladder.

Picture two of our characters, let's say Aderholt and Gaad, interacting over a point—whether Aderholt will pull a stakeout on Saturday over something not related to Soviet espionage. The interaction can resolve in one of two ways. Aderholt likes the resolution of not doing the stakeout so he can concentrate on drinking and thinking about Martha, while Gaad likes the resolution of Adherholt on the stakeout. Nothing too mind-blowing there. Each knows their own preferred resolution, and if they had perfect information, they'd also know the preferred resolution of the other agent as well. But it's rare that agents, whether we're talking about states or people, have full, perfect information. We live in a world of imperfect information. In an imperfect-information world, you can have private information. Maybe that private information is what your preferred goal is; or if interactions are iterative, where in that series of interactions you are in relation to goals. Or, and here's where things get really interesting, you can know the private information of the other party and the fact that you have their private information is your private information. There's a pretty common term for all these types of private information: secrets. Who finds out these secrets for you? Spies.

Secrets can be very powerful in these games between two players. You want to keep yours hidden while revealing the other player's. It's even better when you can reveal their secrets without them being aware that you did so, clandestine revelation. When you can do this, you've brought your level of information a bit closer to perfect compared with the other agent. As the Clark Task Force would say, you now know everything, or at least a bit more of what you need, to make a decision. With this information advantage you should be able to resolve the game closer to your preferred solution.

This is where Elizabeth, Philip, and even Stan come into play. Elizabeth and Philip are trying to get those secrets on behalf of the USSR so that the Kremlin can reach its preferred resolutions when dealing with the US. Stan tries to keep those secrets hidden by catching anyone seeking to reveal them. This is why Center sends Soviet agents to live and operate undercover in America for decades, and why they crack down harshly when Nina betrays them by revealing Soviet secrets ("Chloramphenicol"). This is why, since the dawn of civilization, governments have sought out the secrets of others and desperately try to keep their own secrets hidden away: it provides decisive advantage in interactions with another nation in whatever "game" they happen to be playing. Is this really any different from other functions of a government?

Not Exactly Like Defense

Okay, we need to talk about goods theory. In economics, there are different categories of goods based on whether the item in question is exclusive or non-exclusive (Can anyone access and benefit from it, in theory?) and rivalrous or non-rivalrous (Does it get used up after access?). With two states for two variables, we get four possible categories. The obvious first one is non-exclusive and non-rivalrous, the pure public good. Stan's undercover work against white supremacists in Arkansas is a good example: bringing justice to those who are trying to do harm to the society. The average US citizen might not be affected by the white supremacists being off the street but the society as a whole sees benefit. If it's non-exclusive, but rivalrous, think of the coal that Elizabeth's father mined, this is known as a common-pool good. Anyone can access it, but it gets used up. We're not really interested in this one now, so let's move on. If it's excludable and rivalrous, it's a private good; like Philip's Camaro. Only Philip owns that particular vehicle and no one else can purchase it unless he sells it to them. If it's excludable and non-rivalrous, it's a club good. The traditional example is the toll road; you only get to use it when you pay, but using it doesn't mean others can't.

So governments generally create public goods by providing services to their citizens. The services may not be effective or desired, but they are still a public good. As an example, defense is a service provided to all citizens. You could opt out of military service, but you can't opt out of being defended by the nation's military. You can't say, "Oh, no thank you. Let the Canadians invade my house." To mix pop culture references, it's a Bedford Falls Savings and Loan, only with things that go boom. So is intelligence a public good? In the intelligence literature it's generally considered that. The logical leap is not that great: it's a government service and there's an inseparable linkage between intelligence and the other pillars of national security, defense and diplomacy. But there's something else in play here.

Here's what I'm proposing: intelligence isn't a public good as is commonly thought, it's a club good. Let's compare with defense, a public good. The general public consumes this good, whether they like war or not. But who is the customer for intelligence? Based on the definition from earlier, it's the decision maker. Yes, the public will benefit from the decision maker making a hopefully good decision but that public benefit is a secondary effect. Okay, but does that really make it excludable? Yes, it does. Not everyone gets exposed to the good; by definition, only some people will have access to the secrets so that it can remain private information. Intelligence only has value when it aids in the decision making process, if it was a public good the general public should be able to use it within their own decision making. But they don't, they only benefit from intelligence as a second- and third-order effect. The general public doesn't get to see the intelligence unless a leak occurs. The leak makes the private information public. The enemy now knows that you know what he knows. Any advantage is lost.

Now we need to talk about a special feature of club goods, congestion. When too many people take that toll road that we mentioned earlier, the traffic builds and you can't go any faster than if you were on a public road. What's the point of paying tolls? That's congestion. For intelligence, that would mean a leak or a penetration by a hostile intelligence service. Either way the information is no longer private information. Remember the value of intelligence is granting decision advantage. If a decision maker decides to pay to get access to this club that is intelligence, they want that information for their decision advantage. If fellow club members have the same basic goal as you, having access to that information doesn't really congest the system. But when a club member doesn't have the same goal, or perhaps the opposite goal, then that information loses its value.

Let's make this concrete by looking at the Jenningses. The KGB orders the Jenningses to acquire some information so Soviet agencies can use that information for their purposes. No problem, right? Well, until Stan recruits Nina to get insight into what is occurring within the Rezidentura: What information is the KGB looking for? What information do they have? Who is giving that information to them? Suddenly that information the Jenningses acquired has lost its value because the FBI knows what the Soviets know. The FBI became a member of the club with the opposite goals of the traditional club members! Of course, this new member is free riding, they aren't paying the costs of the club, just enjoying the benefits. For right now, the interaction game has moved closer to a perfect information situation for that most recent member and they get the added bonus of not having to pay. Sweet deal for the FBI!

The Tension

Knowing that intelligence is a club good explains why agents act in seemingly crazy ways, the behavior suddenly makes a lot more sense. With a public good, like defense, a country "buys" military forces that it thinks it needs, or at least what it can afford. This doesn't guarantee that their defense is effective or can actually keep the country safe when challenged, but by buying the tools (fighter jets, soldiers, bombs) the good is out there being non-exclusive and non-rivalrous.

The same can't be said of a club good. While they start out as non-rivalrous, as they approach the congestion point, the value of the good diminishes. This leads to two distinct behaviors. The first is that a club member will seek to maximize what they get out of their investment in the club just shy of that congestion point. The second is that club members won't seek to continually expand investment in the good because of the possibility of congestion; loss of the investment is always hovering over the club member's head which would provide no incentive for "doubling down."

Some of our Soviet characters demonstrate behaviors that we would associate with a public good, while others seem to act like they're dealing with a club good. The Jenningses think they provide a public good to the whole world. But, to Center, intelligence is a club with the Jenningses simply providing that club good. This creates a disconnect between the Jenningses and Center and that can lead to problems.

The illegals program is pretty limited. Beyond the Jenningses, there is Robert in Boston ("Pilot") and the Connerses ("Comrades"). But Center is careful about how much it invests in Directorate S. If intelligence were a public good, Center would flood the US with Philips and Elizabeths. Instead, they just task the Jenningses one more time, squeeze just a bit more out of that investment. This even extends to the possibility of expansion: don't pay more for more couples, use organic expansion. It's cost-saving! Organic expansion in this case meaning to recruit the children produced as part of cover stories. That's a pretty ingenious way to keep club membership costs low. Why pay for all the things you'd need in hiring from the outside when the employees are just making new employees for you? Sounds good in theory, but then again sometimes you wind up with a hotel room full of bodies and a lot of loose ends to clean up. Yikes.

The Jenningses don't see themselves this way. Elizabeth has a calling. Her sense of purpose motivated her to leave her mother behind and take on this life of an undercover spy. Heck, it's why she's willing to report to Center on her concerns about Philip enjoying the American lifestyle ("Trust Me"). Their marriage is purely a matter of appearance, but surely it's not too much to expect loyalty to her partner? Philip thought so, but for Elizabeth who sees her job as part of a public good, that's too much to ask. Tension between providing the public good and loyalty to the partner gets resolved in favor of the USSR and the public good she believes she's generating.

Of course it's not just Elizabeth. Both Philip and Elizabeth are shattered when they find out that the information they stole about the submarine propulsion system was faulty ("New Car"). For the USSR, this is a great use of club membership. They get to benefit from the research investment without having to pay for it, another great example of free riding. They can then use this club investment to improve a public good: improving their submarines. It turns out that the information was flawed, and the prototype sub sank with the loss of all hands. It really doesn't matter if the information was flawed on purpose by sneaky Americans or if Philip and Elizabeth simply got the previous version of the data from a prototype that hadn't been tested. For Center, there was no true loss to the public good; the rest of Soviet submarine fleet was still there, they just didn't get a full free ride from the club. And yet, Philip and Elizabeth feel they failed the USSR and made it less safe by providing that intelligence. They see their work as a public good, increasing the defense of the country by stealing information and secrets.

And so we have the Jenningses seeing their work as a public good and Center seeing it as a club good. With two different definitions, a tension arises and that can be a problem. The problem really manifests itself in how much the Jenningses get tasked. Because Center sees this as a club good they wish to maximize their investment and get as much as they can before congestion takes over. Because the Jenningses think they're providing a public good, they won't be able to see that congestion could even occur and will stumble backwards into it resulting in the complete loss of the good for all parties. In the world of spies, this issue of congestion becomes very real, very quickly.

For every new asset that the Jenningses have to take on, for every nefarious activity that Center has them undertake, the Jenningses expose themselves to the risk of being caught by Stan and the FBI. That's true congestion for this club good. This risk is cumulative, not only from just an increased operational tempo but from the fact that mistakes are more likely to occur. As risk and mistakes, like taking off your disguise so that Martha sees your real face, start to pile up then the chance that you'll hit the congestion point begins to rise ("I Am Abassin Zadran"). But the Jenningses, seeing this as a public good, won't be able to see the congestion occurring and perhaps advise Center that it could preserve the investment for longer if immediate demands were reduced. There's no guarantee that Center would listen, but such advice would be cause for determining what course of action truly maximized the investment: short or long term returns.

This is the biggest problem if one party doesn't truly understand the nature of the good in question, especially in the case of a club good: misidentifying the good jeopardizes the ultimate delivery of the good. Center will attempt to squeeze the club for its investment just shy of the point of congestion. But the Jenningses will not recognize that congestion point until it's too late: if the timing with Martha had been off by just a hair, it would have all been over for the Jenningses and for Center's intelligence flow. Perhaps if the Jenningses recognized intelligence as a club good they would approach their operations slightly differently—not taking so many risks, not taking so many operations, making sure they can continually provide the good. But then that wouldn't make for quite such exciting television.

Intelligence is a club good, and the behaviors of Center and the FBI, show they understand that. The Jenningses don't and so they are run ragged by Center. There's an irony here. The Communists back home in Moscow best understood the value of investments in other-than-public goods and economic incentives while their agents living in the land of capitalism haven't really grasped that.

23
The War to Save Humanity

JAMES LAWLER

The viewer cannot help but situate *The Americans* in the larger perspective of history, a history that is continuing in the viewer's present. This is, first of all, the history of the relation between the United States and the Soviet Union during the early 1980s. But more deeply considered, this is the history of humanity and its survival under the threat of global nuclear catastrophe.

The Americans rejects any simplistic viewpoint on the Reagan and Brezhnev era in which its story takes place. In the episode "March 8, 1983" we see on the TV President Reagan's denunciation of the Soviet Union as "the force of evil in the modern world," while the teenager Paige in her bedroom tearfully reveals the secret identity of her parents to Pastor Tim over the phone: "They're Russians." But we the viewers have become sympathetic to the two perpetrators of this alleged evil, Paige's parents. Partly because of what they're doing, partly because of the courage and intelligence of their actions, and partly because of the kind of people they are, we see that they are essentially good people with deep moral values.

So there is a complexity of viewpoints: that of the viewer who knows the historical outcome, and that of the principal players in the story, Paige's parents Elizabeth and Philip, who don't know this outcome. Their perspective on the drama, their point of view, is that what they are doing is not in itself good, from a moral point of view, but necessary, from the larger perspective of history. Their tragedy is that they must cross a line that they normally would abhor. Killing an innocent person—that is something that good people would not willingly do. At the same time they see their actions as necessary for the survival of their motherland, and, above all, necessary for the survival of humanity. They must perform what they consider to be evil deeds. They must reject their ordinary morality in view of a higher moral standpoint, the standpoint of history in which the very existence of a human world is at stake.

The viewer however knows that their particular conception of how mankind will be saved is doomed to failure. We know that their Soviet Union, the country for which they are sacrificing their lives, will fail. But they don't see that; they can't see that. This is the tragedy that weighs on *The Americans*, like that of Oedipus who doesn't know that the man he kills at a crossroads is his father.

Doing Their Duty

Is it ever right, can it ever be even a moral duty, to kill an innocent person? This is a question acutely posed by *The Americans*, whose main characters, Elizabeth and Philip Jennings, believe that the fate of the world hangs on such killing. They are spies for the Soviet Union implanted in the United States during the Regan era of the 1980s. They're indistinguishable from their neighbors by accent, behavior, and work. They have been carefully groomed to provide crucial information to their home country in its Cold War with the United States.

From their point of view, Philip and Elizabeth are acting from moral motives even when they kill innocent people. For Kantian morality, which focuses on the inner sphere of consciousness, it is clear that what they are doing falls under the heading of a moral duty. It is not a matter of inclination or desire or self-interest. They don't *want* to kill an innocent person. It's not in their personal interest to do so. Meanwhile they have to live with themselves and their children as they perform actions that they personally find repulsive.

For example: Philip, in his persona as Clark, has a sexual relationship, and then a pseudo-marital one, with Martha, a lonely and emotionally vulnerable secretary in the FBI office. Led on by Clark, who first supplies a plausible, patriotic rationale—he claims to be working for a higher US government agency that oversees the FBI—she plants a microphone in the Bureau's office to provide crucial information regarding the actions of the intelligence organization. It's important for Philip to know, for example, whether a possible contact is being staged to entrap them. Has their identity been revealed? What are the secret plans of the American government toward their own? We see that valuable information is obtained through such means, such as the scientific impracticality of the "Star Wars" proposal to create a nuclear shield in space. In "The Colonel" a US army colonel supplies this crucial information from humanitarian motives, to prevent the extension of the arms race into space.

But the mic has been discovered, and so a search begins to find the mole in the office who planted it. Martha is vaguely suspected, and informally put under surveillance. So Philip must find an alternative perpetrator to deflect attention from Martha. He chooses a technician who has access to the office, kills him efficiently and painlessly, and forges a suicide note in which the spying is confessed ("March 8, 1983"). The problem is solved, at least temporarily.

Philip is torn up by his action. He notes childish toys in his victim's apartment, innocent games his victim has been playing. But he proceeds with the killing because he believes in its necessity during a time of Cold War between the two superpowers whose weapons are capable of producing a nuclear winter and the near-annihilation of the human race. It is therefore for him a matter of moral duty to kill this hapless, essentially innocent human being.

249

Justifying Murder?

But is this really a morally justifiable action? A utilitarian might say yes, since far more lives would potentially be saved at the expense of only one death. But such numerical calculation implies that individuals are expendable. If however we believe in the intrinsic dignity of the human being, we should turn to Kant's ethics which rejects such moral mathematics. Certain aspects of Kant's ethics are well-known— his Categorical Imperative in its various formulations: always act on maxims or rules that you can will as a universal law, respect the humanity both in oneself and in others, and put the dignity of the human being above all other values, economic as well as aesthetic or cultural. But how could the killing of innocent people be stated as a law, and, moreover, a law in which the humanity of the individual is respected?

There are applications of the Categorical Imperative that would allow certain kinds of killing. The same God who commanded, "Thou shalt not kill," urged war and killing—but based on justice, on self-defense, as when David kills the unjust aggressor, Goliath. Thus the moral law against killing does not say, Never kill a human being, but Never kill except in self-defense, Never kill except when humanity itself is at stake and is violated by the perpetrator. A human being is not a predatory animal living at the expense of others, but a being who respects a higher standard of human values.

Kant did not consider capital punishment—the killing of criminals by the state—to violate the Categorical Imperative. It is possible to respect the humanity of the individual while killing him. Morality is about respecting the humanity in the individual, not the individual as an individual. "A human being is indeed unholy enough," Kant writes, "but the *humanity* in his person must be holy to him."

But killing a criminal or an unjust aggressor is one thing; killing an innocent person is another. The person whom Philip kills is not consciously threatening anyone. He is, to be sure, a participant in the Cold War. But Philip is far from considering Americans as expendable on account of their country's policies. He kills an innocent human being who deserves to live as much as anyone does and never tries to diminish his victim's humanity.

Kant considers problematic situations in which it might seem *necessary* to kill an innocent person. He does not think highly of the argument that "it was necessary." Under the heading of an alleged "law of necessity," Kant considers the case of "a man who, when shipwrecked and struggling in extreme danger for his life, and in order to save it, may thrust another from a plank on which he has saved himself." The death penalty should not be imposed in such an instance, he comments, because such a law would hardly deter anyone else in a similar situation. This is hardly a ringing endorsement of such an alleged "law."

What Kant considers here are necessities of personal survival, not the sort of impersonal sacrifice that is required of Philip, who must throw an individual overboard to save the human race itself. Philip himself gains nothing by this action. He sacrifices his own personal moral code itself, because for him there is a higher code in which the very holiness of humanity itself is at stake.

The Immorality of Secrecy

Another aspect of the moral tragedy afflicting these "Americans" is the fact that they must keep their activities and their rationale secret. Secrecy essentially contradicts the nature of moral consciousness, which consists in maxims that can be proclaimed publicly.

Moral hypocrites say one thing, generally proclaiming a moral perspective, while secretly intending something that cannot be openly affirmed because of the immoral nature of their purposes. But our heroes are not hypocrites. They would like to proclaim their goals and moral reasons—which eventually they are able to do with their daughter Paige, once she understands who her parents really are. They are trying to "make the world a safer place for everyone," Elizabeth tells Paige in "Glanders"—just as Paige's Christian church proclaims. But in general, they cannot be open about their beliefs, and suffer from this secrecy.

The Higher Purpose of History

To understand the morality of *The Americans* we have to turn from Kant's examination of the morality of individual actions to his moral approach to human history, which is detailed in his historical essays. The foundation of this approach to history is laid out in his third Critique, the *Critique of Judgment*, which justifies seeing the history of humanity as having an over-all moral purpose or teleology.

On such teleological grounds, Kant defends the French Revolution as a progressive movement of history in which the higher goals of humanity are being realized, despite the violence, the terror, and the wars that are collaterally mixed in with this realization. The French King, followed not only by enemies of the revolution but by friends who had fallen out of political favor, lost their heads to the guillotine.

But there is an important caveat in Kant's endorsement of this event in which much blood is shed in the cause of human progress. The fact that immoral deeds lead to a morally praiseworthy result is not a reason for acting immorally. The teleological approach is a justification after the fact, not an excuse for killing *as a means* for promoting the higher goals of humanity. Marx might have had Kant's position in mind in his eleventh "Thesis on Feuerbach" (words inscribed on his tombstone): "The philosophers have only *interpreted* the world, in various ways. The point, however, is to *change* it." Philip's Communist Soviet Union no doubt instilled this Marxist thesis in its cadre to justify the sacrifices and costs, including the collateral damage of innocent lives, of changing history for the better.

In "Idea for a Universal History from a Cosmopolitan Point of View," published in 1784, Kant wrote of the "hope finally that after many reformative revolutions, a universal cosmopolitan condition, which Nature has as her ultimate purpose, will come into being as the womb wherein all the original capacities of the human race can develop." But if this perspective seems to justify revolutionary actions for the sake of human progress, Kant made it clear, writing after the French Revolution of 1789, that "there is no right of sedition, and still less of rebellion, belonging to the people. And least of all, when the supreme power is embodied in an individual monarch, is there any justification, under the pretext of his abuse of power, for seizing his person or taking away his life."

This rejection of revolutionary violence is a double-edged sword, applying both to the revolutionary overthrow of governments, and to the overthrow of the revolutionary government itself. The success of the revolution, however morally unjustified in the violent overthrow of the previous government, "binds the subjects to accept the new order of things as good citizens . . ." Hence the main thrust of Kant's critique of revolution, looked at in historical context, is directed at the French counter-revolution, the reactionary movement which at the time of his writing aimed to forcibly restore the old monarchy.

Kant paradoxically expresses his deep sympathy for the French Revolution, despite what he regards are its crimes. The spectator of the events of history can see the progress that is working its way through sometimes grisly events. That too can be our point of view, the spectators of *The Americans* who can now breathe a sigh of relief at the outcome of the conflict of the two superpowers. Humanity has survived thanks to actions such as those of Philip and Elizabeth Jennings. We can join with them in the achievement of the higher cause for which they acted, while distancing ourselves from the actions they considered to be necessary.

The Coming International Moral Order

When Kant writes of the coming cosmopolitan order he is prophesying a time when nations come together in a common agreement founded on mutual respect. This will be a time when nations can finally proclaim their goals openly to one another, and must no longer secretly hide their intentions from one another behind moral platitudes—the characteristic situation of international relations still in our own time. Looking at this international scene then as it is now, we can agree with Kant that "civilized peoples stand vis-à-vis one another in the relation of raw nature," acting on principles that "no philosopher has yet been able to bring into agreement with morality."

The deeper goal of Philip and Elizabeth, which they cannot openly express, is the creation of a political world order in which nations can be forthright about their goals. Like Kant they look forward to a time in which an authentic moral consciousness actually characterizes the international order. But our time is still one in which the citizens of all countries, represented by governments that must hide their real intentions behind moral platitudes, are effectively in the position of Philip and Elizabeth.

Morality and Hope for the Future

There is a fundamental flaw, and even a contradiction, in morality itself. Kant calls this "the Antinomy of Practical Reason." The ultimate moral goal, the implicit end of every moral action, is the creation of a just world—a world in which good people are rewarded and happy, while evil is punished.

The world in which we actually exist is hardly such a just world. The selfish, the egotists, all too frequently rise to the top, and tend to occupy the highest places. Meanwhile, honest working people barely scrape together a living, and sink to the bottom. But if a just society is impossible, Kant argues, then morality itself, which issues in this ultimate moral goal, must be regarded as an illusion.

To counteract this contradiction between morality and the actual world that we see around us, the moral person must *believe* that the just world is in fact being realized. Morality rests on belief, not knowledge. The moral individual must believe in the freedom of action that makes morality possible, but also in the power to realize its ultimate goals. This power is traditionally called God.

Traditional religion holds that God ultimately realizes the moral demand for justice in the next life, after death. The cost of admission into the just world after death is persistence in morality in this life, despite the injustices, despite all the unjust suffering. Hence, Rousseau wrote that if there were no other proof for the immortality of the soul, the fact of injustice in our present world would require it, for otherwise human life would be senseless. Thus, as a partial solution to the Antinomy of Practical Reason, Kant argues that the moral person needs to believe in, or "postulate," freedom, God, and immortality.

But such beliefs must be somehow grounded in reality to be truly plausible. Kant's first Critique, the *Critique of Pure Reason*, demonstrates the possibility of the postulate of free will by showing that the determinism of the causal laws of science is an assumption or presupposition, an *a priori* framework of the scientific mind, rather than a demonstrated truth about reality. Free will is then the operative assumption of morality, whose features are defended in the *Critique of Practical Reason*. The third Critique, the *Critique of Judgment*, opens up a teleological perspective on nature and history that complements the mechanistic, deterministic perspective of science. Whereas science looks for the determining causes of actions, the teleological perspective looks for goals implicit in nature and human history, the purposes that are being realized if only unconsciously.

Philosophy then has three spheres, corresponding to three questions. The first sphere responds to the question, *What can I know?* The second sphere responds to the question, *What ought I to do?* The third question of philosophy is, *What may I hope?* This question is addressed in the *Critique of Judgement*, which lays the grounds for looking at the purposes of nature and human history in such a way as to provide a ground for hope—hope in the creation of a just world, not in the next life, but in *this* one.

Equipped with the teleological perspective of the third Critique, we can look at the movement of history and see that it is indeed progressing, moving in the direction of a just world. We can see the "reformative revolutions" that have succeeded one another bringing us closer to that better world to which our moral actions aspire, culminating in Kant's time in the American and French revolutions, replacing monarchies with republics. But if the most advanced countries have taken this step, the world as a whole is still divided, nation warring against nation, whether in hot wars or cold ones. The "Idea" of a cosmopolitan order, a republican world condition, inevitably arises, along with the *hope* that it will one day be realized.

Philip and Elizabeth clearly realize the limits of the moral point of view pointed out by Kant himself. Paige's church epitomizes this limitation. Good Christians do what they can within the framework of the existing world order which they recognize nevertheless to be unjust. Learning of the work of Paige's parents, Pastor Tim is reassured in "Clark's Place" by the alleged Jesuit priest from El Salvador, who tells him that thanks to the work of Philip and Elizabeth his own life was saved from death squads doing the dirty work of the dictatorship that is supported by the American government.

Philip and Elizabeth recognize that the world order itself must be changed if real progress, and not just cosmetic amelioration, is going to be achieved. They see themselves as working for this real change. We the spectators of their work know that they have tragically pinned their hopes on a system of government whose failure their leaders themselves will shortly acknowledge with the economic and political reforms initiated by Gorbachev. But however misdirected is the agency in which they place their hope, we the spectators can still share with them that hope itself.

Bibliography

Adorno, Theodor. *Minima Moralia: Reflections from Damaged Life*. Verso.

———. 2016. *Minima Moralia*. Tenth edition. Suhrkamp.

Anscombe, G.E.M. 1963. *Intention*. Blackwell.

Archard, David. 1993. *Children: Rights and Childhood*. Routledge.

Bach, Kent. 1981. An Analysis of Self-Deception. *Philosophy and Phenomenological Research* 41:3.

Bartley, William Warren, III. 1978. *Werner Erhard: The Transformation of a Man, the Founding of est*. Potter.

Bellah, Robert N. 1967. Civil Religion in America. *Daedalus* 96:1.

Benatar, David. 2006. *Better Never to Have Been: The Harm of Coming into Existence*. Oxford University Press.

Benatar, David, and David Wasserman. 2015. *Debating Procreation: Is It Wrong to Reproduce?* Oxford University Press.

Bok, Sissela. 1989. *Secrets: On the Ethics of Concealment and Revelation*. Vintage.

———. Bok, Sissela. 1999. *Lying: Moral Choice in Public and Private Life*. Vintage.

Bykvist, Krsiter. 2015. Review of L.A. Paul's *Transformative Experience*. *Notre Dame Philosophical Reviews*.

Butler, Judith. 1993. *Bodies that Matter: On the Discursive Limits of "Sex."* Routledge.

Cavanaugh, William T. 2002. *Theopolitical Imagination: Christian Practices of Space and Time*. Clark.

———. 2009. *The Myth of Religious Violence: Secular Ideology and the Roots of Modern Conflict*. Oxford University Press.

———. 2011. *Migrations of the Holy: God, State, and the Political Meaning of the Church*. Eerdmans.

Chang, Ha-Joon. 2012 [2010]. *23 Things They Don't Tell You about Capitalism*. Bloomsbury.

Clark, M. 1955. *Intelligence Activities: Commission on Organization of the Executive Branch of the Government [the Hoover Commission]*. Tech. Rep.

Cole, August. 2014. *Just War and the Ethics of Espionage*. Routledge.

Critchley, Simon. 2012. *Infinitely Demanding: Ethics of Commitment, Politics of Resistance*. Verso.

———. 2014. *The Faith of the Faithless: Experiments in Political Theology*. Verso.

Critchley, Simon, and Peter Catapano, eds. 2016. *The Stone Reader*. Liveright.

Critchley, Simon, and Jamieson Webster. 2016. The Gospel According to Me. In Critchley and Catapano 2016.

Dawson, Lorne L. 1996. Who Joins New Religious Movements and Why: Twenty Years of Research and What Have We Learned? *Studies in Religion / Sciences Religieuses* 25:2.

De Beauvoir, Simone. 2015. *The Ethics of Ambiguity*. Philosophical Library.

DeBrabander, Firmin. 2016. Deluded Individualism. In Critchley and Catapano 2016.

Dewey, John. 1922. *Human Nature and Conduct*. In *John Dewey Middle Works*, Volume 14.

Felix, Christopher [James McCargar]. 2001 [1963]. *A Short Course in the Secret War*. Rowman and Littlefield.

Friedman, Milton. 1968. *Capitalism and Freedom: A Leading Economist's View of the Proper Role of Competitive Capitalism*. University of Chicago Press.

Friedman, Milton, and Rose D. Friedman. 1980. *Free to Choose: A Personal Statement*. Houghton Mifflin.

Fuller, Mathew. 2007. *Media Ecologies: Materialist Energies in Art and Technoculture*. MIT Press.

Galliott, Jai, and Warren Reed, eds. 2016. *Ethics and the Future of Spying: Technology, National Security, and Intelligence Collection*. Routledge.

Hayek F.A. 1994 [1944]. *The Road to Serfdom: Fiftieth Anniversary Edition*. University of Chicago Press.

Heidegger, Martin. 2013. *The Question Concerning Technology and Other Essays*. Harper.

Hobbes, Thomas. 1994. *Leviathan: With Selected Variants from the Latin Edition of 1668*. Hackett.

Jagger, Gill. 2008. *Judith Butler: Sexual Politics, Social Change, and the Power of the Performative*. Routledge.

Jeremiah, Emily. 2006. Motherhood to Mothering and Beyond: Maternity in Recent Feminist Thought. *Journal of the Association for Research on Mothering* 8:1–2.

Johnson, Loch K. 2004. Congressional Supervision of America's Secret Agencies: The Experience and Legacy of the Church Committee. *Public Administration Review* 64:1.

———. 2005. A Framework for Strengthening US Intelligence. *Yale Journal of International Affairs*.

Kavka, Gregory S. 1982, The Paradox of Future Individuals. *Philosophy and Public Affairs* 11:2.

Kant, Immanuel. 1963 [1784]. *Idea for a Universal History from a Cosmopolitan Point of View*. In Lewis White Beck, ed., *Kant On History*. Bobbs-Merrill.

———. 1991. *The Metaphysics of Morals*. Cambridge University Press.

———. 1993. On a Supposed Right to Lie because of Philanthropic Concerns. In James W. Ellington, ed., *Grounding for the Metaphysics of Morals*. Hackett.

———. 1996. *Practical Philosophy: The Cambridge Edition of the Works of Immanuel Kant in Translation*. Cambridge University Press.

———. 1996. *Religion within the Boundaries of Mere Reason*. In Allen W. Wood and George di Giovanni, eds., *Religion and Rational Theology*. Cambridge University Press.

———. 1997. *Critique of Practical Reason*. Cambridge University Press.

———. 2012. *Groundwork of the Metaphysics of Morals*. Cambridge University Press.

Kember, Sarah, and Joanna Zylinska. 2014. *Life After New Media: Mediation as a Vital Process*. MIT Press.

Kowalewski, David. 1980. Protest for Religious Rights in the USSR: Characteristics and Consequences. *The Russian Review* 39:4.

Krull, Catherine. 2011. Destabilizing the Nuclear Family Ideal: Thinking Beyond Essentialisms, Universalism, and Binaries. In Catherine Krull, ed., *A Life in Balance? Reopening the Family-Work Debate*. UBC Press.

Lawler, James. 2010. *The God Tube: Uncovering the Hidden Spiritual Message in Pop Culture*. Open Court.

Bibliography

Locke, John. 1987. *An Essay Concerning Human Understanding*. Wordsworth Classics.

———. 1996. *Some Thoughts Concerning Education and Of the Conduct of the Understanding*. Hackett.

Lofland, John, and Rodney Stark. 1965. Becoming a World-Saver: A Theory of Conversion to a Deviant Perspective. *American Sociological Review* 30:6.

Lowenthal, Mark M. 2014. *Intelligence: From Secrets to Policy*. CQ Press.

Machiavelli, Niccolò. 2003. *The Discourses*. Penguin.

———. 2004. *The Prince and The Art of War*. Barnes and Noble.

Marx, Gary T. 1998. Ethics for the New Surveillance. *The Information Society* 14:3.

Marx, Karl H. 1998 [1845]. *The German Ideology, Including Theses on Feuerbach*. Prometheus.

Mendoza, Abraham O. 2011. Soviet Atheism. In *World History Encyclopedia*, edited by Alfred J. Andrea. ABC-CLIO, LLC.

Mill, John Stuart. 2001. *Utilitarianism*. Hackett.

Nietzsche, Friedrich. 1954. *The Antichrist*. Tribeca.

Parfit, Derek. 1984. *Reasons and Persons*. Oxford University Press.

Paul, L.A. 2015. *Transformative Experience*. Oxford University Press.

Piccirillo, R.A. 2010. The Lockean Memory Theory of Personal Identity: Definition, Objection, Response. *Inquiries Journal / Student Pulse* 2:8.

Plato. 2002. *Five Dialogues: Euthyphro, Apology, Crito, Meno, Phaedo*. Hackett.

———. 2012. *The Republic*. Penguin.

Rockefeller Commission. 1975. *Report to the President by the Commission on CIA Activities within the United States*.

Rousseau, Jean-Jacques. 2003. *Émile, Or Treatise on Education*. Prometheus.

Sandel, Michael J. 2009. *Justice: What's the Right Thing to Do?* Farrar, Straus, and Giroux.

Sartre, Jean-Paul. 1956. Bad Faith. In *Being and Nothingness: An Essay on Phenomenological Ontology* [1943]. Philosophical Library.

Schmitt, Carl. 1985. *Political Theology: Four Chapters on the Concept of Sovereignty*. The University of Chicago Press.

Sudaplatov, Pavel, and Anatoli Sudaplatov, with Jerrold L. Schechter and Leona P. Schechter. 1995. *Special Tasks: The Memoirs of an Unwanted Witness—a Soviet Spymaster*. Little, Brown.

Thompson, Graham. 2007. *American Culture in the 1980s*. Edinburgh University Press.

Tolle, Eckhart. 2004. *The Power of Now: A Guide to Spiritual Enlightenment*. Namaste.

Turner, Stansfield. 1985. *Secrecy and Democracy: The CIA in Transition*. Houghton Mifflin.

———. *Burn Before Reading: Presidents, CIA Directors, and Secret Intelligence*. Hyperion.

US Joint Chiefs. 2001 [as amended through 2005]. *JP 1-02, Department of Defense Dictionary of Military and Associated Terms*. Joint Staff Directorate for Operational Plans and Joint Force Development (J-7).

Walzer, Michael, 1974. Political Action: The Problem of Dirty Hands. In Marshall Cohen, Thomas Nagel and Thomas Scanlon, eds., *War and Moral Responsibility*. Princeton University Press.

Weinstein, Allen, and Alexander Vassiliev. 1998. *The Haunted Wood: Soviet Espionage in America—The Stalin Era*. Random House.

Williams, Bernard. 1981. *Moral Luck*. Cambridge University Press.

Winner, Langdon. 1978. *Autonomous Technology: Technics-Out-of-Control as a Theme of Political Thought*. MIT Press.

Woodward, Ashley. 2013. Deleuze, Nietzsche, and the Overcoming of Nihilism. *Continental Philosophy Review* 46:1 (April).

Expendable Assets

FRAUKE ALBERSMEIER, MA, purports to be a research fellow at the Heinrich Heine University in Düsseldorf, working in philosophical methodology and ethics, while she is actually devising a scheme to bring the repetition of history to an end through the ultimate antinatalist revolution.

ROBERT ARP, PhD, works as an analyst for the US Army attempting to thwart any Ruskie plans for world domination. He also researches, publishes, and teaches in philosophy, humanities, and world religions. See robertarp.com.

ADAM BARKMAN is an associate professor of philosophy and chair of the philosophy department at Redeemer University College. He is the author or editor of eleven books, including *A Critical Companion to Tim Burton*, *C.S. Lewis and Philosophy as a Way of Life*, and *Making Sense of Islamic Art and Architecture*. Occasionally Barkman feels like a double agent, sometimes using his Canadian passport, sometimes his American one.

GREGORY L. BOCK, PhD, is Assistant Professor of Philosophy and Religion at The University of Texas at Tyler. His research areas include ethics and the philosophy of religion, and he has co-authored several pop culture and philosophy chapters with his brother Jeff, including chapters in *The Devil and Philosophy: The Nature of His Game* (2014) and *Psych and Philosophy: Some Dark Juju-Magumbo* (2013). He bemoans the fact that it seems easier for spies to spend time with their kids than for university professors to do so.

JEFFREY L. BOCK teaches History, Theory of Knowledge, and Psychology for the International Baccalaureate program at Longview High School, in Longview, Texas. He received his master's degree in History from the University of Texas at Tyler. As a boy, he used to dream about working for the CIA in Russia, but the lack of low-fat non-dairy organic pistachio ice cream on the store shelves made him change his mind.

MATTHEW BRAKE has a Master of Divinity from Regent University and Masters in Philosophy and Interdisciplinary Studies from George Mason University. He's training for a secret undercover mission that if he told you about, he'd have to kill you. Unrelated side note, check out his blog (or else): www.popularcultureandtheology.com

ALEXANDER CHRISTIAN is a research fellow at the Düsseldorf Center for Logic and Philosophy of Science working in general philosophy of science and research ethics with a particular focus on scientific misconduct, questionable research practices, and bias in medical research. Alexander obviously thinks that what he's writing about here is classified, since there's all of this blacked out writing.

CHRISTOPHER M. COX has interests in personhood, autonomy, and espionage. Wait. Did we just print that last one? Forget you read it. Nothing to see here.

CHARLENE ELSBY is Director of the Philosophy Program and Assistant Professor in the Department of English and Linguistics at Indiana University—Purdue University, Fort Wayne. She specializes in Ancient Philosophy and Phenomenology. She keeps a copy of *The Complete Works of Aristotle* in the basement behind the laundry machines.

JAI GALLIOTT is a Research Fellow at the University of New South Wales in Sydney, Australia. His work revolves around the ethical, legal, and social implications of emerging military technologies, including those that peer into your kitchen and see what you're having for breakfast. Those eggs look tasty.

KEVIN GUILFOY, PhD, is Associate Professor of Philosophy at Carroll University and has interests in Medieval philosophy, philosophy of language, and metaphysics. Like Paige, when Kevin was younger he followed a spiritual and intellectual path. And like Paige's parents, Kevin's parents were not happy!

DAVID LAROCCA is Visiting Assistant Professor in the Cinema Department at Binghamton University, and the editor of, most recently, *The Philosophy of Documentary Film: Image, Sound, Fiction, Truth*. Because of a translation error, David wrote about the est organization instead of the impact of the EST (Eastern Standard Time) protocol on clandestine transatlantic communication models. Fortunately, his training in est made it easier for him to recognize that "error" is a non-experience—and a necessary outcome of maintaining a faulty perception of reality. More details at www.davidlarocca.org.

JAMES LAWLER's cover story is that he works as a professor of Philosophy at SUNY Buffalo. He tells his children that he's interested in the history of modern philosophy, but they don't seem to buy it. Searching to verify this account, you'll probably find books on early modern philosophy, Immanuel Kant, Karl Marx, and Jean-Paul Sartre, as well as a book called *The God Tube: Uncovering the Hidden Spiritual Message in Pop Culture* (2010). No doubt this is all fake news.

ROB LUZECKY is an agent from Canada, who is lecturing on philosophy at Indiana University—Purdue University, Fort Wayne. When he isn't busy teaching students about the fun and revolutionary aspects of aesthetics and metaphysics, he spends his time petting cats and wondering if his neighbor is an FBI agent.

DANIEL P. MALLOY teaches philosophy at Aims Community College in Greeley, Colorado. Although he was raised in the Washington, DC, area during the 1980s, he feels reasonably sure his parents weren't Russian spies.

KEVIN MEEKER is Professor of Philosophy at the University of South Alabama and has interests in Ethics, Epistemology, Philosophy of Religion, Philosophy of Logic, and Early Modern Philosophy. His first job in the 1980s was computer programmer. He can neither confirm nor deny that he programmed a mail robot.

When his bosses are looking for him, LOUIS MELANÇON suddenly becomes Henry: never around. He is an Army Professor of Strategic Intelligence at the National Intelligence University, a PhD candidate at the George Washington University, and the lawyers require that anything he says doesn't reflect the views of the Department of Defense, yadda yadda yadda. Lawyers suck.

TALIA MORAG is a postdoctoral research fellow at Deakin University, Australia. She is the author of *Emotions, Imagination, and the Limits of Reason*. She learned her spying techniques from watching *Spies Like Us* some 136 times.

NILS RAUHUT, PhD, is Professor of Philosophy at Coastal Carolina University. He is author of *Ultimate Questions: Thinking about Philosophy* and his philosophical interests include Ancient Philosophy and Virtue Ethics. He was born in West-Germany during the Cold War and he and his East-German born wife have been busy raising three children in the US who are as yet unaware that they are perfectly placed to become future spies for German intelligence.

MASSIMO RONDOLINO, PhD, is still allegedly serving as part of a sleeper cell working for the establishment of the USA as a satellite Soviet republic. He is believed to act undercover as professor of philosophy and religious studies. See https://massimorondolino.academia.edu.

SABINA TOKBERGENOVA, a Russian-speaking philosopher who witnessed the end of the Soviet Union from "that side," has written book chapters for *Wonder Woman and Philosophy* and *Alien and Philosophy*.

SETH M. WALKER is a doctoral student at the University of Denver, studying religion, media, and popular culture. He regularly writes on topics in these areas—including volumes in the popular culture and philosophy genre on *Jurassic Park*, *Orange Is the New Black*, *The Walking Dead*, and the *Alien* franchise—and edits an online magazine that engages the intersection between religion and popular culture: *Nomos Journal*. His marked irreverence—and propensity to always hesitate and blink—is designed to keep the risk of indoctrination at bay.

Expendable Assets

DAVE WOLYNSKI is a military officer who enjoys philosophy, strategy, science, and Cold War-era roller skating rinks. Living in Washington, DC, he enjoys discovering old Soviet dead drops while teaching FBI agents how to correctly parallel park in the city.

ANDREA ZANIN has forgotten who she is. No, really. We've asked around but no one seems to know anything. One guy did say that he's seen her fraternizing with philosophers and loading up with caffeine in front of laptop screen saying Rantchick.com. Maybe you can figure it out?

Index

ORPHAN BLACK

AND PHILOSOPHY

GRAND THEFT DNA

Edited by
RICHARD GREENE
and RACHEL
ROBISON-GREENE

ALSO FROM OPEN COURT

Orphan Black and Philosophy
Grand Theft DNA

VOLUME 102 IN THE OPEN COURT SERIES,
POPULAR CULTURE AND PHILOSOPHY®
EDITED BY RICHARD GREENE AND RACHEL ROBISON-GREENE

In *Orphan Black*, several unconnected women discover that they are exact physical doubles. It turns out they're illegally produced clones, and someone is having them killed. Thus begins a rich saga of deception, double-dealing, twisted science, politics, religion, and violence. The staggering philosophical implications are explored in *Orphan Black and Philosophy*.

"Did Dolly feel like Sarah Manning? Did she look at her clones and contemplate her identity, the metaphysics of it all, or the absurdity of the universe? Did she wonder how many of her clones were out there or why the scientists didn't make her wool purple? Of course not, silly, Dolly is a sheep. *Whether they be like Narcissus or Sisyphus, Sarah and all her clones (and you and yours too!) should read this book, to figure out whether the grazing fodder really is greener on the clone side."*

> —DR. KIMBERLY BALTZER-JARAY, author of *Doorway to the World of Essences* (2011) and writer for *Things&Ink* magazine

"If a human being isn't born, do they still bleed? Is a life predestined to be cut short better than no life at all? Orphan Black and Philosophy tackles these and other questions through the eyes of the clones in the Clone Club. While the story is told via the lives of duplicate humans, the conclusions are sharp and original from the first page to the last."

> —CHRISTINA A. DIEDOARDO, ESQ., author of *Lanza's Mob: The Mafia and San Francisco* (2016)

ISBN 978-0-8126-9920-3

**AVAILABLE FROM BOOKSTORES AND
ONLINE BOOKSELLERS**

For more information on Open Court books, go to
www.opencourtbooks.com.